Delinquent Girls in Court

PATTERSON SMITH REPRINT SERIES IN
CRIMINOLOGY, LAW ENFORCEMENT, AND SOCIAL PROBLEMS

A listing of publications in the SERIES *will be found at rear of volume*

PUBLICATION NO. 67: PATTERSON SMITH REPRINT SERIES IN
CRIMINOLOGY, LAW ENFORCEMENT, AND SOCIAL PROBLEMS

Delinquent Girls in Court

A STUDY OF THE
WAYWARD MINOR COURT OF NEW YORK

Paul W. Tappan

Montclair, New Jersey
PATTERSON SMITH
1969

SBN 87585-067-7

Library of Congress Catalog Card Number: 69-14950

TO
Linda
and Our Wayward Minors

Foreword

"CORRECTION" IS A FIELD of activity not only of peculiar interest but of peculiar difficulty. That we all know.

One begins with an individual whom the less official lines of training and pressure have failed to channel and shape into patterns of behavior acceptable to the community: "he has gotten into trouble"; "he is always getting into trouble."

If he is "always" getting in, we are faced with an individual already structured on trouble-making lines, already in tension with his environment, commonly already equipped with a variant set of values some of which represent rebellion against, or negations of, the more generally accepted values and which are also dear to him because they serve to defend his self-respect. "Correction" here means the re-making of a personality, against entrenched resistance.

If on the other hand he—or she—has just "gotten" into trouble we may have a sound working base of personality, but we run promptly into the negative effects of society's own defensive measure, the "stigma." The individual is judged, classed, and labeled according to the single action if the single action is objectionable enough: he who commits a felony is "a felon," he who commits a crime is "a criminal." Gossip and general attitudes join to thrust him—or her— out of the in-group bound together by loyalties, coöperation, and the social values, to thrust him out and away and into another group where self-respect, like the respect of others, grows precisely out of successful challenge to the accepted social values. And we meet the familiar problem of how to keep any "treatment" procedure from bringing our delinquent into association, familiarity, sympathy, with the more or less organized body of those whom we have thoroughly failed to "correct." "Treatment" may lead even to the patient's schooling in the skills of those others.

Against this background plays the whole movement for individualized, "salvage"-treatment of delinquents, the very term being a device to lessen stigma and to enlist and focus the "education"-attitude we associate with youth as contrasted with the "retribution"-attitude we associate with "public enemies." Against this background plays in particular Tappan's detailed and effective study of the Wayward Minors Court.

That study has immediate value for anyone who is interested in the "correction" problem. It has immediate value for anyone who is interested in the future of that court, or interested in the organization of a system of courts. Tappan's report is curiously satisfying in its analysis of changing structure and function; its analysis of the interplay of the individual officer—judge or other officer—with the scheme of the officially controlling law and with the often very different actually controlling practice of the court; its analysis of the relation of facilities to effectiveness and especially to equality of the protection offered by this institution of the law. Here is original, informative stuff, soundly and objectively gathered and presented with a quiet unusual in this field of slogan, attack, reform, and interest-ridden controversy.

The implications of the book reach of course far beyond the single case, the single institution whose growth and groping are the direct subject matter. Consider the spotty, disintegrated cross-purposing results left behind when the delinquency problem has been approached by way of a sequence of legislative acts each carried in its own day by its own small wave of reform, but with never an over-all view at work. That is typical of all our government, but rarely does one get a view of process, problem, and result as neatly highlighted as here. Or consider the problem of what kind of "trouble" affords wise ground for intervention. Official "correction" is a concept which calls forth an attitude. The values to be officially announced are our "Sunday" values by which we preach, not our workaday values by which we live. Or else, if we approach the matter from the "humane" and individualized angle, we may find ourselves, like Ben Lindsay, "conniving" at things which render the whole institution vulnerable to attack and destruction under the banner of men's "Sunday" values. The curious self-limitation of the Wayward Minors Court to girls and to matters of sex delinquency is particularly interesting in this connection, as are a number of those concrete applications of the standards which Tappan cites. No less interesting is the problem of how far the allegedly "wayward" minor may require counsel's assistance in challenging the allegation. Too much is written about young "delinquents," as too much is written about adult "criminals," which simply assumes the aptness of the label as applied to the person. Tappan's material is a healthy corrective on this point, following into case-detail the lines of thought so well developed by Dession and by Michael and Wechsler.

Finally, I find the study of peculiar value in its bearings on the eternal problem of structure, function, and personnel in any institution. Except for the Supreme Court of the United States few of our legal institutions have come in for sustained studies of the sort; and legal institutions are a neglected mine for study, rich in good ore. Almost nowhere else does the official pattern which is supposed to be followed stand out so clear to see; almost nowhere else is the effort so vigorous to make the result equal and even, irrespective of the officer. It is, then, fascinating to observe, for instance,

that the single steadiest and most reckonable line of operation depicted in the book: to wit, the limitation of operations
to girls and to matters of sex delinquency, rests neither on
the text of the law nor on any seemingly conscious policy-
decision of the court, but appears instead to have developed
by practice or inertia resting partly in the accidental "par-
entage" of the court. Surely the processes and causes of
institutional self-limitation, quite as much as the processes
and causes of institutional development, are central to a
sociology that seeks to come to grips with men at work in
daily living. We need such a sociology, and this study takes
us a step along that road. I could indeed have wished that
the author had done something to organize his material more
explicitly around the concept of "craft." At least two crafts,
that of the magistrate and that of the probation worker,
gather great portions of the material into interesting and
significant bodies of contrast and interaction. Tappan's
Gestalt of thought moves along these lines; but I think its
range of significance appears more clearly and more fully
when the "craft" concept is present to suggest the wider
bearings of this particular coöperative conflict in work-
methods, outlook, training and ideals.

In sum, whether as a study in history or as one in
criminology or as one in court organization or as a contribution to the general sociology of institutions, this book is
welcome. It adds. And it stands up.

K. N. LLEWELLYN

Columbia University School of Law

Note of Acknowledgment

THE AUTHOR WISHES to acknowledge the aid and courtesy of
the numerous individuals who have been of invaluable assistance in the preparation of this work. To the personnel of
the Magistrates' Courts of New York City who gave fully
of their coöperation and assistance in the gathering of the
information on which this study was based he devotes his
hearty appreciation. It is impossible to mention all those
working in and with the girls' court who contributed of their
time and experience to this effort to understand and
interpret that tribunal. Without their friendly and sincere
aid this study could not have been made. Despite the fullness
of their help, they are not responsible for any of the final
appraisals which the author has drawn. To the faculty of
Columbia University, and more particularly to Professor
Karl N. Llewellyn, of the School of Law, he is indebted for
the inspiration and critical guidance of this work. Several
publications mentioned specifically in the footnotes have
kindly consented to quotation from their materials; for this
the author expresses his gratitude. He has drawn deeply and
with appreciation from the counsel of university colleagues
and associates of the bar. Finally, the author expresses
appreciation to the Social Science Research Council: its
postdoctoral fellowship for interdisciplinary research, 1943–
44, made this study possible.

PAUL W. TAPPAN

New York
September 5, 1946

Contents

Tables

1

Introduction

How DO WE TREAT the young girl of "easy virtue" in New York City? What standards of morality do we observe—in theory, in fact, and in our courts? Where are we seeking to go and by what vehicles shall we arrive? Wherein does the "bad bad girl" of the court or training school differ from the "good bad girl" who is spared judicial attention? What do we mean by "moral depravity" in this day of conflicting ethical codes? What legitimate purpose, if any, is served by a morals court? How effectively can it aid the girl or protect the community? Is the girl made better or worse by the manipulations of a specialized experimental court? These are a few of the questions which are considered in this work. In a general way they represent the basic issues which the writer seeks to appraise and partially to resolve.

METHODOLOGY AND PURPOSE

More specifically, this study proposes to consider the judicial, administrative, and social processes of the Wayward Minor Court in New York City, an experimental tribunal for adolescent girls.[1] Its aim is to understand, in so far as possible, the means and ends of the Court, the adaptation

[1] The court for wayward minors is now known officially as Girl's Term. Its name was changed in 1945, apparently to escape some of the odium which has attached to the name, Wayward Minor Court. However, the defendants who go through the Court are adjudicated to the status of wayward minor under the Wayward Minors' Act and are known officially by that term. Since the tribunal in its history has become fixed in the public mind as the Wayward Minor Court, the author applies the statutory term in this work as one that is more clearly and familiarly descriptive of the nature and approach of the Court.

of the means used to the ends ascribed, and, tentatively, to recommend methods better adjusted to the accomplishment of some of its objectives. In stressing some of the social, psychological, and generally interactional elements which occupy an important—if not ponderably prominent—part in the "living law" of the Court, it endeavors to go deeper than would a simple study of procedure. It purposes, further, to stress the relation of the Court as such to other community agencies through which the Court's goals are achieved and their realization is limited and directed.

Broadly, the approach is functional, but it seeks as well to be genetic, cross-sectional, and evaluative—to show the developmental history of an institutional organization, to analyze and appraise its current operation, and to project its possible course in the future. If no greater result is accomplished, it is hoped that the data here set down may increase our understanding of the numerous variables and complex interactions which go into the functioning of modern adolescent tribunals in particular and of judicial processes in general. It is hoped that it may direct the way toward further, more intensive analyses of courts as dynamic mechanisms of social control.

Special attention may properly be devoted to the treatment of adolescents in the New York City courts for several reasons: The pre-adult period is of great significance in the prevention and treatment of crime, since criminal "character" is generally developed during childhood and adolescence; the late adolescent years are, moreover, not only crucial, but the most serious as measured by the commission of felonious crimes.[2] The recent increase in what was already a strikingly

---

[2] See especially Sellin, *The Criminality of Youth*, on the relation of criminality to age and developmental factors. Also see Alexander and Staub, *The Criminal, the Judge, and the Public* for a psychoanalytic interpretation of the etiology of the "normal criminal," and Alexander and Healy, *Roots of Crime.* More generally see Reckless and Smith, *Juvenile Delin-*

high rate of adolescent delinquency merely adds point to the need for careful rethinking of means and methods applied in the treatment of this age group.

Youth is the period when, if at all, effective work of reformation and rehabilitation may still be carried on so that the continued, aggravated criminal careers of adulthood may be prevented. Moreover, in displaying a drive toward humanization in the treatment of offenders who may be rehabilitated, the courts dealing with adolescents already show numerous adaptations of the summary process as it operates on the magistrates' level. The practices of these courts may indicate that the institutions are in transition, directed to the solution of old problems by new judicial and social methods. Fortunately, the material available for understanding the adolescent and the procedures which he experiences is fuller than the data on the adult who passes through the district magistrates' courts: the probation records cover a greater number of cases and contain more informative detail. The limitations upon information concerning adult offenders at the stage of the preliminary hearing in the lower courts are more confining than those existing in the adolescent courts because the latter are still experimental and partially self-critical.

Several methods have been employed in the effort to gain as complete an understanding as possible of the institutions of the Wayward Minor Court. Other methods which suggest themselves have not been pursued, not only because of the element of time, but also because of the limited insight which

quency, and Carr, *Delinquency Control.* For statistics on law violation, see any of the Uniform Crime Reports, bulletins published quarterly by the Federal Bureau of Investigation since 1930. For the increase in delinquency during the war, particularly in the sex offenses of girls, see the New York *Times* for March 21, 1943; September 17, 1943; October 7, 1943; October 10, 1943; April 12, 1944; May 15, 1944; July 9, 1944 and December 11, 1945. There is an apparent increase of nearly 200 percent in female delinquency and an increase of more than 100 percent in venereal infection.

they were believed to offer. Chiefly, the techniques used were the following:

1. Court observation.—The need has been expressed in the literature, both by sociologists and by jurists, for an understanding of judicial processes which may come in part from direct observation in court. Since the courts of the magistrates' system are not courts of record, such an approach may be especially useful for information concerning unwritten institutional processes of the court and the duties peculiar to particular officers in it which can be derived only from observation. Moreover, the summary process in adolescent and adult courts is peculiarly revealing because the phases of that process, recurring rather rapidly in the continuum of business, can be apprehended, analyzed, and compared more readily than in the higher courts.[3]

2. Statistics.—Statistical data on the wayward minor gathered from a detailed study of court records and reports, together with comparative data on other courts of the magistrates' system derived from several sources, have been assembled and analyzed to clarify the methods and objectives of the Wayward Minor Court.

3. Interviews.—Consultation has been held with personnel

[3] The limitations of the method of courtroom observation are also apparent: the accuracy of observation is colored by the subjective reactions of the observer; the adequacy and balance in the samples of process observed are so much less easily checked than in statistical samples; the importance to the "law in action" of much that goes on behind the scenes is neither measured by any precise scientific devices, nor observable with any degree of nicety in the courtroom; and one must reckon with the presence of other imponderables of considerable importance, such as the influence of "politics," of traditions of the bench, of instrumental and ultimate values at work, and of personality factors. The intuitive or subjective element is large, yet it is unwise to neglect the factors which cannot be precisely measured with full objectivity or even be precisely determined to exist, for such factors are present and at work. They vitally affect the processes of "justice," and both their existence and their range and intensity can be checked in some measure by other techniques used in the study.

of the Wayward Minor Court who are most familiar with
its history, methods, and purposes, and with observers who
have attempted to study the court system objectively. Those
officially attached to the Court have been particularly helpful in giving insight into the imponderables which operate
"behind the scenes," and those not officially associated with
the Court have been extremely useful in checking the writer's
critical reactions to the established form and procedure.

4. Case studies.—From the records of the probation department of the Court the writer selected 300 cases for intensive study to determine the methods used in processing
offenders and to explore the relation of those methods to
various factors present in the cases which came before the
Court. A continuous complete series of 150 such cases was
taken from the records of 1938, consisting of approximately
the first half of that year's cases; a similar group was selected from the 1942 files.[4] Therefore they picture rather
fully, within the limitations of the data recorded, the procedures then employed. These data reflect, of course, only
the years intensively studied, 1938 and 1942, but they serve
also to point up significant transitions during the short life
history of the Court. This information has been supplemented, as indicated above, by observation of the current
functioning of the Court.

5. Bibliographic research.—Information has been gathered from research in the legal literature on statutory and
case law related to the development of the Wayward Minor
Court. The writer has also read rather widely in the materials of sociology, psychology, and jurisprudence which re-
late to the adolescent offender, criminology, and judicial
process. It is believed that some of this literature is richly
instructive in analyzing this court's application of judicial
procedures to personal and social problems.

[4] See statistical tables, *infra,* Chapter VI.

THE SOCIOLEGAL APPROACH

The attempt has been made in this study to combine a sociopsychological with a legal approach for the fuller understanding of the judicial institutions and processes of a particular court. It may be possible thereby to view the legal and social controls of the Court less as distinct or conflicting systems than as parts of an interdependent totality. What, if anything, may the sociological and psychological methods add to the study of the adjudicative processes at the levels of fact determination and treatment? Their contribution is more in manner of approach, or frame of reference, than in a set of specific laws, theories, or concepts to be carried over from one field to another.

The need of the social scientist is to utilize whatever technique may be empirically appropriate to increase the depth and scope of his understanding of social institutions.[5] He attempts to see the specific and the concrete in relation to the broader framework of the culture. His interest in personality and society leads to an emphasis upon relationships and interdependence in the processes of personal and social interaction, upon the interpersonal and intergroup relations which are basically important in our courts. In his effort to understand the operation of human institutions through objective, disinterested analysis he tends—within the limitations of self-restraint upon his own biases—to apply relativistic, nonmoralistic standards in his study. Where it is necessary—as in the interpretation of norms in the normative field of the law—to consider established "oughts," his

---

[5] The term "institution" is used in this study in its sociological sense to refer to the habits, attitudes, techniques, and ideas which center in the community's adjudicative practices. This idea of institutions and their evolution is to be distinguished from such structures as the "commitment institution." It is unfortunate that the same term must be used for both; however, when the latter is meant, some qualifying adjective will generally be used to avoid possible confusion.

endeavor as a social scientist is not to evaluate these "oughts," but to understand them, their genesis, their effects. In that sense the purpose of the social scientist is observational: he is concerned with determining the existence and consequences of his social data. In so far as he may ascribe ethical values to his data, however, he does so not as a scientist, but as an individual, and must make clear the introduction of his personal judgment and its criteria. In addition, he will bring to his consideration of social institutions some postulates, hypotheses, and concepts derived from social science. Often these do not approximate the limited exactness of physical laws and are sometimes little more verifiably valid than metaphysical presumptions. His certainty increases with the accumulated evidence of the consonance of his theory with the full data derived from, and tested by, the variety of empirical methods which may be at hand, checked too by the congruence of that theory with what is already known about the social universe within which he works.

No less significant, certainly, than the attempt to interpret legal and adjudicative matters through social science is the converse goal of seeking through the processes and data of the courtroom to shed more light upon sociopsychological theory, understanding, and knowledge. For the scribes of social science have frequently sought employment as handmaidens to the law. Yet the opulent materials of the latter field remain largely unexploited for their potential contributions in return. One set of values that may be recommended by the legally trained involves methods of thinking: precision of concepts, careful and logical analysis, impartial weighing of conflicting claims, a viewing of the particular against a background of the general, a searching for significant differences. These and other juristic thought-ways may serve to sharpen and clarify social investigation and theorizing. Moreover, the content of social science may be enriched by studies of legal processes and institutions. Courts and court-ways lend themselves admirably to functional analysis. The detailed study of a concrete, dynamic system of institutions in a court with its normative patterns, established procedures, and its continuing personnel to deal with rapid sequences of similar but individually different problems in adjudication is, it is believed, pregnant with meaning for the social scientist. Here, for example, are specific data of value to the criminologist, a flood of untapped information on the purpose, method, and consequence of court operation in relation to the criminal and the public. Here also, and of broad significance, are implications for the understanding of social processes—especially social control—and social institutions. The subject matter of social control, wherein growth has been insignificant, for the most part, since E. A. Ross's exploratory volume of 1901, can be deepened and refined by court studies.[6] The areas of formal control particularly may be more adequately appraised for students of society, and the relation of those controls to other forms and methods of group constraint may be scrutinized. Indeed, the study of legal phenomena can itself reveal much concerning the nature and operation of other social controls. Too, the institutional dynamics of growth and change may be investigated here; surely the Court as a set of sociojudicial institutions, crescive and evolutionary, deserves further analysis in terms of the development of the means and ends which it seeks. Or, observing the Court in cross section, the interrelationships of parts within the control structure may be seen, and current operative efficiency in adjudication may be appraised.

The study of a court in operation may serve further to illustrate the institutional and functional relations in what Karl N. Llewellyn calls crafts, craft traditions, and techniques by revealing the interrelationships of the law-trained

[6] See Ross, *Social Control.*

judge in a socially motivated court, employing techniques traditional and novel, legal and sociological, to accomplish the court's objectives. It is hoped in this study of an experimental court, which uses an interdisciplinary approach to data which are both legal and sociological, that some addition may be made to our understanding of the development, operation, and potentialities of institutions, judicial and social.

LIMITATIONS ON REFORM

Increasing awareness of the peculiarities in the processes of adjudication and disposition of the criminal has grown out of modern legal and sociological realism. Contemporary attention has been concerned more and more with what courts do, what their methods and results are. Considerable research has been devoted to the processes of the criminal court as well as to pre-trial and post-trial agencies of criminal law administration and to the interrelationships of the agencies dealing with the criminal in their day-to-day activities. As thought has become explicit and ideas have achieved the sanction of approval from interested groups, new devices have been introduced tentatively and experimentally to improve the administration of the criminal law. While effort has been sporadic and diversified, it has displayed a cumulative pressure, not only toward reform and humanization, but also, though less strikingly, toward speed and effectiveness in handling the unreformable.

The adolescent group has received a large share of recent consideration and experimentation, especially in regard to reform and the prevention of crime.[7] Partly, this is because it has been shown that the chronic criminals who commit the most serious offenses developed their antisocial patterns dur-

[7] See Sellin, *op. cit.*, and Findings of the Subcommission on Causes of Crime, New York State Crime Commission, *The Young Offender and the Law*, pp. 148–52, Legislative Document No. 114, 1932.

ing the years of youth and that innoculation against criminality may thus be most easily and successfully applied in
this period. Moreover, from a practical point of view, it is
realized that the retributive disposition of the public is less
dangerously assaulted by selective and preferred treatment
of the adolescent for whose "peccadilloes" there is a considerable amount of group tolerance. Frequently it is believed
that the youth is not "morally responsible" for his behavior
to the degree that is the hardened and habitual offender of
adult years. The current lay attitudes in regard to moral
responsibility are useful to the criminologist in permitting
clinical treatment methods where they may be used most effectively and least expensively.

It appears, however, that those who seek to encourage the
introduction of "socialized" and "humanitarian" methods
into judicial and related processes are not wholly clear about
either the inherent limitations or the desirable directives which
should guide their actions. Preliminary to a consideration of
the Wayward Minor Court as a specific illustration of the
attempt to humanize the processes of law in dealing with
adolescent girls, a few of the general limitations which restrict
reform may be mentioned:

1. Finances.—Restricted finances, a serious brake upon
any experimental work, must affect judicial change acutely.
The limitations which operate through the city budget and
the inadequate resources possessed by related social agencies
may narrowly restrain a program of change. Cost, however,
is frequently but an excuse to justify the perpetuation of
the institutional *status quo.* Thus active opposition has often
been directed against methods proposed to limit public expenditures while improving the efficiency of service, e. g., the
suggestion that unnecessary judgeships be eliminated, combined with an assertion that for the salary of one underworked
judge, three fully occupied and competent psychiatrists could

be hired. Again, it is a familiar but disregarded truism that careful and reformative treatment can be performed by a probation service at a small fraction of the cost of penal institutionalization. Then, too, expensive, maximum-security prisons are constructed to confine those who might more effectively, and at much less cost, adapt to social responsibility on a prison farm or in a prison colony. Hence, in a society which probably loses at least fifteen billions of dollars annually through its criminals, far more serious than the problem of financial limitations upon reform is that of procuring an intelligent reallocation of social funds so that they may be used effectively and in planned, integrated programs rather than haphazardly; and so that special effort may be directed to critical groups which promise some successful return upon the investment. More is lost through dispersion and duplication of effort and facilities, through lack of planned coördination (at least in the efforts toward prevention and treatment among the young), than should be required for effective work.[8]

2. Personnel.—Too often personnel may be an acute limitation upon successful social action. Related to financial lacks, the problem is chiefly one of getting trained as well as willing workers placed, and placed firmly, in a system where a great deal may be spent for buildings and figureheads, little for those who must do the real work of selecting the reformable potential criminal for treatment and treating him. The difficulties are accentuated when the public service is heavily weighted with the tenure of incompetent deadwood such as incumbents resulting from politically inspired appointments. Here again, however, the problem is very largely one of allocation rather than of insufficiency. Even where there is an ade-

[8] See Samuel Seabury, *Report of the Joint Committee on Probation in New York City,* and special reports of that committee on the various courts of the city. See also Report to the Legislature, 1933, quoted in Breckinridge, *Social Work and the Courts,* pp. 67–74.

quacy of total talent it may be diffused in wasteful or futile expenditures.

3. Official attitudes.—Closely allied to restrictions in personnel and budget is the impossibility of rising materially above the level of official opinion, whether informed or ignorant. Not the least of the difficulties is the heavy leaven of conservatism which restrains the politician; for him, the *status quo* is safer than experimentation. Even a "reform administration" must cleave to conservative reforms; its changes must be popular changes, or at least those which have received an overdue public acquiescence. The established order is an obstacle thwarting reform in that its officials cling tenaciously to the interests which have vested in them. To change an institution vitally is to change its powers and personnel. Reform must cope with the resistance of those whose authority it threatens.

There are, moreover, peculiarities in attitudes of key officials which may facilitate or impede change. The interest and value systems of those who matter may well be seen in the tangibles of fine buildings and machines, extravagant and attention-alluring structures, or in certain public departments (e. g., police, fire, street-cleaning) whose political "visibility" is high. The importance of intangibles, of personnel, of institutional subtleties, or even of traditions, may be derided.

4. Public attitudes.—Neither the public official, his budget, nor his personnel can safely deviate too obviously from the circumscriptions of public attitudes. The direction and degree of change must depend in great measure upon the value systems of the culture and the degree of public enlightenment. In the administration of the criminal law, retributive public attitudes are particularly wont to limit legislative and, to a lesser degree, administrative changes.

5. The experimental approach.—There are further difficulties intrinsic to the experimental approach itself which militate against the achievement of broad and lofty goals, such as those often sought in dealing with the criminal. Central is the complication of motives and emotions generated in the attempt to apply objective thought to situations fraught with feeling. Man's affective states are obstacles to intelligent dealing with social problems. There is, moreover, a considerable cultural repugnance to dealing with human beings experimentally. For the most part the conscious purposive manipulation of man is taboo.

Finally, even within the range where experimentation may be permitted it is generally unwise—at least during the early stages of trial and error—to attempt experimentation on a large scale. The complexity of the human being and of his social environment makes it important that attempts at experimentation be conducted under conditions as carefully controlled as possible. More may be accomplished by a discriminating selection of cases for intensive exploratory and experimental work than by the dispersed effulgence of a good will flowing in all directions or by working on patterns inadequately adjusted to particular needs.

STANDARDS OF COMPARISON AND EVALUATION

A final and important preliminary consideration remains: to state briefly the evaluative purposes of the writer and to point up some of the problems associated with the formation of policy. Let it be understood first that it is not the aim of this work to establish a specific norm of conduct to be used by the Wayward Minor Court in adjudication. The desire is rather to see whence the norms and objectives of the Court have derived and how they have developed into their present form, and to appraise them in relation to the mores of our culture and community. We seek to observe the developing methods used to attain the objectives of the Court and to evaluate these techniques in terms of what they do and can accomplish; in other words, to consider the limitations and potentialities of legal and court method in moralization of the young. Finally, we suggest minimum generic standards essential to an honest, fair, and effective operation of a specialized court for the young girl—both in the formulation of norms of conduct sought to be controlled and in methods of processing—to avoid the dangers involved in current court handling.

A basic problem confronting the analyst of any social problem is the establishment of standards. The facile denigration of objectives, methods, and accomplishments, though not uncommon, is an altogether naïve and unconstructive approach to social change and planning. Yet a more positive approach will present numerous difficulties. In evaluating efficiency of personnel, institutions, methods, and the like, the critic may easily be deflected by the absence of any objective criteria of measurement. Appraisal of institutional effectiveness involves qualitative and largely nonquantifiable norms: judgment as to the success of a method may be made highly questionable by the imponderability of its products. On the other hand, the hazards of evaluation are often increased by the seeming objectivity and accuracy of concrete data which may be used to "measure" performance; for simple statistics do not reveal functional quality. Indeed, any statistical estimation of a wholly quantitative character—when figures are available—may be a snare if no basis for comparison has been or can be established. And further complication enters when data used are inexact, subjectively derived, or noncomparable.

The difficulties thus inherent in the analysis of social problems and institutions are abundantly represented in the investigation of court behavior. Two special and crucial lacks may be noted. First, there are, for the most part, no objective terms for the statement of current performance. Thus, for example, we lack the means by which to determine accurately the specific effects of probation, commitment institutions, and parole. In so far as estimates of success are made, they often reflect the partisan interpretation of an organization which evaluates its own work with rough-hewn statistical tools and with no satisfactory criteria of achievement. Secondly—and here is a difficulty even greater to overcome if one's purpose be to evaluate—we possess few norms to which the existing performance may be compared. Hence, even if there were available some index of the accuracy of adjudication and treatment by a particular court, operating under a particular statute or statutes with given personnel and institutional facilities, we should seek in vain for a standard of expectancy, of average performance, or of ideal functioning. The multiplicity of variables which enter into "success" or "failure" and, equally difficult, the task of defining those terms in standardizable fashion, should generate considerable skepticism concerning statistics dealing with the criminal and the interpretations of those statistics.

The illustration of treatment success data is merely suggestive of the dilemma of evaluation in the field of criminal law administration. There are many other striking instances of phases of that administration where statistics are questionable or lacking. Consider the often publicized figures on prosecution by which the efficiency of the prosecutor's office is tacitly suggested.[9] However accurate the data may be, they are often—taken alone—worse than useless for rating "justice" or "success" in dispositions. One source of serious

[9] See, for example, the Annual Report of the District Attorney's Office, New York County, for 1943, especially pp. 2–5 wherein a conviction rate of 97.5 percent, claimed with pride, is compared to the inferior record of prior years (and of prior district attorneys). See "Highest Percentage of Successful Prosecutions in 42 Years," New York *Times,* June 21, 1944; August 9, 1944; May 29, 1945; and March 14, 1946.

error in the numerous prosecution and court studies of recent years has been the implication that the "mortality of criminal justice," or its success, can be measured simply through conviction rates. That the layman should be led by widespread publication to believe that a conviction rate of 95 percent or 98 percent by the prosecutor's office is evidence of effective justice and a sound basis of political preferment highlights the dangers of statistical naïveté. Quite clearly the accuracy of adjudication depends upon the number of innocent defendants who are discharged and convicted, an unknown and (within the present limitations of our ability to determine facts) largely unknowable quantity. We do know, however, that the proportion would vary greatly with time, place, personnel, statutes, rules of court, values, and other factors.

Similarly, though less seriously perhaps, error is invited by a comparison of figures on arrests or court appearances, figures which apparently reflect many factors, but especially the size, quality, and equipment of the police force; the offense involved and the attitudes, public and official, toward it (whether sympathy with nullification of the law, crusade against crime, or moderate enforcement of the law be currently characteristic); the statute and the ease or difficulty of its enforcement; and finally—and again an unknowable factor—the actual amount of violation. Other illustrations might be given, but these may be sufficient to indicate that quantifiable data where available may be dangerous as well as helpful in evaluation and that considerable care must be exercised in interpretation. Comparisons are more apt to be valid where controls among the related factors may be held constant. Variations in statute, offense, personnel, procedures, policies, and attitudes are among the important influences which affect the statistical data of the court. The scramble from a simple statistic to a broad conclusion too often ensnares the unwary criminologist in the familiar traps of particularism and unicausality.

To narrow down our consideration to processes of the Wayward Minor Court, a central problem is the standard of adjudicative accuracy which should be expected from that tribunal so that it may accomplish its greatest benefits and to do the least amount of damage. As we examine the possibilities, it appears that an ideal of 100 percent accuracy might be established. That would clearly not imply a 100 percent rate of conviction, but rather a figure dependent upon the number of girls brought into court who were in reality not wayward minors. It would be both variable and unascertainable, as indicated above; therefore, the ideal could be used only as a conceptual standard. Also, it would be a wholly unattainable ideal, of course, even under optimum conditions. The conceptual standard might still be used, however, if it is realized that only approximations to the ideal could be effected. It must be remembered too that the closer any court attains to 100 percent conviction of the guilty, the larger the proportion of innocent defendants it will tend also to adjudicate. It should be noted that the establishment of such an ideal standard does not suggest the methods or areas of change by which perfection is to be approached.

A second, alternative norm might be considered—less idealistic, more practical, though even further removed from statistical ascertainability: a standard determined by as high a degree of adjudicative accuracy as would be possible within the limitations of reasonably efficient operation by the Court's potentially and feasibly attainable facilities, statutory, personnel, institutional, etc. Prescience would be required for the statistical discovery of such a rate, but as a conceptual standard it constitutes an ideal toward which the Court might well strive. It is useful in this study as a theoretical norm, but one which does not inform in very concrete terms.

A third basis of comparison might be used through which some statistical contrasts could be drawn. No concrete standard for performance being established, comparisons may be made between adjudication and disposition rates in a given court under a given statute with continuing personnel features and at different periods in the court's history. Further comparisons could be made, as they have been in this report, to other courts where similarities and dissimilarities make comparison relevant. They may serve, in part, to point up the difficulties involved in translating techniques used for given purposes in one court to another where the purposes and consequences are quite different. The inherent limitations of this method are apparent when there are numerous variable factors insufficiently revealed or controlled. However, in conjunction with these statistical data—despite their restricted utility—other methods of study and observation may be combined, as the writer has attempted to do, using as an ideal reference point the second conceptual standard suggested above.

The various factors in the processes of the court which conduce to excessive inefficiencies and inaccuracy may be "spotted" by careful and long-continued observation. Then the court may be directed toward changes in the realms of most obvious and remediable weakness first, looking to a gradual improvement of its processes, as extensive in the long run as possible. Perfection should not be anticipated, to be sure, because of the inevitable and continuing limitations of budget, personnel, institutional establishments, public enlightenment, and other factors. Success would be measured in terms of changes through the elimination of useless, inefficient, and inaccuracy-producing procedures and personnel.

Though it is impossible to tell in any absolute sense who

among the defendants in court are innocent and who need certain types of treatment, it is possible to assert on the basis of experience and observation that some procedures are better adapted to getting at the facts of a case more quickly, that trained personnel in sufficient number improve institutional performance, that a given statute functions well or poorly and why. It is possible to recognize the relative inappropriateness of existing means to ends which a court may seek. Therefore, wherein the material which follows may be critical in nature, it means to counsel no impossible perfectionism of administrative attainment, but seeks rather improvement in areas in which practically reducible weaknesses appear. Then too it stresses the basic principle that an institution or agency should not attempt to perform functions for which it is unqualified by its nature and its continuing limitations.

2

Legal Process and Social Objectives

IMPATIENCE WITH MATTERS of "mere" formal procedure—
with what are popularly known as legalistic technicalities
and obscurities—is a common reaction. It compels thought
about the importance of legal process in the attempt to
arrive at projected social goals. The feeling among laymen
that the red tape of technical formalities should be abolished,
particularly in dealing with the young offender, is understandable. It proceeds from the belief that the spirit of social
amelioration is lost in the form of legal procedure; that in-
direction, delay, and distortion derive from circumlocutions
required by law; that the objective sought is often not attained because of seemingly absurd technical requirements.
The inclination, then, is to cut tape, abolish form, by-pass
the rule, and take the direct route to utopia. So common is
this tendency, shared by some men of law, that its implications must be considered.

Let it be granted first that the fact of a traditional legal
procedure and its long-continued use does not establish its
perfection. It cannot be assumed that a given procedure,
however ancient, is adapted to the requirements of new social
problems which demand solution or to the requirements of
new ideologies about social change. On the contrary, it must
be recognized that a change in the definition of a problem
must require some change in its method of solution. Thus, in
so far as a court attempts to achieve novel goals, it must
expect to work in some degree with novel tools or to use the
accustomed tools in novel ways. It is natural that such an
institution as the Wayward Minor Court, trying to deal

with a narrowly defined age-group and to meet its peculiar problems, has found the given methods of trial procedure somewhat ill adapted to its work.

Moreover, it will be clear that new issues and new ideals will develop more rapidly—particularly on the idealistic frontier of reform—than will the problem-solving techniques of an institutionalized system of law, operated largely by practical and often conservative judicial engineers. The consequence may be termed a juridical lag, as the ultimate values defined by the socially "progressive" are thwarted through the instrumental inadequacies to which the legalistically "conservative" cling. The nice adaptation of means to ends is peculiarly difficult in the province of criminal law, as it is, indeed, in the whole field of social reform. Yet it is a truism that the objectives to be attained from any program cannot be divorced from the techniques that are used: the ultimate ends are conditioned by the immediate means. Hence, if the methods applied by the law are in conflict with each other or are unadapted wholly or in part to accomplishing the predicated social goals, only frustration of purpose can result.

The crucial problem is, of course, the finding and establishing of procedures which lead most surely and efficiently toward the desired objectives without foregoing such persisting values as are embodied in the older procedures. Success in doing so is often thwarted by the conflicting pressures of those who are interested in solving other and often irrelevant social problems. The visionary theorist projects his finespun plans to attain logical perfection, and the reactionary clings to any and every tradition. Each is often helpful and often damaging to our evolving social institutions. Much that the conservative would protect is worth preserving. Yet too often an indiscriminate conservation blocks the forward-thrust of much needed change. Energy which might be devoted to pulling together in compromise toward a community of achievement is lost in mutual vilification and misunderstanding. In similar fashion the social scientist proceeds too often without knowledge or understanding of the law, suggesting that to attain "justice" we should cut through the circuitous legal process. The jurist follows slowly, insisting on the preservation of "proper procedure," lest in abandoning the means of justice the ends too may be lost.

There is one telling argument against wholesale abandonment of legal rule and procedural form to accomplish social objectives: wholly to free the law from the "dead hand of the past" one must entrust unlimited discretion to judge, reformer, or clinician and his personal views of expedience. Unless he be circumscribed in some degree by established instrumental or traditional rule and form, the fate of the defendant, the interest of society, the social objectives themselves must hang by the tenuous thread of the wisdom and personality of the particular administrator. The implications of judicial totalitarianism are written in history. The flood of facile recommendations from the impatient must, then, be carefully scrutinized to determine whether the gain that is promised by dilution or evasion of the established law is greater than the loss which it involves.

In a period of widespread public and political concern about the increasing volume of delinquency with which our courts must deal, there is an especially strong pressure by various interest groups and social agencies for the prevention and remedying of the problem. A part of the campaign customarily involves a legislative program that is aimed to meet the presumed requirements of the children and adolescents who get into trouble. Since the reform groups are generally made up predominantly of representatives of social agencies and sectarian organizations, and other lay persons, they tend to stress both the removal of "unnecessary technicalities" and the institution of social work and clinical methods in place of the customary adjudicative process.

It is important, therefore, to consider the questions raised concerning the conduct of trials of adolescents: Should we, for example, abandon the rules of evidence, allowing hearsay and the testimony of a witness who has not been cross-examined? Does the offender need the protection from "improper" testimony when the very function of the court is his protection? Are a prosecutor and/or a defense attorney necessary? Do they serve to protect the interests of the community and of the defendant, or will they actually tend only to slow and impede the process of "real justice"? Why require formal proof and an early trial of the issue? Is not the defendant's problem apparent by his presence in the court or clinic and his willingness to plead his guilt? Why apply formal legal rights and remedies? The offense involved is a social one, and simplified social procedures and treatment are necessary. *Et sequitur.* Questions of this sort must be considered and at least tentatively answered in connection with the Wayward Minor Court and its methods.

There are telling arguments against legal forms preserved for their own sake, divorced from a utilitarian perception of the objectives sought. No brief can be held for wooden formalism; the life of the law is in its adaptability to changing needs. Procedure and rule are the instruments of justice, but only when they are precisely adjusted to the ends which the socially intelligent have defined. The issues involved in deciding what techniques and forms are or should be applied by a court—specifically, the Wayward Minor Court—are difficult. They have no comfortingly easy solution. Yet the following may become clear:

1. Sufficiently precise principles of substantive law are required. The nature of the behavior proscribed must be

clearly apparent in the statute in order that the normative purposes of court action may be clear-cut: the justification for the court's "taking hold" in official action needs to be explicit. Thus, partially through statutory statement, the ends sought through the adjudicative process may inform and direct into reasonably similar lines of action the various personnel entrusted with achieving those objectives. One by one or as a body they may thereby be restrained from too broadly extending or too narrowly limiting the functions which they perform. Through definite norms the potential delinquent may be informed, too, of the conduct which he is to avoid; the educational and possible deterrent value of the rule rests partially therein. The possibility that a well-defined course of conduct rather than—or in addition to—a specific offense-category should be used in the statute is discussed below.[1]

2. Rules that will meet the social objectives of the court, intelligently conceived, must be designed and applied. Procedural rules are required in order that the determination of legal issues may be carried on with some efficiency and predictability. For adequate speed and effectiveness there must also be a rather uniform method of dealing with cases. System is needed too to accomplish the conflicting purposes of sufficiently protecting at once the possibly innocent defendant and the security of the social group. Methods recommended by the benevolently motivated must be carefully scrutinized, not only for their legality and constitutionality, but for their potential ultimate effects upon the institutions sought to be changed. There is grave danger that we may experience large-scale loss from the efforts of experimental courts as a result of their determination to apply methods recognized as legally invalid or to carry out schemes of immediate ex-

[1] See *infra*, Chapters V and VIII.

pedience which culminate in problems more serious than those sought originally to be solved.

Human personnel is neither omnicompetent, omniscient, nor perfect in patience or justice. Hence, the procedural rules of the court should be adapted to the accomplishment of the social purposes established in the substantive norms. There is but one pragmatic test of their value: do the rules, procedural and substantive, do the job? They have no intrinsic value other than that of regularizing action, no other purpose than to operate as instruments for the attainment of the social objectives defined. It is necessary, however, that great care be used, both in defining those goals and in measuring the consequences of the rules, including their by-products. And the problems lie much deeper than even legal technicians commonly perceive.

3. The processes used in dealing with the offender must be considered as an interdependent whole, not as a series of independent stages. For the proper operation of the machinery of justice each part must work efficiently; it must be geared to the operational requirements of every other part; and the total mechanism must be designed for optimum performance of its functions. Many of the failures in the administration of the criminal law result from loose coördination and the cross-purposes of its semiautonomous agents and from the forgotten interstices of procedure. This is frequently and easily overlooked in the operation of the law because there have evolved specialized stages of procedure: detection and apprehension, prosecution, adjudication, disposition, and treatment.

Since separate governmental divisions have developed with varied political and geographic jurisdictions, they often function with a jealous minimum of communication and co-operation, frequently operating in virtual isolation, each setting its own policy, doing its own job, seeking its own public recognition. And as the processes of legal administration are studied, these agencies tend to be considered divisible units of the whole, to be analyzed and criticized as separate functionaries. The result strengthens the attitudes of independence. It is obvious, however, as we view the processes of criminal law, that all must work together if they are to achieve the common purpose. Unless suspects are apprehended, there are no defendants whom the court may adjudicate. Though he may be apprehended, the offender will escape, or the innocent be condemned, if the courts fail effectively to discriminate the guilty from the innocent. Though cases may be skillfully adjudicated, the functions of apprehension and adjudication are nullified if unwise dispositions are made. If the methods of penological treatment applied are ill adjusted to the objectives sought, no prior procedural efficiency can secure the ends of law. Hence the persistence of independent attitudes and consequent operation in near-isolation can and do contribute heavily to the ineffectiveness of an inherently interlocking process. Consequently, when the processing of offenders falls short of desirable and possible accuracy, this may be due to the ineffectiveness of personnel, institutions, and statutes, operating at any one or on several of the levels of administration which touch the defendants. Frequently it results from poor articulation of goals and lack of coördination among the processing agencies.

CENTRAL ISSUES IN THE PROCESSING OF THE ADOLESCENT GIRL

The majority of delinquency studies have considered the male offender only or have suggested that no differentiation need be made between boy and girl in court processing, presumably implying that the traditional and partial institutional separation of commitments by sex is sufficient.[2] It is believed that further specialization is warranted by the peculiarities of female delinquency and their consequences, chiefly because the most frequent offenses are sexual, which sets a type; and then because of the peculiar danger of the spreading of venereal infection and of the impregnation of the unmarried. Although these offending girls are rarely hardened and habitual criminals of the type who threaten the community's security of person and property, their delinquency leans in a direction which can readily develop into more serious crimes such as, for example, blackmail, abortion, or drug addiction. Hence there is peculiar justification for their separate processing and treatment to avoid their contamination through court or detention contacts with older and more dangerous offenders. By differentiating the girl delinquent in adjudication it is also possible to apply more systematically the special objectives, judicial machinery, and treatment facilities which the character of their offenses and, usually, of their personalities requires.

Yet the female delinquent in New York City may, under present practice, be treated by any one or more of a number of legal and social agencies with no assured reference to the norms of trial and disposition which would be relevant to her rehabilitation.

Preliminary to a more specific consideration of the Wayward Minor Court as such, we shall observe the several methods by which, depending upon a variety of circumstances, the adolescent girl may be treated:

1. *Processing for behavior problems, sex delinquencies, and petty offenses.*—If a girl is a behavior problem without known serious criminal involvement, she may—through re-

[2] For example, the Youth Correction Authority, the Youth Court Act, the youthful offender division of the county criminal courts in New York City, and even the early proposed plans for extension of the Wayward Minor Court proposed no differentiation for purposes of court processing.

ferrals in the community—come under the care of a non-
judicial and noncriminal agency, thus being spared the
stigma of court or custodial contact. Such agencies, for
example, as the Community Service Society, the Jewish
Board of Guardians, the Salvation Army, Catholic Charity
Societies, Community Organization Society, Departments of
Welfare and Health, the Isaac Hopper Home, and several
hospitals of the city assist in the care and rehabilitation of
"unfortunate girls." Many of the agencies designed to aid
the adolescent in trouble refuse their assistance if she has
become involved with the law to the extent of exposure to, or
adjudication by, a court. There results an invidious discrimination between the "bad bad girls" who have been to
court and the "good bad girls" who have been spared that
experience. Whether the girl is considered merely unfortunate or delinquent, whether she be given the advantages of
unstigmatic aid by a private agency or the disadvantages
of disposition by a court, may depend upon the fortuitous
source of often insufficiently informed advice concerning the
available community facilities.

If the police who picked up the girl (or a magistrate in the
court to which she has been brought) believe her to be a
serious behavior problem or a noncommercialized sex offender, she may be referred to the Wayward Minor Court.
Even without police intervention, a guardian or a social
agency may bring the case to that court. There, depending
upon a variety of factors but chiefly, in theory at least, upon
the nature and extent of her misbehavior, she may be placed
under unofficial supervision without an adjudication of wayward status, or she may be adjudged a wayward minor and
put on probation or committed to an institution.[3]

If apprehended by the police as a commercialized prosti-

[3] For fuller details as to dispositions from this court, see *infra*, Chapter
VI.

tute, she will be brought to, and tried in, the Women's Court; thence her case will be disposed of, generally, by suspension of sentence, commitment for a definite term, or probation, depending primarily on the judge she "draws" and, to some degree, on the number and frequency of her prior convictions.[4]

For any other alleged petty offense, such as vagrancy, disorderly conduct, fortunetelling and gaming, she will be brought by the police to one of the numerous magistrates' district courts,[5] according to the locus of her offense, there to receive a public trial along with adult and habitual offenders. Or she may be exposed to any one of a series of specialized magistrates' courts—Night Court, Week-end Court, Probation Court, or Traffic Court—according to her offense or the hour of her apprehension and the place where the offense was committed.

2. Processing for misdemeanors.—If she has been arrested for a misdemeanor, the police will bring the girl for preliminary hearing to the magistrates' district court for the precinct of the offense, prior to her trial in a special sessions court. Though the girl is alleged to have committed a criminal misdemeanor, the magistrate may in his discretion, and with the approval of the prosecuting attorney (if there be one in his court), reduce the charge to an offense triable before him, thereby mitigating the penalty imposed.[6] More frequently the offender is sent to trial in special sessions before three judges where she may, if convicted, receive a suspended sentence, be fined, given a commitment, or placed on probation. Theoretically, the determination of treatment de-

[4] See Marsh, *Prostitutes in New York City; Their Apprehension, Trial and Treatment,* pp. 46–68, for a discussion of the lack of any unifying principle in the dispositions from this court.

[5] Discussion of certain areas of overlapping between the jurisdiction of the magistrates' and special sessions courts is omitted as unnecessary to this discussion.

[6] Code of Criminal Procedure, sec. 342-a.

pends upon the mitigating or aggravating circumstances of her crime and character. In practice, much less careful consideration appears to be given to the offender's merits in these general courts than in the specialized tribunals for adolescents, and the penalty imposed reflects the varied inclinations of the judges, requiring an agreement between two of the three. As in other unspecialized courts any specific consideration given to the adolescent tends to take the form of simple, unsystematized leniency.

If the offender is sent to special sessions for trial as a misdemeanant, and if, after a routine probation investigation, she is considered by the judge and prosecutor to be of corrigible character, she will be given, upon her consent, a private hearing before one judge as a youthful offender; the criminal charge will be dismissed.[7] Generally, from this court, she will be placed under probationary supervision, though commitment may be made to one of the institutions to which girls are sent from the Wayward Minor Court and Women's Court.

If the girl is accused of a misdemeanor and is recommended for treatment as a youthful offender, but wishes to protest her innocence, she will be sent to trial in private session before judges of the Special Sessions Court. If found guilty of the misdemeanor, she will then be returned to the Youthful Offender's Court for sentence.

3. Processing for felony.—If the girl is accused of a felony and is held by Magistrates' Felony Court, and if a true bill be found by the grand jury, she may, upon recommendation from the assistant district attorney or the grand jury, be considered for treatment as a youthful offender without a jury in General Sessions Court or in a county court, depending upon the locus of her crime. The probation in-

[7] Code of Criminal Procedure, sec. 252-b. See also Appendix A of this study.

vestigation and supervision, if such be the disposition, will be considerably more detailed in General Sessions than in any other court in the city, since this is the only criminal court of New York City with a probation department of fairly adequate staff and standards.[8] (This is not, of course, a criticism of the diligent efforts or able capacities of many overburdened probation officers of other courts for whom the diminutive budgetary appropriations provide.) Too, in the General Sessions, the offender will be given the automatic examination conducted by the psychiatric division established for this court. She may, though she probably will not, be sent to an institution.

In the event that she is not recommended for treatment as a youthful offender, or does not consent to receiving such treatment, the girl will go from the grand jury to trial before judge and jury. In this instance a longer delay will be involved, and she will experience the full force of the criminal procedure at the higher trial level. The likelihood then is that, if convicted, she will be committed to a state penal institution. In a very small proportion of cases, the girl may be tried by the Supreme Court, First or Second Judicial District, whose disposing powers are similar to those of the other specifically criminal courts.

Without considering in detail the implications of the heterogeneity of agencies, courts, custodial institutions, techniques, philosophies, and purposes to which any adolescent girl may thus be exposed, it may be enough here to stress the

---

[8] See *Report of the Joint Committee on Probation in New York City* (Seabury Commission) and special reports on the Magistrates' Court in 1936, Special Sessions in 1939, Domestic Relations in 1942, and General Sessions in 1942. The General Sessions probation department was set up by Cardinal Hayes, of the Archdiocese of New York, as an experiment in correctional treatment. In two years a quarter of a million dollars was spent in its development and operation. When this department was succeeded by a publicly maintained probation department in 1927, the funds appropriated more closely approximated the need than in the other criminal courts in the city. See Cooley, *Probation and Delinquency.*

fact of great disparity. The qualitative and quantitative nature of treatment depends upon vast systems of largely autonomous, uncoördinated facilities; upon the diverse personalities and prejudices of numerous individuals who may exert wide discretion in her disposition; often upon the fragile and tenuous balance of fortuitous circumstances. There is, moreover, virtually a complete lack of ordered purpose or philosophy in the application of means to ends in the whole of the picture and in many or most of its parts.

THE WAYWARD MINOR STATUTE AND ITS APPLICATION

The Wayward Minor Court plays a particularly important role, in comparison with the other tribunals mentioned, since it handles a larger number of adolescent girls than does any other single court. This results from the jurisdiction of the Court, which is city-wide and covers types of misconduct most characteristic among young female offenders. The "wayward minor" is defined under Title VII–A of the Code of Criminal Procedure, Section 913–a,[9] as follows:

Any person between the ages of sixteen and twenty-one who either (1) is habitually addicted to the use of drugs or intemperate use of intoxicating liquors, or (2) habitually associates with dissolute persons, or (3) is found of his or her own free will and knowledge in a house of prostitution or assignation or ill fame, or (4) habitually associates with thieves, prostitutes, pimps or procurers or disorderly persons, or (5) *is wilfully disobedient to the reasonable and lawful commands of parent, guardian or other custodian and is morally depraved or is in danger of becoming morally depraved may be deemed a wayward minor.* [Italics not in the Statute.]

A finding against the defendant results in the adjudication of the status "wayward minor," not in conviction for a crime. Consequently, the girl has not the stigma of a criminal

9 See Appendix A for this statute. Since 1944 the legislature has added two clauses in definition of the wayward minor. See Appendix C.

record in the traditional sense, is not fingerprinted, and is not so greatly discriminated against in employment. It should be noted that this status concept—like that earlier applied to the juvenile delinquent and, more recently, to the youthful offender—is distinctly advantageous as a device to permit the application of special, experimental adjudicative and treatment facilities and as a means of preventing the establishment of a criminal role at an early age. However, it must be stressed, the meaning which comes to be attached to that status depends upon the methods and results of the processing of the defendants. The concept easily becomes the basis of a distinction without a difference if personnel, institutions, and attitudes are like those of the traditional criminal court.

In practice only subsection 5 of the statute is used in the complaints in the Wayward Minor Court, largely because of the difficulties of securing sufficiently specific proof under the other provisions. The central issue under the rule in operation, then, is the imminent or existent "moral depravity" of the defendant. The connotation of that term is obviously very broad and general and its denotation quite vague; it leaves open the question of the type or types of behavior over which the Court may properly take jurisdiction. The need for statutory rules which proscribe behavior in rather specific terms is discussed elsewhere. It is enough here to indicate again that the terminology of the rule upon which the Court's jurisdiction depends is so indefinite as to leave unclear the scope of the Court's control. It is apparent that something more than willful disobedience to the parent's commands is necessary to confer jurisdiction, but the need to interpret the "danger of becoming morally depraved" imposes upon the Court a legislative function of moralizing character. Is anything more implied than sexual misbehavior? If so, what? What is sexual misbehavior—in a legal sense— of the nonprostitute of sixteen, of eighteen, or of twenty, when fornication is no offense under the criminal law, and statutory rape applies only to one under the age of eighteen? This problem of drawing lines delimiting the area of "moral depravity" is peculiarly acute when moral, religious, national, and cultural biases may direct discretionary interpretations. This makes for considerable conflict and confusion in the Court.

Whether or not the fact is welcome, this is in many respects an age of moral relativism. Moralities cannot but change and conflict in response (usually, of course, in delayed response) to the many serious modifications of other segments of the culture. A nice question may be raised at any given time as to what is the general *mos*, if any, which governs a particular form of behavior and, also, to what extent legal control can be effectively established in this area of conduct. The position has been expressed on too many occasions to require extended reiteration that law—as an art of the possible—should not endeavor to establish more than an ethical minimum, preserving to the primary groups their legitimate function of moralization.[10] Some jurists have gone so far as to maintain the desirability of complete divorcement between the functions of law and morality.[11] It is suggested here merely that, as two forms of social control, law and mores may well reënforce each other. But legal penalties are stringent. The formal punitive devices of the law may do more damage than benefit to the offender and his associates, and it is impossible with the formal, crude tools of law to control numerous forms of behavior having moralistic implications. Therefore, the attempt to legislate or adjudicate on a very high plane of ethics or morality is doomed to fail-

[10] See Del Vecchio, "The Homo Juridicus and the Inadequacy of Law as a Norm of Life," *Tulane Law Review*, XI (1937), 503, quoted in Hall, *Readings in Jurisprudence*, pp. 277–80. See also Cardozo, *The Paradoxes of Legal Science*, pp. 35–37.

[11] For this separation of law and morality see, for example, the works of Kant.

ure. At the very least, when the law offers to impose a higher standard than does the morality of the time, the result must be either frequent nullification or injustice to individuals.

Where careful studies by biologists and social scientists have indicated that a large and increasing proportion of girls during their adolescent years experiment in premarital and extramarital relationships—girls of "good families" in our high schools and colleges as well as those from under-privileged homes—by what justification does a court specialize in penalties for the nonprostitutional (and frequently nonpromiscuous) sex behavior of girls from sixteen to twenty-one? [12] In practical effect the result may be to subject to punishment merely those individuals among the sexually active who are so inept in their expression as to be "trapped" by parent, police officer, or nature. In the latter case it frequently means that the pregnant unwed girl enters motherhood as a wayward minor and is fortunate if her child is not born in custody.[13] Where pregnancy has not resulted, the stress which the court experience adds to the frequently exaggerated reaction of parents to their discovery of their children's behavior may be expected utterly to destroy the possibility of the adolescent's development of a normal and healthy heterosexuality.[14] When the girl is committed—as

[12] See Waller, *The Family; a Dynamic Interpretation,* pp. 223–25, where he discusses the disappearance of community controls and the "almost incredible moral confusion." Ira S. Wile (editor of *The Sexual Life of the Unmarried Adult*) and Dorothy Dunbar Bromley (co-author of *Youth and Sex*), discuss the increasing frequency of premarital sexual intimacy. Terman, in his study of 792 couples, revealed that of those born after 1910 only 13.6 percent of the men and 31.7 percent of the women stated that they were virgins at marriage; in contrast, among those born before 1890, 85 percent of the women and over 50 percent of the men asserted their virginity at the time of marriage. See Terman, *Psychological Factors in Marital Happiness,* Chap. XII. See also Dell, *Love in the Machine Age,* and Lindsey and Evans, *Companionate Marriage.*

[13] For instances of this, see *infra,* Chapter V.

[14] As Frankwood E. Williams has stated: "There are good, social reasons for guarding carefully the developing sex life of adolescents and guard them, wisely, we should but if in the difficult process through which they

may occur even though she is a corrigible offender, if her parents demand that she be put away [15]—the consequent distortion of her experience may easily lead to frigidity or into perversion or prostitution, for both of which our commitment institutions for female delinquents afford excellent training.

When, as is frequently the case, the Court goes beyond the attempt to control the sex behavior of the unmarried pre-adult and wields its authority to penalize or terminate filial insubordination, questions of equal difficulty arise. In an era of increasing emancipation of youth, to what standard of obedience should the daughter be held? In other words, what are parents' "reasonable and lawful commands" today? Surely, the parental criteria of reasonableness are often most irrelevant, though in effect the Court may be used to impose them. It is significant that the statute establishes disobedience and depravity conjunctively as the basis of adjudication. Yet it has frequently happened that the Court has required testimony only as to the former. It is clear that from an administrative point of view the value-system of judge or officer may have undue weight in determining standards which properly lie in the field where views of morality

are going things do happen, it is better that they do and hetero-sexuality be established than that they should not happen and ill health and abnormality be the result. I do not say that only one of the two things can happen, but if in this highly charged situation something does happen, nothing really serious has happened until we make it so. Parents should keep that in mind. By our present methods we frequently offer a child but one of the two alternatives." See Williams, "Confronting the World; the Adjustments of Later Adolescence," in *Concerning Parents* (B. Gans, ed.) pp. 156–57. See also Butterfield, *Love Problems of Adolescence,* and Kimball Young, *Personality and Problems of Adjustment,* pp. 419–25.

[15] See *infra.* The Court is frequently used by parents in an attempt to break up their daughters' relationships with boys of whom they disapprove. Though there are relatively few girls of Jewish faith who go through the Court, a common reason for their arraignment is their affection for Gentiles. In these situations the girl is usually not committed unless she is obstinate, but she may be remanded for fairly extended periods and then endure the persuasive influence of unofficial probation.

diverge and which, if justiciable at all, should therefore be established concretely and specifically in the law.

To summarize and sharpen the issues central to the writer's proposed analysis: It must be apparent from the above observations that one basic issue in the operation of the Wayward Minor Court is that concerning the type of conduct which the tribunal can and legitimately should control. Can the Court perform a preventive function by defining a course of conduct which, unrestrained, might produce serious delinquency? Or must it await the commission of a distinct offense before its machinery is called into action? It must be stressed here that a decision as to the purposes and area of control of the Court—its ends—should precede a determination of the methods or means best adapted to those ends.

Oversimplifying the situation to some extent, it may be said that two opposed points of view exist as to the objectives of the Court: One, derived from legal tradition, would require a statutory pronouncement of rather specific offenses to give the Court jurisdiction. This would imply that the force of the law should not be brought into application until after the defendant had become delinquent and would, therefore, foreclose the Court from a function of preventing merely incipient or predelinquent antisocial behavior. The other expresses the view of social work—that the goal of the social tribunal should be prevention primarily. Under this ideal, mature delinquency should be anticipated and forestalled by dealing with the child when his conduct points toward crime, requiring therefor substantive statutory provision which would establish merely general principles or a course of conduct to permit the Court to take hold. Its aim would be to prevent the development of serious misconduct rather than to penalize the behavior defined in the law. Toward that end the social worker in the Court tends to demand that the tribunal operate as an agency for the solution of a wide variety of social problems that conceivably may be associated with individual demoralization and community disorganization. It may be noted that the use of the status concept "wayward minor," with its noncriminal implications, may be applied under either view—to one who has been adjudicated for a specific offense or to one who has followed a certain course of conduct—though adoption of the concept in the law has largely grown out of the social work view in the children's court movement.

The second fundamental inquiry then involves the techniques which the Court may employ justifiably and with some success in approaching its objectives. As suggested above, the methods of processing are inextricably linked with the outcome of court action. It will be necessary to postpone discussion of these methods until consideration has been given to the procedures actually in use. Here it is sufficient to raise in advance one vital and knotty question: Is it legitimate and/or effective to permit investigation by probation officers of the defendant's social history prior to hearing, for the purpose of obtaining facts upon which both adjudication and disposition may be determined?

Again, with some oversimplification, two contrasting procedural philosophies may be discerned. The legalist is inclined to require the full unimpaired and unmodified traditional rights of due process for the adolescent so that the defendant who risks conviction for an offense and possible incarceration in a reformatory institution may be amply protected. The social work view, on the contrary, resists the "legal technicalities" and proposes that the Court operate freely as a quasi-administrative agency to perform its preventive function, assuming trial rights to be unimportant when they impede the reconstructive tasks of the probation officers. More specifically, it is urged under the latter view that the Court, acting as a clinic, should require a social investigation prior to diagnosis and prescription of treatment; this is interpreted to mean that there should be an investigation before a hearing is held.

A more explicit consideration of the issues involved in these competing ideologies of ends and means must wait upon the fuller elucidation of court development, personnel, and methods. It will be our purpose, then, to analyze the philosophies struggling in the Court and to determine in so far as possible what compromises of legal and social views may be made for fuller functional effectiveness in the attainment of the Court's ends.

3

Institutions of the Court in Transition

THE WAYWARD MINOR COURT furnishes an instructive example of the evolution of legal institutions and court-ways. It is impossible to trace the details of a court's development accurately without experiencing its growth through close association. But in that case the evaluative judgments of a participant observer (as to the influences diffused within the legal and court systems and the social inventions derived from experiment and experience) are subject to considerable distortion through errors of interpretation and memory. As is natural, moreover, those who grow with institutions are frequently least conscious of the changes which occur or least aware of their causes.

The Women's Court.—The origin of the Wayward Minor Court—with much of its philosophy, jurisdictional limits, and procedures—may be detected in the development of the Women's Court and the Children's Court, with both of which it has had a continuing kinship. Some insight into the plan of operation of the new girls' court may also be drawn from the evolution within the system of inferior courts.[1] In 1907 the first night courts in New York City were established for men and women, to hear cases of prostitutes as well as of many other types of offender. These courts were points of congregation for morbidly curious spectators and entertainment-seekers; it is said also that men of small enterprise sought women of easy virtue in the courts' environs. These night courts with their inadequate privacy and lack of sex segregation were an object of special attack by the Page Commission

[1] See Kross and Grossman, "Magistrates' Courts of the City of New York."

in the report of its investigation of the magistrates' courts issued in 1910.[2] One result of the report was the establishment in 1910 of a separate night court for women in Manhattan and one in the Bronx—to avoid the association of female offenders with incorrigible men and "to limit the number of doubtful male characters who are seen from time to time among the spectators at the night court." [3] Chief Magistrate McAdoo in his 1910 report said of the changes that were made in dealing with prostitutes:

The new law made radical provisions with reference to new courts. It provided for two night courts, one for men and one for women, thus separating the sexes and doing away with the disgraceful conditions which formerly prevailed in a single court where promiscuous throngs of degenerate and wretched unfortunates, professional criminals, and minor offenders of both sexes, sometimes only partly sobered from the effects of alcohol, were herded together nightly. . . . I deemed it best in order that we might get consistency, arising from experience, that three magistrates should be specially assigned for this work, instead of allowing the usual rotation of all the magistrates to this court. This plan has worked admirably. . . . My own idea has been to the effect that fines in these cases are practically useless; that when there is any chance of reformation, probation or commitment to a reformatory is the best course to pursue. But where the defendant, convicted, is an incorrigible professional, the best punishment is a determinate sentence to the Workhouse. This court has practically killed the business of the professional bondsman, and, as the fines were usually paid by the keepers of the assignation houses, . . . to fine them only encouraged the vice.[4]

In 1916 a similar night court for women was established in Brooklyn.[5] In 1918 the Women's Night Court of Manhat-

---

[2] Page, Final Report, April 4, 1910, Assembly Document 54. The investigation of the inferior courts by the Page Commission was the basis for the Inferior Criminal Courts Act. For a criticism of its accomplishments, see Nathan Fine, *The Collapse of the Seabury Investigation*, pp. 100 ff.

[3] Laws of 1910, c. 659, sec. 77.

[4] Annual Report of the Magistrates' Courts, 1910.

[5] By authority of the Board of Magistrates.

tan became a day court,[6] and provision was made for the
remand of female prisoners for observation and study after
conviction and before sentence.[7] Finally, in 1934, with the
abolition of the Brooklyn court, the Manhattan Women's
Court became city-wide in jurisdiction, as it is today. Two
years later, some thirteen years after the passage of the
statute which defined its jurisdiction, the Wayward Minor
Court was inaugurated as a special part of the Women's
Court by authority of the power vested in the Board of Magistrates to establish specialized courts for the handling of
specified offenses.[8] The new court met one day each week at
300 Mulberry Street, where "experimental procedures" were
followed "in the effort to establish a new technique for handling wayward minors." Until that time it had been customary to handle all female violators of the Wayward Minor
Statute, along with prostitution cases, as a part of the routine procedure of the Women's Court at Jefferson Market. It
has been observed of that court that,

During court hours the main entrance to the building is thronged
with women offenders, shyster lawyers, professional bondsmen,
men who appear to be pimps, etc. Inasmuch as this entrance serves
both courts [the Women's Court and the district Magistrates'
Court], the rule of the Women's Court against curiosity seekers
does not apply to this entrance.

In 1941, with the opening of the new criminal courts building, the Women's Court remained at Jefferson Market for a
time, but its adjunctive division for wayward minors was
moved to 100 Centre Street; the latter was benefited by
larger quarters with adequate courtroom and probation
office space separate from the other criminal courts. The
transition marked a new, formal recognition of the distinctive character of the Court and the attempt to substitute

6 Laws of 1918, c. 419.   7 Laws of 1918, c. 418.
8 Inferior Criminal Courts Act, sec. 100.

more systematic procedural methods for the experimental ones. Finally, by order of the Board of Magistrates in March, 1944, the Wayward Minor Court was established as an entirely separate, specialized court.[9] Its province continued to be limited to incorrigibles under the Wayward Minor Statute and, as a practical matter, largely to sex delinquents. Specialization, which in itself was desirable, thus came about at the expense of limiting the range of action which was needed for the care of adolescent girls. In July, 1945, the Court was rechristened Girl's Term.

The Children's Court.—In 1893 the New York Legislature established a rule under which separate trials for children might be held, and in 1902 it more specifically provided that some of the judges of the courts of special sessions should be specially assigned to try children's cases exclusively. Criticism by the Page Commission of conditions in the special sessions children's division resulted in the establishment of a new children's court division after the passage of the Inferior Criminal Courts Act (1910) ; again, however, the division was to be a part of the Court of Special Sessions. The act provided for a probation department to work with children, and in 1911 the judges began to appoint officers to fulfill that function. The political character of appointments led the Court of Appeals, in 1912, to require that probation workers should be selected competitively by civil service. In 1915 the legislature provided for the establishment of a separate children's court with assignment by the mayor of five special sessions justices to that court. The year 1924 saw the passage of the Children's Court Act, which established a separate and independent tribunal in New York City, taking the court out of the jurisdiction of the criminal law. Six justices were appointed for a period of ten years each, and a probation department staffed by fifty-nine officers

9 New York *Times,* for February 23, 1945.

and equipped with clinical facilities was organized. By 1928 the Court had eight judges. In 1933 the Family Court, which had been a part of the magistrates' system since its origin in 1921, was combined with the Children's Court to create the Domestic Relations Court. This new court combined both divisions for unified service to the family and its children.[10]

Thus, briefly, these courts evolved. Through their presence and experience the functions and jurisdiction of the Wayward Minor Court have been both limited and directed. It is proposed now to consider in more detail the relation of the Wayward Minor Statute and its administration to the evolution of the courts.

The statutory definition of the wayward minor has been quoted above.[11] The central provisions of the law as passed in 1923, and as amended in 1925 and 1929, do not differ greatly from earlier "incorrigibility" statutes, and they resemble the juvenile court statutes of many states.[12] Apparently the earliest direct predecessor of the present statute is to be found in an act of 1882 [13] designed to control those girls from fourteen to twenty-one who, charged with being prostitutes, had professed a desire to reform; such persons might be detained in one of the sectarian institutions of the city as specified in the statute. The law was modified in 1886 [14] to cover any female over the age of twelve; the list of offenses, moreover, was extended so that the law covered any such person who was found in a reputed house of prostitution, frequenting the company of prostitutes or thieves, or associating with vicious and dissolute persons, or who was willfully disobedient to parent or guardian, and in danger of

[10] Laws of 1933, c. 482.
[11] See *supra*, Chapter II and *infra*, Appendix A.
[12] See Lou, *Juvenile Courts in the United States*, pp. 53–54, for a summary of the specifications of delinquency from court statutes of several states.
[13] Laws of 1882, c. 410, sec. 1466. See Appendix for its terms.
[14] Laws of 1886, c. 353, sec. 1466, subd. 1. See Appendix A.

becoming morally depraved; also included were prostitutes or persons of intemperate habits who professed a desire to reform. Incarceration was to be in the same sectarian institutions as those previously indicated. The laws of 1903 broadened this statute to include any girl over the age of sixteen who had been convicted of petit larcency but had not previously been an inmate of the penitentiary.[15]

It becomes apparent upon closer inspection that these earlier laws differed from the Wayward Minor Statute in the following respects:

1. Under the provisions of all three of the earlier statutes the offender might be convicted by her confession. This is not true under the present law, which requires that adjudication be based upon "competent testimony." (It appears, however, that decisions are, in fact, based upon defendants' admissions in numerous cases.)

2. The age range of the earlier laws included the juvenile as well as the adolescent delinquent, and the laws of 1886 and 1903 established no upper age limit. The jurisdiction of the Wayward Minor Court is specifically limited to girls from sixteen to twenty-one years of age.

3. In the new statutes, language varying slightly from that of the older laws was used in defining the coverage of offenses, though there was great similarity and some identity in the terminology. In the earlier years of the Wayward Minor Court, complaints founded in larceny, especially shoplifting, and other serious crimes and offenses were heard in the Court. More recently some narrowing of its control has resulted from interpretation, since only subsection 5 of the act is now applied generally. As indicated above, chiefly sex complaints are received by the Court today, though numerous other types of minor misbehavior are occasionally alleged in the cases brought before the Court.

15 Laws of 1903, c. 436. See Appendix A.

4. The Wayward Minors' Act more specifically differentiates the status of "wayward minor" from that of a "criminal" and indicates the court process to be an adjudication rather than a conviction. This expresses the contemporary belief that helping a delinquent to avoid a criminal record is in itself a crime preventive, and that therefore the full force of criminal procedure should be shunned when possible.

5. In practice the Wayward Minors' Act is applied only in cases where complaints can be obtained from parent, relative, or guardian—apparently because of the statutory provision concerning willful disobedience. The operation of the earlier statutes was not so restricted, and the police occasionally brought in girls who had been found in circumstances which would subject them to criminal court treatment. For the most part, however, complaints were made under the earlier laws by parents or guardians.

6. Finally, the modern statute, evincing the trend toward extra-institutional though official treatment of the young, declares probation to be the preferred form of treatment. Yet all the statutes have had a common basic purpose: to control the disobedient and unmanageable child who has eluded parental control. Just as in the administration of the Wayward Minors' Act it is subsection 5 which is used almost exclusively in complaints and adjudication, so in the earlier statutes the "willful disobedience of the child" was the chief point in issue: they were primarily "parents' laws," designed to assist in disciplining the child and adolescent and, in that connection, chiefly to restrict and punish sexual misconduct.

The laws of 1882, 1886, and 1903 were enacted during the period of relatively undifferentiated courts and were applied in the ordinary police courts of the day. Later, after those tribunals had been established, young girls were taken into the night courts and into the Women's Court. Until 1917 separate hearings, dockets, and records for children's cases were not even required by statute. As noted above, distinct and specialized children's courts were rather slow to develop, and in consequence the incorrigibility laws were applied for a number of years to child and adolescent without systematized methods for differentiating in procedure between age levels. It thus developed that the various age groups and their behavior problems (disobedience and sex offenses) were treated without any clear enunciation of the specific offenses designed to be controlled.[16]

Clear statutory differentiation occurred, however, in 1922 and 1923. In the former year the passage of sections defining juvenile delinquency in the penal law confined this status to individuals below the age of sixteen [17] (though control once established could be continued up to the age of twenty-one). It is interesting to note the striking similarity between the last four subsections of this law and the provisions of the earlier incorrigibility statutes. The delinquency status was designed to accomplish similar purposes of controlling the "ungovernable" child and of providing a remedy for the contaminating associations of juveniles; the status therefore provided, in addition, for the separation of children from older offenders in trial and treatment. The statute preserved and advanced the earlier purpose—in new language—of preventing the moral impairment of the child.

The Wayward Minors' Act of 1923 resembled even more closely the incorrigibility statutes, specifically incorporating the provision (implicit in the judicial construction of the Children's Court Act) for treatment of the disobedient adolescent who was deemed in danger of becoming "morally

[16] It appears to have been rather commonly true of the statutes defining delinquency and incorrigibility which were enacted around this time that the substantive norms were very vague. The motivation was a protective reaction against legalism as applied to youth, with as yet little appreciation of the counter-values of order and system. See American Law Reports Annotated VL, 1533.
[17] See Laws of 1922, c. 547.

depraved." These later laws are obviously of comparable indefiniteness as to the substantive offenses designed to be prohibited. Indeed, though the necessity of a definite charge and specific proof has been iterated by the higher courts, both for juvenile and for adolescent adjudication under the statutes, little has been added in concrete definition by the case law, save through the exclusion of certain conduct declared not to be a ground for bringing the laws into force.

From 1923 to 1933 the wayward minor law was applied in the criminal courts of the magistrates' and special sessions systems to defendants who differed from the usual offender in chronological age. Then further development in the courts tended to segregate more completely the classes of offenders and to specialize their treatment. In 1933 the charge of juvenile delinquency became the exclusive province of the children's division of the Domestic Relations Court. And in 1936 the Wayward Minor Statutes came to be applied chiefly, though not exclusively, by the wayward minor division of the Women's Court. This institutional bifurcation tended to concentrate sexual offenses within the province of the Wayward Minors' Act, partly because the jurisdiction of the Women's Court was mostly confined to prostitutional offenses.[18] Some of the adolescent girls brought into the court, nevertheless, had merely been disobedient to their parents; many, however, were pre-prostitutes.

There has thus continued among the wayward minor complaints a substantial proportion based upon truancy, running away from home, and keeping late hours. These charges, however applicable to the status of juvenile delinquency, were

---

[18] It is interesting to note that as the application of the Wayward Minor Statute evolved, its elastic terms permitted the corruption of practices in the Women's Court; the Seabury investigation revealed that alleged prostitutes who refused to pay "tribute" for protection were sometimes adjudged to be wayward minors in the absence of evidence to support a complaint in prostitution.

of questionable weight in proving the "danger of moral depravity," in terms of sexual misconduct, which Section VII–A was commonly thought to require. Such charges were and are supported in the Court, however, since the influence of the earlier association of jurisdiction and offense persists in current practice. Cases appear in which, though there is no evidence of direct sexual misconduct (or other moral depravity, if that expression have legal definite reference to nonsexual conduct), the girl is adjudicated a wayward minor and either placed on probation or committed.

In the days of the incorrigibility statutes, venereal examinations were given to prostitutes after conviction and, occasionally, to convicted minors, but only upon request from a relative or a probation officer. In 1936 the Women's Court began giving examinations before trial under the provision of Article 17b of the Public Health Law; since that law had been passed in 1917, this was a somewhat belated procedure. As in the instance of those charged with prostitution, it became customary to give the Board of Health examination to adolescents against whom sexual misconduct was charged. In the development of procedures in the Wayward Minor Court, however, that court has not been consistent in requiring an examination, even where sex offenses are alleged. Such a requirement has been more common during the administrations of some judges than of others, and it is not entirely standard procedure even today.

Whereas in the Wayward Minor Court the health (V.D.) report is submitted at the hearing, the method used in the Women's Court appears to be a fairer compromise. There tests are taken before trial, but the information contained in the Board of Health reports is sealed until after trial. Discharged defendants, then, who are found to be diseased may still be treated noncorrectionally under the public health law. Thus, theoretically, the mind of the judge is not prej-

udiced during trial by information on the defendant's health
which is certainly not conclusive as to guilt, and yet treatment of the infected is still assured. Unfortunately—and unnecessarily—the positive report papers differ appreciably in
bulk from the papers of negative report, so that the protection of the defendant against this prejudicial information is
somewhat illusory. In conformity with the changing statutes
and general practice, and in the interest of rehabilitation, the
courts have also extended their use of probation. Both lines
of growth reveal the developing faith in the ameliorative influences of official but extra-institutional procedures and the
disillusionment which has resulted from the effects of in-
carcerating children and adolescents. Thus from the Children's Court practices were diffused an emphasis on probation and an associated inclination to deal with broadly
familial and social problems. The Women's Court, in contrast,
directed more consideration toward sex offenses, health examinations, and a more distinctly punitive approach.

   Further influence from the historical association of these
courts and the continuing spread of ideas among them, some
of which are of highly dubious value, appears in the adaptation by the Wayward Minor Court of methods which have
been developed in the Children's Courts: for example, that of
social intake coupled with unofficial treatment, and of social
investigation prior to a hearing of the issue. (The intake
process in the Children's Court involves the obtaining by an
adjustment board of social data concerning the defendant
and her family from parent, relative, or guardian, the information being secured at the time the complaint is originally presented. Frequently, then, informal treatment is
applied without court action. In the adolescent court the
intake information is received by a probation officer.)

   In the children's courts there has been an extensive development of "unofficial probation," applied to juveniles not

adjudicated by the court; thus official court treatment is frequently avoided, and the case remains at the intake and adjustment level. This technique has been borrowed by the Wayward Minor Court and integrated with other procedures drawn from the juvenile court level. Justification is sought on the grounds that these methods that have been used by children's courts for a generation in their attempts at individualized and preventive therapy constitute progressive, socialized justice for adolescents as well as for children. It is such rationalization which encourages the perpetuation of error and its spread from existing institutions to new and emergent ones. The argument forecloses criticism by the implicit assumption of the validity of established techniques that have been denoted liberal. Unfortunately, this sort of projection of the practices of one court to another is especially congenial to the reasoning of court personnel; hence the adoption of the precedents of unofficial procedure. It makes for uncritical formalization and diffusion of practices in our crescive institutions.

This trend toward unofficial work is one of the extremely important and challenging phenomena found generally in the modern tribunals for the young. Most courts are proud of their informal, extralegal supervision, which they usually rationalize on the grounds that thus is accomplished all that a court proceeding can achieve, while at the same time the child is protected from official court contact. Yet, as Frederick A. Moran has said in summarizing some of the problems of juvenile courts before the National Conference of Social Work,[19] these unofficial cases are usually ones that are recognized as not meriting judicial action because of their trivial character. "Issues that can be solved by voluntary adjustment obviously should not be brought to the

[19] "New Light on the Juvenile Courts and Probation," reprinted in the *Year Book,* National Probation Association (1930), pp. 66–75.

attention of the court." Such social work should be carried on under noncourt auspices.

There has thus been a forcing upward into the adolescent level of methods used in judicial processing of children. These techniques developed in the children's courts from the theory that when a social problem exists, the court should deal with it for the protection of the child and that, since the primary purpose of the court is such protection, it need not regard seriously the strict civil rights of the alleged offender as is required by formal due process in the criminal courts. The same principle is being carried over to the adolescent courts.

In contrast with this trend, the Association of Juvenile Court Judges of America at its conference in May, 1940, formulated a resolution expressing in clear terms the need to preserve the rights of the child-defendant:

The juvenile court is designed, within the scope of its legal powers, for the care and protection of dependent and neglected children; for safeguarding their interests and enforcing the obligations of responsible adults; and for the correction, re-education, rehabilitation, and redirection of delinquent youth. *Although operating as a socialized court, it must recognize and protect the rights of those brought before it as provided by law and the Constitution.* [Italics not in the original.] [20]

Even in administrative proceedings, substantial conformity with these due-process rules is required. Thus in a case in New York involving the removal of a policeman by the Commissioner it was stated that:

While the hearing may be more or less informal, the trial must be fair in all substantial respects. Some latitude is allowed as to rules of evidence, methods of examination and the like, but no essential

[20] See Cobb, "Social and Legal Aspects of the Children's Court," address delivered on February 6, 1945, before a joint meeting of the committees of the Court of Domestic Relations, of the Association of the Bar, and the County Lawyers Association.

element of a fair trial can be dispensed with unless waived, and
no vital safeguard violated without rendering the judgment of
conviction subject to reversal upon review. A fair trail, according
to existing practice, requires that the accused shall be confronted
by the witnesses against him and given an opportunity to hear
their statements under oath, and to cross examine them to a reasonable extent. Hearsay evidence cannot be received; evidence cannot
be taken in the absence of the accused and trier of the fact can find
the fact only on the evidence and not on his own knowledge.
Greenebaum v. Bingham, 201 N.Y., 343, 347.[21]

Chief Justice Cobb, of the Court of Domestic Relations,
has trenchantly criticized the numerous practices of children's courts whereby the basic rights of due process are
denied to the young. Particularly and effectively he attacks
the procedures of pre-trial investigation, adjudication based
on the "total personality" rather than on specific conduct,
and informal or unofficial probation supervision without
adjudication. The trend of these tribunals he describes in
these words:

Become legalistic for the occasion, the supporters of unre-
stricted social processes in a court of law for children and their
parents, have embraced the catchwords *"parens patriae"* and
"chancery" as something equivalent to little or no legal restraint
so they may cast the beneficent safeguards of due process of law
into the limbo of forgotten things. Nothing could be more fallacious. As we have seen, children must be duly adjudicated before a
children's court can assume authority. The flesh and blood parents
may not be lightly thrust aside in favor of the state as a foster
parent.

The appallingly perverted doctrine of *"parens patriae"* so
specious that it has wheedled the judiciary and even cast its spell
over some courts of appeal, has in it the germ of case work domi-
nation. It has led to the legal baptism by legislatures of youths up
to the voting age as children, and has made a rubber stamp in some
states of the judicial function to the point that it has well nigh
surrendered to social processes in the guise of "probation," in-

21 *Ibid.*

stead of jealously protecting both child and parent from infringement of their constitutional rights and personal privileges. Both children and insane are wards of the state, but are they to be prejudged by determining them to be such without regard to forms of law? [22]

At this pont should be stressed certain basic differences which make inapplicable to the adolescent some of the principles and methods which, beneficially or otherwise, are applied to children:

1. Whereas the Children's Court also has some jurisdiction over errant parents through its Adjustment Bureau and the use of orders of protection to guard the child from abuse or exploitation,[23] the Wayward Minor Court lacks the official power to control or punish them.

2. Behavior of the pre-adolescent child which warrants social investigation and supervision does not necessarily establish a standard for adolescent conformity under the law. The extent to which the adolescent should be permitted by law to assert independence of parental controls, for example, is certainly greater than that safely permissible to children.

3. The Adjustment Bureau, as a central agency of the Children's Court, functions through informal supervision and treatment to aid a majority of alleged delinquents without official court action. The court for adolescent girls lacks many of the facilities available to the Adjustment Bureau. There too, however, the practice of placing the offender on unofficial probation without adjudication, in circumventing judicial determination of the child's conduct and rights entrusts excessive discretion to the probation staff in dealing with cases which may not merit treatment by court per-

[22] *Ibid.*
[23] Penal Law, sec. 486, 494. See *In re Carl,* 22 N.Y.S. 2d. 782, Dom. Rel. Court, 1940: "Children are to be protected against their own parents when the parents exceed reasonable bounds in correcting them."

sonnel or which may need treatment different from that given
by the bureau.

4. Finally, it is significant to note that, in accordance
with Justice Cobb's emphasis upon the preservation of the
procedural rights of the alleged delinquent, the Children's
Court has abandoned the technique of probation investigation and report prior to adjudication. The child may be
found delinquent today only if he be legally proven so by
proper evidence. Thus has disappeared from the juvenile
courts of the city a method which had been rationalized on
the ground that the tribunals were civil, not criminal, and
that they dealt with children whose rights of due process
need be considered less seriously than those of adults. The
Wayward Minor Court, lacking either excuse for its anti-
legal "socializing" of its procedures, not only borrowed the
method, but has persisted in applying it within the framework of a criminal court system to legally adult individuals.

In addition there are factors which apply to both situations, but even more vigorously in the case of the wayward
adolescent. Neither the Children's Court nor the Wayward
Minor Court is equipped with the necessary diagnostic and
treatment facilities or staffed with sufficiently trained personnel to operate as a general social agency in behalf of
family welfare. The Wayward Minor Court, particularly in
view of its material and jurisdictional lacks, needs to avoid
attempting the impossible in social and familial adjustment
when investigation reveals problems which are beyond the
skill or the power of the Court. Moreover, institutional facilities and probation resources of the Court are unsuited to
carry out effective prevention and reform. Certainly, too,
the trial practices of the domestic relations court system do
not justify depriving the adolescent defendant of the most
basic protections established in the law.[24] Moreover, the chil-

24 See *People* v. *Slater,* 29 N.Y.S. 2d. 164, 176 Misc. 641.

dren's courts are civil, not criminal courts; their treatment facilities are not so tinged with punitive assumptions. The criticisms, on social and legal grounds, which are made of these children's court procedures apply with even greater force to tribunals for the adolescent. It is perpetuation and aggravation of error to spread methods which are rooted in a false philosophy.

CURRENT COURT PROCEDURES

The procedures used by the Wayward Minor Court are briefly outlined here to indicate the major stages and the ordering of them which have evolved in this court: [25]

Intake.—All complainants are interviewed by a probation officer in order to determine the basis of the complaint and numerous facts concerning the social history of the defendant and her family. As indicated above, the complaints are ordinarily made by parent or guardian. The judges usually insist that when a case is brought in by the police or by a social agency the legal guardian's signature must be available before a complaint will be issued.

Arraignment.—Arraignment generally takes place on the next court day, at which time the defendant is informed of the charge against her and of her rights under the law. An adjournment is then customary to permit investigation of the case history by the probation department.

Interim disposition.—During the period of the adjournment a temporary disposition is made in one of three ways:

1. Parole: the girl is returned to her parents, relatives, or friends, or to an agency.

2. Remand: the girl is sent to one or more institutional shelters or to a hospital for custody, diagnosis, or the beginning of treatment.

[25] For more complete analysis, see *infra,* Chapter VI.

3. Parole and remand: occasionally it is found that both types of interim disposition are required in a particular case, usually one involving a series of adjournments.

Hearing and adjudication.—At this time testimony is given by the complainant and by the witnesses, if any, in support of the complaint; the defendant may answer if she wishes. Generally the judge confers with the probation officer concerning the latter's findings on the social history and offense of the case. Some of the judges actually read the officer's reports, though at least one judge pursues the policy of avoiding such possibly prejudicial information from report or officer. If the Court finds against the defendant, she is "adjudicated" to the "status" of wayward minor rather than convicted of a crime.

Final disposition.—Upon adjudication the defendant may be subjected to either of two general types of treatment:

1. Official probation: The offender is placed under the supervision of an officer of the Court for a definite period. If the girl fails during that period, the probation may be revoked, and the girl will be committed.

2. Commitment: the girl is sent to a private, sectarian, or state institution, as provided by statute, for an indeterminate period up to three years. If she fails at the institution of original commitment, the sentence may be revoked and the girl recommitted to another institution or, rarely, put on probation.

If the girl is not adjudicated, some control over her may still be retained through "unofficial supervision," [26] either by an officer of the Court or a representative of a social agency. Thus the stigma of a formal adjudication may be avoided, and since the duration of treatment is indefinite, it may theoretically be made to depend upon the discovered

[26] For further consideration of the operation of unofficial supervision, see *infra*, Chapters II and VI.

need. This procedure, it has been indicated, tempts the Court to deal with nondelinquency cases.

A noteworthy characteristic of the Court is its administrative flexibility in processing. Inasmuch as the legislature has established only very general standards limiting procedure and policy, much is left to judicial discretion in the methods of detailed implementation. Consequently, in the establishment and execution of its norms, the Court has operated somewhat informally and administratively after the fashion of a quasi-judicial tribunal.[27]

Yet it must be borne in mind that this court is not an administrative agency but a part of the criminal court system, functioning under an inadequate statute of the criminal code, and with narrowly limited facilities of treatment. It is not free to operate with the informality, freedom, and resources of a noncourt agency. The Court and its agencies carry the stigma of the criminal system. If it were strictly an administrative agency, of course, the Court would be warranted in applying some methods and procedures inappropriate to a court and might well also have the fuller coöperation of public and private social agencies, and probably a fuller integration in the entire processing of cases.

[27] Thus it is necessary, in order to achieve a readjustment of the individual offender, to establish rules for her conduct (especially during probation or parole) which may vary considerably from case to case. Too, there is need in the Court for a careful regulatory and supervisory function in accordance with a generalized ultimate purpose of moralization but individualized to the requirements of the particular offender and her family. In the employment of advisory and informative assistance (e. g., from psychiatrist, probation officer, social agency, shelter representative) and the application of informal procedural methods rather than strict and technical rules, the Court resembles an administrative or quasi-judicial tribunal. To a lesser degree, but in a way quite similar to that of many administrative organizations of modern government, the Court purports to deal with the individual, not only judicially in adjudication according to certain standards, but legislatively in the establishment or specification of those standards and administratively in their execution.

Roscoe Pound has stated the problem of attempting through a court to deal with matters of intimate human behavior:

Child placement involves administrative authority over one of the most intimate and cherished of human relations. *The powers of the Star Chamber were a trifle in comparison with those of our juvenile courts and courts of domestic relations.* The latter may bring about a revolution as easily as did the former. It is well known that too often the placing of a child in a home or even in an institution is done casually or perfunctorily or even arbitrarily. Moreover effective preventive work through these courts requires looking into much more than the bad external conditions of a household, such as poverty or neglect or lack of discipline. Internal conditions, a complex of habits, attitudes, and reactions, may have to be dealt with and this means administrative treatment of the most intimate affairs of life. *Even with the most superior personnel, these tribunals call for legal checks.* [Italics not in the original.] [28]

The Court has attempted to adapt its methods to the putative requirements of the individual case, thus displaying an attempt to follow the clinical ideal of the individualization of justice. Its experience has shown, however, the peculiar difficulties which may thwart the realization of the purposes behind that ideal. The very informality and lack of legislatively prescribed norms have encouraged *ad hoc* devices in experimental attempts to solve the problem represented by each case. It appears that at its inception there was little teleology in the Court more specific than the rather generalized benevolent purpose to aid in the solution of the problems of adolescent girls.[29]

[28] Pauline Young, *Social Treatment in Probation and Delinquency*, Foreword by Roscoe Pound, p. xxvii.
[29] As Patrick J. Shelly, Chief Probation Officer, summarized this point of view: "The Wayward Minors' Act is, perhaps, the most salutary piece of legislation passed in many years by the legislature. Prior to its enactment, a criminal charge of some kind had to be made against a wayward, so-called incorrigible youth. The principle underlying the diagnosis and

The scope of the Court's work was not clearly conceived, and its fluctuating methods appear not to have been harmonized with any specific set of goals. As a progressive court resting on the shoulders of its probation department, its success was to depend in a large measure on the social investigation and treatment carried out by its officers. Yet the staff established to implement the broad purposes of the Court was numerically inadequate to the size of the task and amazingly varied in the propensities and predilections of its members. It had an asset, however, in the sincerity of interest and the diligent efforts of some workers whose training and ability excelled the general run of New York City's underpaid probation officers.[30]

The Court began its operation, then, under a triple handicap: understaffing, legislation vague as to substantive norms and court objectives, and an unspecific procedural scheme, apparently guided by a desire to use social work techniques and to function somewhat informally. A further limitation which is general in our court systems but peculiarly acute in the magistrates' courts was the lack of that coördinated

---

treatment of male and female adolescents is the same, viz., individualization. There are, of course, different inherent motivating influences at work in the lives of all growing boys and girls and it is only after a study of the individual as a whole, that constructive advice and help can be given." Kross, *Procedures for Dealing with Wayward Minors in New York City*.

[30] The entrance salary for probation officers in the magistrates' courts, who are supposed to have had a proper educational training—college work in sociology—and social work experience, is $1680 per annum. The maximum salary is $2399. As a result there has been little interest among those trained in social work in contributing their talents to the field of probation, little coöperation between the probation departments and the social work schools. See the New York *Times* for December 21, 1943, for the difficulty of obtaining probation workers. For recommendations for the extension of probation services, see the New York *Times* for December 11, 1940; January 2, 1942; and January 26, 1942. "Mayor recalls that he has repeatedly attempted to correct conditions in the Probation Division. Especially to reduce the salaries for probation officers, as fixed by the judges." New York *Times* for January 29, 1939.

planning which is essential to the evolution of desirably effective processing of offenders. The special need of the Court was to develop procedures which were reasonably regular and yet varied and flexible: to develop and then to apply comparable techniques in comparable situations of behavior and character, where experience taught the effectiveness of those techniques. No provision was made, however, for self-evaluation, for interchange of information and discussion of problems, for planning of program and redefinition of methods and purposes. So much of this as occurred remained in the field of the haphazard.

Thus the institutions of the Court have grown, not only in crescive pattern, but in one unaccompanied by any consistent effort at building teamwork and an interchange of experience. It has attempted to accomplish conflicting imprecise purposes with inconsistent and often ill-fitting methods. The jealous autonomy of judges, of probation officers, and of institutional officials—and the operational independence among these categories—has continued virtually undisturbed. This, together with the lack, until recent months, of staff conferences or case supervision, has contributed to a developmental confusion. The result—at least at the beginning —is a flexibility that, when viewed as the work of a single institutional system, has had the variation of the capricious.

On the other hand, the very fact of the establishment of a specialized tribunal for the adolescent girl with an attempt to coördinate available facilities has constituted, ideologically, a long step toward more effective treatment of the young. There is, of course, a real value in the availability of versatile methods of procedure and treatment with the readiness of a recently established court to use them. And, despite the lack of formalized channeling of information, the Court has profited somewhat from trial-and-error learning. There have crystallized certain general uniformities of procedure observable in most of the cases. It should, indeed, be possible in the future, through integration of the information which has and will become available from the agents and agencies of the Court, to arrive at informed and more systematized methods of adjusting the available facilities to the requirements of individual cases. Flexibility will become more ordered and more intelligently directed when, instead of depending so largely upon the idiosyncratic preferences of its officers, the Court comes to operate in terms of their combined experiences and judgment.

THE NEW WAYWARD MINOR STATUTE

A bill advocated by the Court was submitted to the legislature for approval, passed the Senate and Assembly, and on April 16, 1945, received Governor Thomas E. Dewey's signature.[31] It aims at providing none of the needed limitations upon court discretion and authority. Rather, like prior amendments recommended by this tribunal, and in accordance with the general trend of institutional development in the Court, it seeks chiefly to make official some of the methods which have been used informally and to extend still further what the Court persists in believing to be its inadequate powers. A study of Assembly bills No. 1938 and 1939 shows the following to be the chief changes sought, their character appearing especially significant in the light of the criticisms directed at the present methods of operation in the Court.

The first and most striking amendment empowers the Court to make institutional remands or parole for fifteen days without the consent of the defendant or her parent and thereafter to add a further fifteen-day period with consent, these periods to fall before adjudication. Thus the trend, so popular and dangerous in the courts for the young in New York, of applying treatment before trial is given statutory

[31] See Appendix C for terms of the new statute.

sanction with little curb upon its use. Indeed, until 1946, a formal technical consent had been required before the Court could order an extended remand. As though the amendment were insufficient, however, further power of the same sort is provided in another section of the law dealing with methods of disposition of the cases. These are, for the most part, methods of final disposition (and, as will be noted below, the bill provides for one needed change), but somewhat strangely the amendment includes provision for another possible period of thirty-day remand during "continued probation investigation" before final sentencing. There is greater merit in this section of the act, if taken alone—or in conjunction with appropriate protections to the defendant—since it would require adjudication before this remand and would allow for treatment of shorter duration than does the indeterminate sentence. In the context of present procedure and the whole statute, however, it merely crystallizes the current informal methods used in the Court—with all the above-mentioned risks of attempting to apply court therapy to the total personality even when (as indicated in the law) the diagnostic investigations are presumably incomplete.

As implied above, the act also provides statutory sanction for the pre-adjudication social inquiry into the defendant's "habits, surroundings, circumstances and tendencies," thus continuing the approach of adjudicating and treating on the basis of personality and social problem. The act provides that the statements made by the defendant during the investigation may not be used against her or against her interest, but they may be considered in applying treatment after her adjudication. Rather an anomaly! The results of the investigation are to be available before trial, but they may not be used "against her interest." It becomes difficult indeed to understand why, then, the inquiry must be carried on at the early stage of processing. If the statement is to mean what

it says why, in the name of judicial efficiency, should the
Court not wait until after adjudication and then study only
those whom unprejudiced evidence indicated will require diagnosis and treatment? If the findings bear only upon official
and final disposition, they need not be sought in advance of
trial; rather, the evidence brought out at trial should serve
to indicate both need and direction of social inquiry. It is,
perhaps, an unconsciously revealing statement in the act
that the information obtained may be used after (not *if*)
the girl has been adjudged a wayward minor.

The statute then proceeds in general terms to assure to the
defendant her legal rights in the hearing and a determination of the results on the basis of competent evidence. In the
light of the act as a whole and current procedures which it
is designed to vindicate, the provision for due process appears to be a perfunctory and *pro forma* declaration of good
intentions, such as that frequently found in statutes of this
sort.

An important part of the act is the section which is intended to widen the methods of final disposition. As indicated above, it provides for the alternative of using a short,
definite term on remand after the defendant is adjudged but
before final sentence. The "further investigation by a probation officer" during remand is scarcely sufficient justification for such a commitment. One might gather from the
words of the act that the section grew out of the need of an
additional month of investigation beyond that provided in
the pre-trial period. This does not make sense. In reality it
would seem that the "remand" is a euphemism for a direct
commitment of short duration and that it would be followed
generally by suspension of sentence, at least in cases where
the girl has "responded favorably" to treatment. The section
provides specifically, too, for suspended judgment as a type
of ultimate disposition, thus sanctioning a device useful to

the Court, but one which some judges have hesitated to use in the absence of specific provision therefor.

Bill No. 1939 to amend the code of criminal procedure by amplifying the definition of the wayward minor is also disappointing when examined in the light of the changes needed. The five clauses defining the wayward minor under the present statute are left intact (except for the elimination of one unimportant conjunction), though only the fifth is used by the Court today. Clause 6 would cover the runaway girl who is also "morally depraved" or in danger of becoming so. Clause 7 is an omnibus clause obviously difficult to apply because of the need to prove a willful endangering of morals or health—all vague, tenuous concepts which by their nature should tend to prevent adjudication but which may easily be used, under a liberal interpretation, to adjudge wide varieties of nondelinquents. The changes fall far short of providing the needed definiteness of conduct-description for fair adjudication. Nor do they make for the real widening of jurisdiction to include trial of girls who have committed serious offenses—an objective which this writer believes to be an entirely natural and desirable direction of court growth. Instead, the new act promises, not only to preserve, but to add to the confusion inherent in the present statute's antiquated, vague, and moralistic foundation.

The present practices of starting treatment under remand, placing an offender on unofficial probation, granting extended adjournments prior to a hearing, and other informal procedures, violate the fundamental principle of case work practice that therapy should not be begun before diagnosis of the case has been completed. The new Wayward Minor Statute will tend to institutionalize this error by specifically sanctioning lengthy periods of remand before a hearing on the case is held; the time is to be spent, presumably, in continued probation investigation, although the practice is apparently designed to perpetuate present procedures of informal supervision. Any argument that these probation periods are necessary to shorten the unduly long indeterminate sentences is clearly absurd: the way to shorten a commitment term is to do so in so many words, by statute and only *after* adjudication, when diagnosis is complete.

4

Facilities

IT HAS BEEN SUGGESTED that the basic difficulties in the operation of the Wayward Minor Court are found in personnel
problems and in other inadequacies of the facilities available
to the Court as well as in the limitations of the statute under
which it operates. Some of these deficiencies may be pointed
up here to show their relation to the confused objectives of
the tribunal and to the methods which are used now and may
be used in the future.

THE MAGISTRATES

There are currently, in 1946, three magistrates, of differing religious faiths, sitting in the Court, each serving for
periods of two weeks. In earlier years there have been times
when only one judge sat there; other times when there have
been as many as six or more. Relative to the case load there
is no problem of quantitative inadequacy in the assignment
of judges to the Court nor, it is believed, is there today such
a problem in regard to the frequency of court sessions, since
the Wayward Minor Court days have been extended from
one to two and, finally, to three days a week. (Some officers
of the Court, however, believe that the load is sufficient to
warrant daily sessions.) On the other hand, serious anomalies
do emerge from the values and traditions of the magistrates,
particularly from the incongruity of these values, both with
some of the ideal objectives of the Court and with the views
of other groups that function in the processing of the adolescent.

The magistrates who sit in this court are motivated—like

other judges—by a series of characteristic attitudes. Most noticeable, perhaps, is the fact that they are swayed by legalistic traditions to which they are conditioned by reason of their formal training in the law and by their bench experience. This bias predisposes the magistrates to hold fast to traditional court procedures, to customary methods of handling cases, and to conservative views concerning responsibility and punishment, and thus to apply within an experimental tribunal the ancient, formal methods of receiving and weighing evidence.

Associated with this legalistic bent are the directives of habit which move the magistrates as members of a political and institutional system; these must affect their thinking, feeling, and conduct on the bench. The judges who sit in the girls' court are among those assigned to the Women's Court. They also rotate through the district courts of the city. To some degree their attitudes and methods bear the marks of the Women's Court: the atmosphere of fatalism, repression, moralism, and an inclination to disbelieve defendants who—in Women's Court—are described as "chronic liars." Similar reactions are apparent in the Wayward Minor Court as well.

This experience in a rotating magistracy appears also to incline some of the judges to treat their duties in the adolescent court as merely another part of the job, something to be disposed of as quickly and as easily as possible in the hurried stream of cases summarily processed. One judge, who prided himself upon the speed with which he disposed of the lengthy court calendar, seemed scarcely to attempt to understand the special problems of the Court and its defendants.

Another related traditional and motivating drive, characterized by a kind of intellectual myopia, is discernible in the Court: a tendency to ignore or to underemphasize the clinical values in personality diagnosis and treatment. The customary lack of training of the judiciary in biological and social sciences—amended by a few judges in later informal study—limits their tolerance for nonlegal techniques of handling offenders. The suggestion that the Court resort to such devices as referral to social agencies, unofficial handling, psychiatric examinations, and probation recommendations for treatment sometimes finds the incumbent judge adamant or, at the least, unsympathetic. The magistrate's legal but non-psychological training, associated with political traditions, apparently inclines him to attempt to handle cases of young girls formalistically, preserving to himself the fullest rights of determining dispositions. (The approach of one judge, who has had psychological and clinical training, is refreshingly different in its emphasis upon clinical investigation and treatment.) As in other efforts to establish treatment-prescription on a more specialized and scientific basis, the judges have sought, for the most part, to preserve their dispositive powers intact.

Finally, there is observable in varying degrees among the different judges a pressure of moralistic righteousness in acute symptomatic forms where—as in this court—sex offenses are adjudicated. This is not, of course, a distinctly judicial characteristic, but reflects a conservative cultural traditionalism in a conservative and traditional profession, and reflects, moreover, our official, public, explicit line of morals. It requires no more than one such pietistic magistrate to unleash the fullness of Hell's fury among the sinful; for by his special zeal and great exertion he is enabled to stamp the Court and its wayward subjects more indelibly than do his more tolerant fellows.

As W. Norwood East, a specialist in this field, has written concerning the problems of judgments on sexual offenses:

Sexual offenses are more liable to be misjudged by prejudice and ignorance than most other forms of criminal behavior, and bias is almost inevitable if conduct is reviewed solely in the light of narrow personal experience and the tastes and distastes of the assessor. Many persons of both sexes are grossly ignorant on sexual matters in spite of the modern tendency to discuss the subject with a considerable degree of freedom. Some husbands, in effect, repeatedly commit rape upon their wives because they do not understand the art of married life, and do not realise that a woman is at a disadvantage unless a psychical approach precedes each physical contact; sexually anaesthetic men and women, who are incompetent to pass judgment upon the inter-relationship of sexes, may be called upon to assess the guilt of a sexual offender; and sexual behavior is often assessed by persons who regard any sexual activity as perverse unless it conforms to their accustomed and restricted pattern of behavior.[1]

On the positive side, the magistrates assigned to the Wayward Minor Court have generally been selected for their interest in the problems of adjustment which come before that tribunal. Too, through a limited rotation in the specialized courts, these judges are gradually and partially trained in dealing with the type of situation that confronts the Court. Despite the predominantly independent operation of court functionaries, the current group of judges has evidenced the desire to develop a clearer understanding of the Court's requirements and a greater uniformity of procedure. They have recognized a need for new legislation and have written bills for possible enactment. Although there is fair promise for future clarification and improvement in court policy and technique through conference of the magistrates, the ideological contrasts among them restrain one's optimism as to an early resolution of the Court's confusions. To a large extent the magistrates are at swords' points in their attitudes.

What qualities should be sought in a magistrate for a girls' court? According to Flexner and Oppenheimer, there are several requirements to be looked for in a good judge for

[1] East, "Sexual Offenders" in Radzinowicz and Turner, *Mental Abnormality and Crime*, pp. 177–78.

the young offender: He should be a lawyer in order that the
rights of the individual may be realized and protected. He
should be able to put himself in the child's place and should
be of such personality as to win his confidence.[2] Justine
Polier, herself a children's court judge, adds that, since
these judges have such extensive discretionary powers, he
must always be on guard not to abuse his authority: He
must be alert to determine the truth between conflicting evidence and sensitive to the emotional nuances that lie behind
the facts. At the same time he must be careful not to expose
feelings unnecessarily or indulge in exhibitionism that may
satisfy a need for power or showmanship but will not benefit
those before him. He must seek a contact with the child, and
yet try not to overwhelm the child or place himself either
between child and parent or between the child and the probation officer designated to carry out the treatment when the
hearing is ended. He must draw on the facts set forth in the
investigation without parading them in such a way as to
undermine the child's confidence in teachers, ministers, social
workers, or parents who have contributed to his knowledge.
The judge's manner must be such as to inspire confidence in
his final decision.[3] These qualifications are certainly among
those needed by a judge in a court for adolescent girls.

PROBATION OFFICERS

Running often against the current of magistrates' traditions, there flows a stream of biases among the social workers
in the Court. The probation officers, like the judges, share in
varying intensities a set of distinctive attitudes toward the
method and purposes of their work. The inclination to make
a broad attack upon social problems in the Court, as compared to the legal drive toward narrowing a problem to its

2 *The Child, The Family and the Court,* United States Children's Bureau
Publication, No. 193 (1929), p. 51.
3 Polier, *Everyone's Children, Nobody's Child,* p. 72.

specific and legal issues, is an important part of their approach. The worker is wont to look widely for the multiplicity of factors which may be deemed germane to the behavior problems in court, attempting then to treat the situation as a social, not a legal, question. Lacking training in legal methods and philosophy, the worker is apt to view the limitations imposed by technicalities of court procedure as absurd barriers to be circumvented wherever possible. Also, since probation officers are poorly paid, they usually lack any extended formal training in social work methods or ideals, and thus they are inclined to function with views of goal and technique that are different from those of the social workers. Limited as probation officers are by institutional and political traditions, the dominant drive of some of them often seems to be to get the job done at a minimum level of performance. Using the tools closest at hand, they work in a practical fashion, but without the guidance of professional training or an integrated experience to develop the needed community of objectives or systematized methods.

Training in social work stresses a tolerant and nonmoralistic reaction to the client, an attitude of particular importance in a court for sex offenders. Unfortunately, where officers are trained neither in the sympathies of applied sociology nor in the objectivity of the law, but are motivated often by the desire to "set the fallen woman straight," their religio-moralistic bias does much to exaggerate that tone in the Court. Similar traits of background and attitude among the workers of remand and commitment institutions extend and deepen this emphasis in the processing of offenders.

According to Pauline V. Young, the worker with delinquent youth needs these characteristics:

Expert knowledge of child nature and child nurture, of the social world in which he lives, and of the larger economic, communal, political, and social forces which shape that world and determine to a great extent his destiny; ability to attract people, which depends essentially on the ability to be genuinely interested in their problems, experiences, interests, and desires; ability to see objectively the situation from the other person's standpoint without any prejudice and emotional coloring; ability to carry on teamwork with one's clients and coworkers; cordiality; intellectual honesty; detachment from own problems and resolution of own conflicts.[4]

The writer fears that these traits are rare in the personnel of the girls' court.

Miss Young also indicates the need for a scientific, non-moralistic approach by the probation worker and the necessity of such exploration as will reveal the "inner life history" of the defendant and his attitudes toward himself and his behavior.[5] The changing of attitudes is a slow process. "An abrupt change can rarely be expected by an intelligent worker, and sudden change will rarely be lasting. People's habits of acting and thinking cannot easily be modified under pressure." [6] Haste and superficiality in probation work inevitably spell failure.

A further quality often found in probation departments and social agencies, clearly expressed in the staff of this court and of many of the metropolitan social agencies which deal with adolescent girls, is the strong in-group sentiment of the organization. Jealous of its own power, suspicious of the power of others, autonomous and noncoöperative, the organization reduces its effectiveness by attempting to do the whole job or refusing to do it at all. The officers of the Court generally have either been insufficiently informed, or they are disinclined to exploit the coöperating agencies of the community which might play a more specialized and successful role in many of the cases than can the Court itself. Conversely, in refusing to handle court cases, the agencies tend

[4] Pauline Young, *Social Treatment in Probation and Delinquency*, pp. 474–75.
[5] *Ibid.*, pp. 15, 54, 124 ff.
[6] *Ibid.*, p. 390. See also Aichorn, *Wayward Youth*, p. 64.

not to coöperate well with the Court toward serving its needs. Moreover, as Robert P. Lane, executive director of the Welfare Council of New York City, has pointed out, there is in New York a "sprawling miscellany" of 1,000 welfare and health agencies of which but few were established on the basis of a careful study of an existing or expected need. Most of them have grown out of "emergency situations, philanthropic hobbies or just a general set of good intentions." Some of them are badly administered and uncoöperative.[7]

A minimum of mutual aid exists between public and private agencies, their traditional hostility often seriously impairing their performance in the community. Judge Justine Polier, of the Domestic Relations Court, emphasizes the failure of coöperative assistance between the social agencies of the city and the Children's Court, quoting from a report of the Welfare Council:

> In writing of the 50 or more voluntary agencies specializing in services to prevent delinquency, a memorandum of the Research Bureau of the Welfare Council stated: "Limitation of intake is widely practiced but no set policy is followed. Both practice and policies shift from time to time, without notice. As a consequence, the work of the private agencies cannot be related in any rational way to the total problem in any part of the city or to the whole of any sectarian or cultural group. Nor can the volunteer agencies be depended upon to carry any definite part of the load on a continuing basis. They move in and out of the picture for reasons that cannot be understood except in terms of their own individual convenience and fluctuating resources.[8]

Roscoe Pound too has pointed to the limitations on the function of probation facilities and the need for securing the aid of specialists:

> But probation agencies of a juvenile court are not organized or equipped to do family case work. Here is a field for coöperation of legal with extralegal agencies. It shows how important it is to have

[7] New York *Times* for November 30, 1944.   [8] Polier, *op. cit.*, p. 111.

a modern organization and an enlightened personnel, equal to utilizing to the utmost the possibilities of such coöperation. If we look only at one type of case the probation officer may have to consult a physician, a psychometrist, and a psychologist. In twenty years of experience as dean with nervous breakdowns, insomnia, and nervous scare on the part of ambitious adult students, I have often wished I could combine the special knowledge and technique of all these. The juvenile probation officer has need of . . . more.

Such reflections must lead us to appreciate the need of method. If in devising methods we are threatened on one side by the Scylla of perfunctory routine, we have to avoid on the other the Charybdis of blundering trial and error on the part of each particular magistrate and probation officer.[9]

Finally, the effectiveness of probation in the Wayward Minor Court has been narrowly restricted by the size of the Court staff and budget. Since its beginning and until 1946 the Court has shared its officers with the Women's Court; consequently, the officers assigned have carried on investigations and supervision for both courts throughout the five boroughs of New York City and, under the procedure used, have appeared personally at the hearings of all the cases assigned to them. To fulfill these functions there has been, during most of the history of the girls' court, a total of eight officers, one operating at intake exclusively, one working largely as a liaison officer in the court, and six doing investigative and supervisory work for the two courts. The proportion of time available for adolescent cases has been variable, depending upon the demand from the magistrates sitting in Women's Court. (Since the establishment of the girls' court, however, the tendency has been to stress the probation work in that tribunal rather than in the Women's Court; the officers are sincerely interested in, and earnest about, their work with adolescents.) A great deal of the officers' time is spent in traveling, the more so because little attempt is made

9 Pauline Young, *op. cit.;* foreword by Roscoe Pound, p. xxix.

to assign them according to area. Attendance at court also
consumes much of their energies. No specialization of function for investigation and supervision has been worked out in
the limited staff. Case loads are variable but heavy. Unfortunately, the officers indicate their inability to estimate the
proportions of time devoted to women's and girls' cases, to
investigation and supervision, and to court attendance and
travel. According to the record, however, nearly three hundred cases are investigated each year for the Wayward
Minor Court alone; about 10 percent of these are placed on
official probation for supervision; an additional 10 to 20
percent are supervised unofficially. In 1939 a larger number
of cases (335) was investigated for the Manhattan Women's
Court, and seventy-four were disposed through official probation. The probation report for 1939 estimated that 1,350
contacts were made for wayward minor investigations, 670
for cases of prostitution; during the same year 1,398 contacts were believed to have been made for supervision of
minors, 1,943 for women.[10] However accurate or inaccurate
may be these data, it is generally conceded among the officers
themselves that the time available is far from sufficient for
careful supervision, a great part of which must be done
through office visits.

In 1945 two new officers were appointed to the Wayward
Minor Court, no doubt because of the extension of court sessions to a three-day week. These officers, above the average
in qualifications, should relieve considerably the pressure of
business. Too, the assignment of one officer exclusively to
Women's Court work promises increased efficiency. It is believed that now the probation problem in girls' court is less
one of the inadequacy of staff size than one involving more
effective utilization of the existing personnel through selection of cases, appropriate referrals, and case supervision.

[10] See Annual Report of the Probation Department, Magistrates' Courts,
1939.

However, one officer has recently expressed her belief that the Court needs a probation staff of twenty-five to perform its work satisfactorily.

To summarize, treatment through the Wayward Minor Court, as is commonly true in probation practice, is a matter of direct and individual handling of each errant defendant. The customary approaches are those of scolding, moralizing, admonition, threats, appeal to authority (generally court authority), policing or supervision to detect violations, and, frequently, short-term incarceration—all of these while the individual remains either in the situation which provoked the delinquency or, more rarely, under temporary removal from those circumstances. Such probation procedures have never produced particularly effective results in reformation or in rehabilitation. Indeed, it is questionable whether it is possible, under present circumstances, to provide through ordinary court probation—without most extensive supplementary aid—for the kind of organized effort required to modify the home, neighborhood, and community influences which generate the delinquency and which must be remolded if there is to be either prevention of delinquency or ultimate regeneration of the delinquent. The methods used by this and by other courts for the young, not only fail generally to reform the offender, but frequently, in this writer's view, contribute to the continuation of delinquency. Occasionally there is evidence of careful effort in case work, either with the family of the wayward minor or in enlisting the aid of supporting agencies. Yet the facilities of the Court inevitably render such instances exceptional.

DETENTION AND COMMITMENT INSTITUTIONS

What of the nature of these facilities? [11] A fond hope has pervaded the development of experimental institutions for

11 For a brief description of the facilities of the Court, see Wayward Minor Court, *An Evaluative Review of Procedures and Purposes.*

the young—the reformatory, training school, industrial
school, shelter, and farm—an illusion that where the prison
has so obviously failed to correct the criminal through its
zoo-minded, machine-gun penologies, new structures for incarceration and novel penal methods might still achieve success. As a result we find the prolific flowering of devices to
tame the offender before he may become the "wild beast" of
popular and, often, official fantasy.[12] Yet in all their profusion they rest on a common foundation of error. Universally
they involve: (1) the mutually interstimulating association
of delinquents and pre-delinquents whose attitudes largely
are directed against society;[13] (2) living under conditions
which differ more or less radically from normal social living
and its motivations; and (3) varying degrees of punitive,
repressive atmosphere and discipline which have persevered
through the penal tradition venerated by penal personnel. To
hope from such roots to redirect and grow sound, socially
directed citizens is to dream. Prevention and reformation are
not there. The dangerous and intractable youth may be re-

[12] See, for example, the quotation from County Court Judge Peter J.
Brancato before sentencing four youths, aged fourteen to twenty: "I can
tell you that they'll be grandfathers by the time they come out of jail.
. . . Fourteen years of age or not, he's the worst of the lot." *P.M.* for
October 8, 1943. See also quotations from numerous notables in the
Proceedings of the Attorney General's Conference on Crime: Police Commissioner Valentine of New York City: ". . . the menace of these mad
dogs and human vultures, preying upon the honest, hardworking, sincere
people of the United States, is a major problem—an infamous, vicious,
cancerous growth, the roots of which must be torn out and completely
destroyed," p. 135. J. Edgar Hoover: "The career of 'Baby Face' Nelson
is over; he died of seventeen bullet wounds while two of the finest men I
ever knew gave their own clean lives that they might serve society by
ending his filthy one," p. 25.

[13] As the Thomases have pointed out in *The Child in America*, p. 96:
"As adults we have a naïve way of thinking of influence as transmitted
from the older generation to the younger, and we appreciate the point
that it is a horrible practice to place young children with old criminals,
while influences seem to spread more rapidly laterally, as between members of a younger generation, than vertically, as between mmbers of
different generations."

strained for a time, and society may be protected briefly from his threat. But to expose to these conditions the mildly delinquent, the hopeful first offender, the morally emancipated, the girl in danger of becoming morally depraved, invites futility. Institutions for the confinement of court-convicted defendants are neither delinquency-preventive nor, in many instances, rehabilitative. As Harry Elmer Barnes has stated:

Children are sex-starved, especially the older adolescent of both sexes, and more particularly the girls. Since most of the girls are put away by the court for sexual irregularity at the most critical age of their lives, it seems little short of insane to deny them wholesome companionship of the opposite sex. If sex is a problem, it will never be solved by locking the girls up in a penal institution. . . . This criticism is made in spite of the good that is done here and there by some of the more progressive schools. As the adult prison is an anachronism and a failure, so is the juvenile reform school. There may be some children who should be sent to these places; but as penal science expands, employing child-guidance clinics, psychiatric services, the techniques of well-trained social case workers and the knowledge and application of medical science, it will be difficult to find a child who will respond better in a cooped-up institution than in his own home or a foster home. The child must be treated where he is found, if that is possible. If the home is definitely depraved, there are other homes ready to receive him. If a child is merely practicing the mores of his neighborhood which are acceptable to his parents, it is the duty of the trained worker to find some plan which is applicable to the situation rather than to pull him away from his family and send him to a school with a stigma attached to it.[14]

The following is an evaluation from a White House Conference Report on the use of institutions for the young:

Furthermore, the court assumes that a child is not fit subject for correction in the penal institution, since during his impressionable years he learns the habits of the underworld easily and uncritically,

14 Barnes and Teeters, *New Horizons in Criminology,* pp. 915–16.

and that the atmosphere of a penal institution stunts his growth and development; that he learns best in the absence of fear and punishment and the presence of encouragement, love, security, and recognition. It is assumed that the proper social environment of an offender is in his own "normal community life and his own home." When such conditions are lacking or are too disorganized to be of benefit to him, other conditions should be substituted.[15]

One of the most serious limitations on the effectiveness of processing in the Wayward Minor Court is the nature of facilities for segregated confinement of the girls. The difficulties in this area are numerous. There is grossly insufficient provision for special types of cases, for those in need of psychiatric examination, for those who cannot be returned home but who do not require confinement in a closed shelter or institution, and for the many for whom no specialized facilities exist, although they are emotionally unstable or psychopathic.

Another basic problem arises out of the use, in a majority of cases, of private, sectarian, and philanthropic institutional resources which are in no way integrated as to policy, coverage, or methods of training or treatment; though these institutions are supported largely by public funds, there is virtually no public supervision, direction, or control but merely the right of visitation, exercised rarely enough. In consequence the facilities for detention and commitment are limited to the structures and standards which have been established sporadically by interested agencies.[16]

Inasmuch as the nonpublic agencies may limit intake and

[15] White House Conference Report, *The Delinquent Child*, p. 198.
[16] The gross lacks in treatment facilities, probation, agency, and institutional servicing in the Children's Court have been noted very frequently. See Polier, *op. cit.;* Harrison and Grant, *Youth in the Toils.* See also the New York *Times* for June 27, 1944, and May 28, 1945, and the New York *Post* for May 2, 1945. The deficient servicing of the Wayward Minor Court has received less publicity, but it is certainly no less a problem.

return to court the cases which they do not choose to supervise extramurally or within their institutions, the Court cannot itself determine, even within the limitations of the existing facilities, those which may be called upon to deal with the needs of a particular case. Despite the character of the Court and its defendants, the attitudes of the institutional personnel appear to be chiefly religio-moralistic and punitive-correctional.

The need, in consequence, is for a series of public institutions, or institutions subject to public standards and scrutiny, for which the community and the Court may take full responsibility to assure as complete and fair a coverage as budget and legislative policy will permit. The quality and type of service rendered to a case would not then depend upon the religious predilections of the defendant's parents, upon intake policies of a racially discriminatory character, nor upon the limited, unplanned, uncoördinated, unsupervised, and frequently contaminating facilities provided by benevolent groups that all too often are poorly subsidized.

The publicity attached to the revelation of abuses committed by the Manhattan Society for the Prevention of Cruelty to Children—to which children had customarily been sent for extended periods of detention—disclosed the uncontrolled outrages which may be perpetrated by publicly supported, privately controlled, uninspected agencies on the court cases delegated to them.[17] The consequent refusal of the city to send children to this shelter so intensified the detention problem that numerous boys under the age of sixteen were confined in the Tombs despite protests.[18] This problem was partially solved by establishing a new Youth Center, under an interfaith administration, for boys referred from

[17] See the New York *Times* for January 23, 1944, and January 27, 1944, and the New York *Post* for September 28, 1943, and October 1, 1943.
[18] See the New York *Post* for March 19, 1945.

Children's Court. The problem of detention and commitment facilities for adolescents is serious and chronic, but thus far it has failed to stir the public conscience.

The chief facilities for segregation available to the Court include:

TEMPORARY DETENTION FOR INTERIM DISPOSITIONS

The Florence Crittenton League maintains a privately supported, nonsectarian shelter, generally used by the Court for noninfected girls during short court adjournments. Occasionally it will accept a remand for a prolonged period of custody if the girl is not a serious disciplinary problem. The institution is in poor physical condition and lacks any adequate provision for recreation, occupational training, or other employment of the girl's time and thoughts. However, the staff has been expanded and strengthened and the League is seeking a better house.

The House of Detention, opened in 1932, is the city prison under the Department of Correction where girls who are disciplinary problems, girls brought in on warrants, and frequently, Negro girls (when the other limited provision for them has been exhausted) are detained prior to hearing. Wayward minors are not committed, but women are committed from other criminal courts on prison or penitentiary sentences. It is largely an institution for prostitutes, vagrants, and drug addicts, although women and girls charged with more serious offenses are held there as well. The intended capacity of this prison was 400, but there are frequently more than 600 in confinement, so that single cells must house two inmates.[19]

TEMPORARY DETENTION AND INDETERMINATE COMMITMENT

Brooklyn Training School, a privately supported institution, accepts wayward minors between sixteen and seventeen years of age. It lacks facilities for venereal treatment. Though its educational, vocational, and psychiatric facilities are good, it reserves the right to reject commitments from the Court.

[19] *An Analytical and Comparative Study of Treatment of Women Offenders Passing through the Department of Correction in the City of New York,* an unpublished dissertation by Herta N. Genz, contains some very informative materials on the Women's House of Detention and the reactions of the women confined there.

Catholic Houses of the Good Shepherd in Brooklyn and in Peekskill, New York, will accept white girls over sixteen years of age regardless of their religion, but in practice Protestants are rarely committed and may not be without their consent and the consent of their parents. There are facilities for vocational training and for the treatment of veneral diseases and limited facilities for pre- and postnatal care. Physical and psychological examinations may be given during remands. Girls failing to adjust to the routine of these institutions are frequently returned to the Court.

Cedar Knolls, maintained by the Jewish Board of Guardians, accepts wayward minors between the ages of sixteen and seventeen, but reserves the right of selection. It has no facilities for cases of venereal disease.

St. Mary's in the Field, maintained by the Protestant Episcopal Mission, has a limited service for girls from this court. It refuses, however, to accept sex delinquents or venereally infected girls.

The Wayside Home, maintained by the Salvation Army, has a small capacity and is limited to girls who are not difficult disciplinary problems.

Westfield State Farm, at Bedford Hills, New York, accepts wayward minors on indeterminate commitments as well as women, up to the age of thirty, from other courts. It has facilities of a sort for vocational training, medical treatment, pre- and postnatal care, and it also has nursery equipment. A large variety of minor and serious offenders is incarcerated at this state reformatory. A substantial proportion of the defendants from the Wayward Minor Court is sent here, as will be shown in a later section. Negro girls are especially apt to be sent to Westfield if their home situation is considered bad and no other provision can be made for them.

SPECIAL FACILITIES FOR DIAGNOSIS AND TREATMENT

Bellevue Hospital accepts for observation a limited and selected group of girls from the Court in cases where a condition of psychosis or feeble-mindedness is suspected. Although the space provided by the institution is really sufficient for only twenty girls, there are usually from twenty-five to thirty on remand for study and short-term treatment, and the waiting list is often long. Recommendations are made by the psychiatrist for disposition of the cases referred for observation. Bellevue also has a mental hygiene clinic to which may be referred neurotic and unstable wayward

minors. General physical examinations and treatment may be given
at court request.

City Hospital and other hospitals of the city are occasionally
used for physical examination and treatment when the girls cannot be cared for elsewhere. The hospitals, with the exception of
Bellevue, generally lack custodial features.

Inwood House is a privately supported institution with facilities
for venereally infected, white, pregnant girls; limited provision is
made for Negro girls. The House will accept wayward minors on
long-term remands when it has the space.

In 1945 plans for an open-door shelter for girls were conceived and promoted by some of the social agencies of the
city, with the understanding that part of the facilities would
be available for court cases.[20] Apparently these plans have
failed or stagnated. The Community Service Society intends
to open a shelter for girls suffering from the results of dis-
rupted homes, personal problems, and emotional disturbances, but it is to be used for the Society's own problem
cases, excluding girls with court contacts.[21] There seems to
be no favorable prospect for the acquiring of needed additional nonpunitive resources. Indeed, the official position
taken by former Mayor La Guardia was to the effect that
there is no acute or increasing threat of delinquency in New
York City.[22] As a result, while delinquency of children and
adolescents has been increasing at startling rates the country
over, New York has pretended officially that no problem exists and, for the most part, has proceeded to curtail public
facilities for dealing with maladjusted youth. Provisions for
psychological, psychiatric, and mental hygiene aid have re-

[20] See the New York *Times* for July 6, 1944.
[21] *Ibid.,* April 9, 1945; June 19, 1945.
[22] See particularly the New York *Times,* June 27, 1944; February 28,
1943; November 22, 1943; and January 26, 1942; the New York *Journal
American,* July 24, 1944; and the New York *Post,* November 24, 1943.
See also Blanshard and Lukas, *Probation and Psychiatric Care for Adolescent Offenders in New York City,* and the Report of the Seabury Committee on Probation in New York City.

ceded to diminutive proportions. The Juvenile Aid Bureau, the Police Athletic League, and the Crime Prevention Bureau—instruments of prevention and of assistance to the young—have usually suffered from financial malnutrition.[23]

[23] See, for example, the New York *Times* for June 29, 1941 (Juvenile Aid Bureau budget cut from 60 to 75 percent); April 16, 1942 (Mayor La Guardia criticizes psychologists' child treatment); April 2, 1942 (La Guardia drops Juvenile · Aid Bureau from 1942–43 budget); and December 12, 1943.

5

Confusion of Purposes

LET US CONSIDER the purposes and philosophy which have
evolved with the growth of devices for processing the wayward minor. In the procedures and attitudes of personnel in
the Court, certain inconsistencies have already become apparent. The earlier concept of "incorrigibility" implied that
the girl had progressed in her delinquencies to a point beyond mere unaided parental control. Yet by statutory definition, the majority of those who came before the courts as
incorrigibles were young girls only "in danger of becoming
morally depraved." The institutions provided for in the
statute, moreover, were designed to protect the girl and to
reform her before returning her to society. Some development of the philosophy implicit in the administration of
these statutes became explicit in the enactment of the Wayward Minor Act. Most marked were the tendency to specialize in cases of sexual offenses and the modification of
methods. The girl was to be known as "wayward," not as "incorrigible"; she was to be treated by preventive and reformative measures through the status concept, with less emphasis
on penitential and moralistic devices.

In the evolution of the Wayward Minor Court, with its
gradual merging and compromise of statutes, procedures,
and philosophies, there has resulted imprecision and a conflict of goals. It is natural that institutions in development,
especially if they change markedly, should display internal
inconsistencies and maladaptations during transition. Special resistances to change may develop within parts of the
institutional system, creating lags and anachronistic sur-

vivals. Particularly in the realms of values, attitudes, and philosophies outmoded traits persist to clog and deflect the operation of the institutional machinery. In this court perhaps the most basic issue has involved the question of ultimate purpose in dealing with the adolescent girl offender: whether the design of the Court is to punish or reform, to deter (from sexual misconduct), or to incapacitate (as a health measure).

Our strongly punitive heritage in dealing with offenders against the criminal law has found continuing, if somewhat diminished, expression in the methods of administering treatment to the adolescent as well as to the adult. Correctionally repressive attitudes are particularly common among those to whom the treatment processes are entrusted. Though the woman is generally treated more leniently than the male in our courts, the contrary is true in cases involving violation of the sexual code. And though the wayward adolescent is often spared serious penalties today, the adolescent sexual delinquent continues to feel the sting of a traditional reproach and repression.

It is probably true that, toward the individual case, the dominant attitude of the majority of those into whose hands the wayward minor is placed during processing and treatment is still retributive and punitive. It is expressed in statements, prior to committing the girl to an institution, that she has had her "last chance," that she has not "learned her lesson," that she must be "incarcerated," that "what she needs is a period of firm discipline." It is found too in the approach often used in probation supervision wherein the supervising officer employs moral judgments, threats, and fears as control devices. In the charge against her, the very statement that she is in danger of becoming a "bad girl" encourages a religio-moralistic tone in the proceedings which is increased by the common commitments to sectarian institutions. This moralism, though it appeals to one sound line of behavior motivation, is most frequently associated with a retributive reaction. The absurdity, psychologically, of the punitive approach is especially obvious in the areas of youthful delinquency and sex conduct. The direct repressive attack protects neither the individual nor the community, and it nullifies efforts at reform.

Side by side, but in substantial conflict with the punitive approach, proceeds a clinical emphasis upon rehabilitation, expressed in the effort to remove the girl, if it is believed necessary, from her risk-creating environment, to find her legitimate employment, to take care of her more obvious physical ailments, and to encourage the development of higher ideals as such. The more constructive purpose and methods of treatment are likely to be applied when contact with a girl on probation has developed the worker's insight and sympathy; especially, therefore, when the girl's conduct has not been too morally offensive to the particular worker, when the girl has conducted herself with docility, or when she is attractive and engaging (though this last appears to produce varied reactions in different officers).

Often entering into this conflicting intermixture of purpose is the added desire to prevent the sex offender, especially when she has become venereally diseased, from spreading her charm or infection further, and so to incapacitate her for a time. In such instances one finds a struggle among philosophies of moralistic judgment and punitive treatment against a violator of the social mores, of a nonmoralistic and clinical effort to cure disease and protect society, and of a reformative attempt to produce a better adjustment to the community and its standards. Court, probation, and institutions, all in varying degrees display the confusion of purposes, emphasizing now one, now another. The diverse value-systems of the individuals or institutions acting upon the girl and her own attitudes and responses to these pressures appear to be the chief elements in determining which purpose and method will predominate.

The temporary incapacitative function of dispositions from this court reveals with peculiar clarity the inequalities in treatment and the disparity of seeming purpose, not only within the Court, but in comparison with other courts of the magistrates' system. Immediately striking is the contrast between Women's Court through which, for the most part, pass habitual prostitutes, and the Wayward Minor Court with its generally younger, less hardened, nonprostitutional, and frequently nonpromiscuous violators of the sexual code. The punitive attitude is somewhat more marked in the former court, where a mixture of moral condemnation and resignation to the inevitability of the commercialization of man's "base passions" is a common reaction. In the girls' court the defendant's behavior is deemed less reprehensible, her character more corrigible; yet, the fact that the same judges and probation officers serve in both courts—and also because the Wayward Minor Court was formerly a part of the Women's Court—affords a natural vehicle for the translation of the retributive attitudes from one court to the other. It is interesting to observe, in the light of the greater corrigibility and lesser seriousness of offenses among adolescents, the dispositions from each court. This is done in some statistical detail in a later section. Here, in summary, it may be said that the alleged prostitute is much less likely to be convicted than the minor is to be adjudicated; this is probably due, in large part, to the requirement in Women's Court of much more specific proof of guilt under the statutes and to the greater desire in the girls' court to solve the social problems which appear. (The conviction rates in the Women's Court are not low compared to rates for various offenses in the other magistrates' courts; the girls adjudication rates are, however, very high.) Moreover, the defendant in the Women's Court, if convicted, is much more likely to escape extended institutional confinement than is the girl in her specialized court. This may reflect the assumed hopelessness of attempting to deal with the prostitute, the uncertainty as to her guilt, and traditions of treatment for commercialized sex offenders. Too, the statutes permit wider latitude in disposition of the prostitute. In the Wayward Minor Court the high frequency of rather long indeterminate sentences may be attributed, in part, to the limited statutory provisions for the alternatives of probation and indefinite commitment and, in part, to the desire of the Court to deal correctively with the problems which appear before it.

We find then, a series of purposes or motives to treatment operating in the Court, marked by some inconsistencies and a predominant leaven of retributive attitudes. Let us consider the place and effectiveness of these in practice:

A temporarily incapacitative function is served by the commitments of the Court. Indeed, the segregation growing out of the dispositions of this tribunal is more frequent and more extensive than that in other courts dealing with more serious offenses. As observed above, the prostitutes, from whom, by assumption, the community needs greater protection, are less frequently convicted and, when convicted, are given shorter terms or no penalty at all. The length of terms for the adolescent is difficult to rationalize for incapacitative purposes. Though a great part of this contrast may be attributed to the statutes under which the courts operate, the point here emphasized is that, comparing dispositions and purposes of the tribunals, the lesser offenders are found to be exposed to considerably more rigorous treatment. Whether the reason lies in statute, attitudes and policy, personnel, or available institutions, the result itself is significant, anomalous, and correctible.

Clinical functions are performed by the **Wayward Minor Court**, particularly in the diagnosis and cure of venereal diseases, though examinations are not given to all defendants as they are in Women's Court. In each court, when disease is detected, an attempt is made to provide for treatment whether the defendant is found guilty or innocent. Extended confinement is not required for cures. One would expect, in fact, that there would be a greater danger of early reinfection in the case of prostitutes, yet when they are confined at all, they are released much sooner than are the nonprostitutes. There appears, however, to be little clinical justification for extended institutionalization.

From the point of view of reformation, it may scarcely be contended that the commitment to Westfield of a large proportion of the wayward girls is even conceivably an effective method of reformation. Indeed, it is generally conceded that young offenders should not be sent there if other disposition can be made of the case. Yet a large percentage of the Court's products is sent to that institution where older and habitual violators of the law have influenced the character and policies of treatment. Though large numbers are sent from the Court to sectarian institutions for indefinite terms, a practice deemed more lenient and beneficial, the much greater emphasis upon moralism and religious observance in these institutions is of dubious reformative value except for a limited group who may find there religious sublimations of their sexual energies. The Jews and Negroes, for whom little other institutional provision has been provided must seek their substitutive habits in the more rigorous environment of the Westfield Reformatory.

As noted above, the retributive and retaliatory motives appear to operate strongly in the Women's Court. Yet the actual practices and consequences of the Wayward Minor Court operation, whatever may be its intention, are more

harshly punitive than are those of many of the courts which
deal with far more serious violations of the law. Though some
justification for this situation may be sought in the futility
of short, definite sentences, yet such short terms might well
do the wayward girl less harm—if commitment is necessary
—than do the longer periods of institutional contamination.

As to deterrent purposes, the Court operates on the assumption that the Wayward Minor Statute, like other provisions of the criminal law, serves the end of inhibiting undesirable conduct. Determination of the extent to which legally
established penalties do, in fact, prevent criminal behavior
awaits empirical proof, but it may now appear rather clear
that the deterring effect of legal penalties will vary greatly
with the type of conduct sought to be controlled, the methods
of treatment set up, the actual penalties imposed (as contrasted with those provided for by statute), the extent of
effective enforcement, and the relationship of the deterrent
to other motives of treatment for the particular offense.[1] It
is suggested that the deterring efficacy of the Wayward
Minor Statute is narrowly limited as a result of several
factors.

Conceding the deterrence brought about by legal penalties
under ideal conditions, its effectiveness may be qualified or
nullified where characteristically emotional behavior is involved. Formal social control is especially difficult in this
area. The standards of behavior affectively conditioned in
early home, church, and school experience are often more

[1] As Llewellyn has emphasized in "On the Good, the True, the Beautiful in
Law," University of Chicago Law Review, IX, 249, ". . . right law must
be intelligibly, intellectually accessible, to the people whom that law is
to serve." It is a point which seems frequently to have been overlooked
or minimized by some who have analyzed the influence of law upon
behavior. The less specifically the public is informed about substantive
norms and the related penalties, the less effective they can be in per-
suading offenders to avoid more serious types of antisocial behavior.
This is what Jeremy Bentham meant in his emphasis upon the need for
"cognoscibility" of the provisions of a criminal code.

significant in controlling attitudes toward authority and specific conduct than are the proscriptions of the law. In the province of sexual behavior rational legal controls are not apt to restrain conduct very effectively if family ethics and community mores fail. Moreover, where penalties are gauged to the presumed requirements of the average, reasonable individual, they are not likely to succeed in constraining the sort of deviant who appears regularly in the Wayward Minor Court, e. g., the psychopath, the emotionally unstable, the intellectually dull, the endocrinologically hyperactive, the morally emancipated—types which often violate the social norms of sex behavior.

From various pressures there has developed a body of emotionally loaded, morality-directed legislation in which a deterrent ideology is fused with a tradition of retribution. Penalties based on moral evaluations and religious conceptions are often established therein. Laws designed to control sexual behavior, such as the Wayward Minor Statute, tend especially to be influenced by these retaliatory drives. Any deterrent consequences of such predominantly retributive legislation are largely accidental; indeed, one would expect to find laws of this type stimulative to many rather than repressive. The problem of moralistic-retributive legislation is rendered especially acute where the law attempts to control behavior which lies within the domain of morality or private ethics.[2] In an age of conflict and change in moral values—when the sophisticated look upon mores as culturally relativistic—particularly at a time when much that has been deemed to involve societal mores is coming to be viewed as involving matters of personal and private ethics (as in sexual behavior), the law which attempts to control conduct is apt to be nullified by rather general resentment.

[2] See Ernst and Lindley, *The Censor Marches On,* for a trenchant survey and criticism of morality and obscenity legislation. See also Ernst and Seagle, *To the Pure.*

It is probable that sex activity in our society lies largely outside the realm of effective legal action.[3]

In sum, we find operating in the Wayward Minor Court an
intermixture of retributive, deterrent, incapacitative, and
reformative purposes. The health measures of temporary
sexual incapacitation and venereal treatment carried on by
the Court constitute, perhaps, its greatest constructive accomplishments; but it is difficult to justify a long-extended
processing through a criminal court and punitive measures
for clinical objectives that might often be applied to the
young girl with less dangerous by-products by social agencies and hospitals. The deterrent efficacy of the statute is
believed to be slight for the reasons mentioned. The strong
retributive drives are especially out of place in a court for
adolescents, and they thwart the reformative goals which are
generally conceived to be its ideal objective. The reformative
purposes are further frustrated by the character of the
facilities, personnel and organizational, that have been described. It is impossible to say what proportion of cases has
received a needed and partially successful rehabilitative
treatment, but it is certain that many defendants have been

[3] Roscoe Pound has said, "No legal machinery of which we have any
knowledge is equal to doing everything which we might like to achieve
through social control by law. Some duties which morally are of the
highest moment are too intangible for legal enforcement. This is brought
out in the experience of domestic relations courts and juvenile courts,
which continually have to take over the methods and aims and points of
view of administrative rather than of judicial tribunals." Pound, *Criminal Justice in America*, p. 62. In the same work he further maintained,
"Organized meddling with individual conduct and even individual belief
and opinion by extra-legal self-appointed groups, more hateful than
any official control, and powerful to deny the legal protection which the
law books purport to guarantee to the individual, has always been a
characteristic feature of American life. In the present century it has
increasingly affected legislation and administration. Extra-legal cen-
sorship in some parts of the country avails itself of administrative machinery and becomes at least quasi-legal," p. 203. See also Cardozo, *The
Nature of the Judicial Process*, especially pp. 15, 35, 48, 54–5, 119;
Pound, *Law and Morals*, pp. 63–6, 72–9, and *Social Control through Law*,
pp. 54–62.

injured through the unnecessary application of processes poorly designed to meet their requirements of health and morality. Ideologically, the Court has developed a rather complete acceptance of the reformative concept and, indeed, has gone beyond to acceptance of a preventive philosophy. But the perseveration of traditional attitudes among treatment personnel tends to deny in practice the values which are accepted in theory.

Another aspect of the problem of purpose and philosophy in the Wayward Minor Court is involved in the question of whom that tribunal is designed to aid. Confusion results from the attempt to assist both parent and child when, as is usually the case, it is the conflict between them which has caused the complaint. As previously indicated, the act is a "parent's statute" which by its terms is designed to support or replace parental control. If assistance is given to the parent it is frequently impossible to help the girl. Thus where the parent is attempting through the Court to acquire all the daughter's wages—a problem of some foreign-born parents particularly; or where the parents demand that the girl terminate her association with a man of whom they disapprove on religious, nationality, or other grounds; or where the mother's complaint is based upon the jealousy incurred by her daughter's sexual competition for a paramour—which happens occasionally—it is impossible generally to serve parent and child at once. The natural and frequent consequence is to impose treatment within the limits permitted by the statute. The frequent frustration of purposes is obvious. There is no jurisdiction over the parent. Therefore parental coöperation cannot be coerced when it is most needed by the Court to help the girl. If the parents are responsible, through neglect or overt act, for the girl's delinquencies, no legal pressure can be brought to bear upon them in this court. Even if the girl has done nothing culpable and the parent alone is guilty of misconduct, no control can legitimately be asserted, yet her adjudication may occur. When "jurisdiction is taken" over the daughter "to protect her" from her parent, harm may be done to the girl by the status-attribution, while no control can be exerted over the parent save through non-legal pressure. The experience of the probation officers attests the frequency with which the parent and the home conditions created by the parent are basic to the social and/or legal problems which confront the Court. The inclination of the tribunal then, is to step in and do whatever it may by reason of its jurisdiction over the child; the dangers and injustice to her in this procedure are not sufficiently considered.

Only if the girl is guilty of legally defined wrong is the Court justified in adjudicating her a wayward minor, and in such instances the tendency is to adopt a punitive attitude and to institutionalize the girl. When little or no blame is attached to her conduct, the Court may adopt the expedient of probationary supervision in order to influence behavior in the family, or it may put her under "unofficial supervision" without adjudicating her in order that some degree of semi-official control may be imposed [4] or some therapeutic work may be undertaken.

The limitations imposed upon the Court's jurisdiction by its place in the magistrates' system and the further diminution of control due to the restricting provisions of the statute together militate against conciliatory efforts in cases of domestic discord. The delegation to the Domestic Relations Court of authority to deal with neglected and delinquent

---

[4] In connection with the problem of the conflict of interest between child and the parent and the need to protect the child's welfare, see the statement by Judge Julian Mack in "Legal Problems Involved in the Establishment of a Juvenile Court," in Breckinridge and Abbot, *The Delinquent Child and the Home,* pp. 181–201.

children up to the age of sixteen, achieved in the face of strong tradition-bound opposition, both from within and from outside the Court, accomplished the desirable goal of submitting to the jurisdiction of one court both the child and his socially and legally responsible parents. The result has been unquestionably to facilitate the effective handling of juvenile cases, within the limitations of court personnel. The difficulties arising in the Wayward Minor Court from the arbitrary separation of juvenile and adolescent at the age of sixteen and from the lack of legal power in situations of flagrant parental neglect and misconduct are obvious handicaps to its effectiveness in dealing with family situations. The need in some situations to use for the solution of a single knotty domestic problem the Domestic Relations and Children's Court, the Wayward Minor, magistrates' district, and supreme courts, as well as numerous social agencies, reveals the inefficiency and waste which have accompanied the unplanned, crescive development of our judicial system. Neither the jurisdictional control nor the facilities for diagnosis and treatment in the Wayward Minor Court is adequate to the purpose of solving complex familial and social problems. Reformatories and other punitive and semipunitive treatment facilities, together with criminal court handling, are not the devices to meet the problems of domestic discord and maladjustment.[5]

The question of treatment purposes brings us, finally, to what is believed to be a most crucial question of policy in the Court: What types of behavior should be used as a basis for assuming jurisdiction? Is a general course of conduct (rather than an actual and specific offense) sufficient for adjudicative purposes, and may the Court thus act preventively in the forestalling of delinquent and criminal conduct?

[5] See the quotation from Roscoe Pound, *supra,* p. 94.

THE COURSE OF CONDUCT AND PREVENTIVE TREATMENT

As previously indicated, the status concept of the "wayward minor" has been, though it need not necessarily be, associated with a "course-of-conduct" or behavior problem as the basis of adjudication: the noncriminal category might be applied to an adjudicated defendant in consequence either of a specific offense or of a course of conduct. The proper grounds for adjudication is a question of central importance, involving the objectives and accomplishments of the Court. More specifically, the question is whether the course-of-conduct principle or some other such general standard of behavior is justified as a basis of establishing jurisdiction in the Court. In considering that question, several serious difficulties appear and require discussion.

The implications of the course-of-conduct principle for legal and political philosophy need more attention than they have commonly been given. The limitation of officials under Anglo-American legal tradition from proceeding against any person on the basis of a specific offense only—an act or a series of acts—has been a price paid for civil liberty against arbitrary abuse by officials of criminal law and procedure. The result has been to limit the attack on crime by official rules which, in the main, labor to exclude from a jury's consideration the nature of the man accused as a ground for conviction. In the development of adolescent procedures, however, the purpose of salvaging youth and the conception of criminal procedure as curative have been at work to modify the traditional philosophy and procedure. Within the existing machinery of criminal prosecution, these ideas have made themselves felt in the growing practice, and then in an ensuing norm, of dealing within the utmost allowable limits —and often beyond—with seemingly hopeful adolescents in some curative fashion. After the informal establishment of practices aimed at prevention, statutory validation has been sought and procured. In general, there is little opposition based upon the possible abuse of the powers of criminal prosecution; for these are nonvoters. Also, there is little danger of political pressure from or through their parents, because it is the parents who bring the adolescents in for correction before the official machinery takes hold. Not infrequently these parents desire to rid themselves of the difficulties and expense of rearing their children. Thus the development of a course of conduct and general misbehavior as basis for adjudication, along with other methods of tribunals for the young, has grown out of reformative purposes and with little opposition. And the present trend of the Court is to seek even greater freedom of discretion in adjudication. The generality of norms in the new Wayward Minor Statute provides such increased elasticity.

There is danger, however, that unless the conduct be defined in clear and precise terms a court will expand its area of control to more and more varied problem situations with which it is not equipped to deal—an observable trend in the Wayward Minor Court. There thus develops a dispersion of court energies in relatively ineffectual or, in some cases, definitely injurious influence in the situations sought to be treated. Consequently, it is important that the behavior—whether an offense or a course of conduct—should be enunciated in the statute clearly enough to limit and direct the discretion of the court. It seems clear that legislative policy on adolescent treatment must go beyond a mere preventive and rehabilitative purposing under vague statutory specifications to a clear pronouncement of the type or types of conduct which must be present in a case to warrant court adjudication.[6]

[6] See Belden, *Courts in the United States Hearing Children's Cases*, p. 11, where she says that "the fundamental purpose of juvenile court procedure is not to determine whether or not a child has committed a specific offense, but to discover whether he is in a condition requiring

If it be assumed that delinquency prevention is possible by court action, the justification for establishing any particular course of conduct as the basis for a court's "taking hold" should rest on a fairly high degree of certainty, not only that such conduct when continued may be followed by more serious irregularities of which the criminal law takes cognizance, but also because the conduct, in the absence of official intervention, is more likely than not to lead to criminal offense. For the facilities available and likely to become available are not so numerous as to warrant attempting to deal preventively with cases unless there is more than average likelihood of future criminality. Too, it is an important credo of our political system that individuals should not be needlessly harassed by the criminal law. Hence, adjudication should be based only on a reasonably sound inference that criminal behavior will eventuate from the incipient misconduct observed. The loss of individual freedom involved in legal constraints should be justified by evidence that more is to be gained by adjudicating for conduct deemed risk creating than is lost by court intervention in cases where no formal restraint may actually be needed.

The difficulty here is profound; for, from the large body of research that has been conducted on crime causation in recent years, one fact clearly emerges: the hypotheses of causation must be treated most tentatively. As Michael and Adler have stated in their critical volume, "the absurdity of any attempt to draw etiological conclusions from the findings of criminological research is so patent as not to warrant further discussion." [7] At our present stage of knowl-

---

the special care of the State." The author's view is that such a criterion (as one, apparently, upon which courts for the young are wont to operate) constitutes a tremendous threat to the welfare of the guiltless child against whom no "specific offense" is proven but who is subjected to quasi-criminal facilities because he is deemed in need of treatment.
[7] Michael and Adler, *Crime, Law and Social Science,* p. 169.

edge it is impossible to settle with any certainty upon noncriminal conduct as deserving of reformative treatment because of its causal relation to crime. Nor do we yet possess sufficient information concerning either the behavior sequence or categories of crime risk which are so highly correlated with law violation as to constitute good indices for preventive treatment. Further understanding of behavior sequences leading into crime must await more research in criminogenetics with the use of control groups; only thus may we be sure that a given factor in conduct which appears frequently in criminal careers is not itself neutral, or of minor importance, and merely associated with other more significant items. We should learn from data of criminal and control groups the comparative frequency with which the conduct investigated is associated with noncriminal careers. Recent research points to the need for multiple-correlational analysis to show those series of factors which, when found in combination, are likely to antecede criminal behavior.

It may prove very difficult to base adjudication as well as preventive and reformative treatment on associated categories of conduct and environmental history—certainly far more difficult than convicting on the basis of specific offenses. Too, as Dession has pointed out, the techniques of psychiatric diagnosis—themselves more precise than those of the sociologist and the psychologist, for the most part—are still too inexact and their results too imperfect to found upon them the trial process of the criminal law.[8] Today, certainly, within the narrow limitations of our knowledge we must be wary in selecting behavior factors in adolescence to use for adjudicative purposes on the assumption that, if unattended, the behavior will probably lead to crime. We simply do not know what factors in conduct, if any, can be treated success-

[8] See Dession, "Psychiatry and the Conditioning of Criminal Justice," *Yale Law Journal,* XLVII (Jan. 1938), 319.

fully by a court in the attempt to prevent delinquency. On the contrary, a respectable body of literature points to the conclusion that delinquency is most frequently correlated with the individual's subjective responses to environment, particularly with his emotional stresses and disturbances.[9] Such factors, varying within the family, will respond, if at all, only to skilled, prolonged case work and psychological and/or psychiatric treatment. Adjudicating the adolescent as a morally depraved person and then applying institutional treatment or office probation is a patently absurd method of attempting to meet the problem.

In the writer's belief it is unwise for the Court to attempt to define a noncriminal course of conduct as a basis for adjudication. Though the matter is primarily a problem for legislative policy-making, if it should be deemed wise to found the wayward minor status upon some specific conduct other than an offense, a further problem must first be met. There should be assurance that the facilities of the Court are adequate and appropriate to the reasonably effective accomplishment of the preventive purposes implied by course-of-conduct adjudication. It has been shown that the present commitment facilities are unadjusted to a preventive function and are of dubious value for reformation. They were conceived for, and are largely dedicated to, the punitive-correctional purposes of punishment for offenses against the law. Nor can the probation department carry on the thoroughgoing type of intensive individualized therapy within the present limitations of its budget, personnel, and attitudes. If these facilities can feasibly be made adequate to the performance of the preventive function, the legislature will then be more justified in attempting to establish upon a sociologi-

[9] See Healy and Bronner, *New Lights on Delinquency and Its Treatment;* Alexander and Staub, *The Criminal, the Judge, and the Public;* Alexander and Healy, *Roots of Crime;* Healy, *Mental Conflicts and Misconduct;* Lindner, *Rebel without a Cause;* Pauline Young, *op. cit.*

cally relevant course of conduct, and the Court will be more justified in applying it. One norm which the legislature might adopt, consistent with the demands of various pressure groups but with greater protection to adolescents against futile and injurious treatment, would be a test using promiscuous and commercialized sex conduct as indicative of "moral depravity."

The sexual offenses now adjudicated in the Wayward Minor Court would seem to fall rather neatly into what Jeremy Bentham called "imaginary offenses," which he defined as "acts which produce no real evil, but which prejudice, mistake or the ascetic principles have caused to be regarded as offenses. They vary with time and place. They originate and end, they rise and they decay with the false opinions which serve as their foundation." He considered, so far as the public is concerned, that sexual offenses in which there is neither violence, fraud, nor interference with the rights of others could be subsumed under this category of "imaginary offenses." [10] Eliot Ness has somewhat similarly defined the problem of the sexually promiscuous girl:

By and large, the promiscuous girl is not criminally motivated, nor is she beyond reclamation as is the hardened prostitute. She is more likely to be a casual, fun-seeking girl, wanting male companionship; a young experimenter, somewhat lonely—immature in her judgment and, perhaps more important, disassociated from the stabilizing forces of family, the church, or any significant groups which strengthen the individual's integrity and belief in herself.[11]

It is probable that so vast a majority of noncriminal adolescent girls who are behavior problems, emotionally maladjusted, and deviant in sex conduct would profit more from the specialized assistance of presently available noncorrec-

[10] East, "Sexual Offenders" in Radzinowicz and Turner (eds.), *Mental Abnormality and Crime*, p. 177.
[11] Ness, "Sex Delinquency as a Social Hazard," *Proceedings of the National Conference of Social Work*, 1944, p. 280.

tional public and private social, psychiatric, and health
agencies that there is rarely justification for applying the
inevitably stigmatizing devices of court and postcourt treatment. Harm may be done to a large group in obtaining improvement among a few of the more intractable individuals
unless careful selection be made. The hospitals in the city,
with their social service departments, appear to be generally
better adapted to dealing with the pregnant or diseased nonprostitutional adolescents; the mental hygiene clinics are
more suited to work with the emotionally unstable; while
family welfare agencies are more successful with the under-
privileged or pathological homes. Finer tools are needed
than those we own if we are to distinguish with any nicety in
advance the noncriminal but incorrigible adolescent girl who
may profit more from court contact than from other types
of treatment.

If the legislature persists in sex and course-of-conduct legislation, the closest approximation to a test for court action
that the writer can suggest is that only those cases should
be court processed which (*a*) involve a definite and statuto-
rily defined conduct problem; (*b*) have been dealt with un-
successfully by the available and appropriate social agencies
of the community; and (*c*) may probably be more aided in
the forestalling of delinquency than damaged by repressive
treatment in the application of the available court facilities.
This last would usually imply that the conduct involved
was of some seriousness and of extended duration. It would
seem that by the time a case has reached this point it is too
late for mere preventive work and that psychological and
social rehabilitation is in order. The point made here is that
the court should not attempt, under idealistic preventive
theory, to hear and treat all manner of problem cases. Court
action and the authority of judicial organs are required for
the reformation of individuals truly delinquent in conduct.

In essaying preventive measures with pre-delinquents, the tribunal may do them infinite harm.

Again, a preventive function would imply the use of careful clinical diagnosis, understanding probation supervision, adequate psychiatric and medical care, and the continued use of other community resources. It would imply too that the facilities used should carry no stigma or blame. At the present time the Court tools are not adequate nor are they well organized for the purpose; no specific courses of conduct have been defined; coöperation with social agencies is insufficient; and the Court is too easily disposed to take control regardless of the availability of more appropriate social facilities that have not yet been called into use in the case.

As Sheldon Glueck has said, in deprecating the use of court and correctional agencies for attempted prevention of delinquency:

> In most instances, children should be kept away from the typical contacts with police stations, courts, and correctional institutions until more scientific and sympathetic efforts have failed. As Fulton puts it, "An official affidavit should be used only as a last resort when all other methods have failed. The respect and dignity of the court should be maintained by a reputation that court action is something which should be feared and avoided." [12]

Our conclusion must be that neither the Court, with its existing paraphernalia, nor our present stage of knowledge warrants the attempt at preventive work through the course-of-conduct principle of adjudication. And it is very doubtful that we can come to operate preventively through the Court in the future. (This conclusion implies, of course, that the present philosophy and function of the Court are founded in error in so far as it operates on the principle of preventive adjudication for behavior problems. That is the inevitable

[12] Glueck and Glueck (eds.), *Preventing Crime*, p. 6.

conclusion to which our data and observation point. More
constructive suggestions for a differing function will be discussed in Chapter VIII.)

Despite conflicting values in the Wayward Minor Court,
there is an outstanding and hopeful trend. Developed in recent years among social workers and criminologists, popular-
ized even more recently—and hastened by conditions of wartime delinquency—considered seriously at last by legislature
and court, there is today an earnest concern for the prevention of delinquency and the rehabilitation of the young offender. Despite the conflicts in philosophy, in means and ends
erected, the ideal of clinical treatment and rehabilitation is
in the ascendancy. By and large, the other purposes and motives which operate in and through the Court in individual
cases reveal chiefly a natural perseveration of attitudes within
a formalized social institution, powerful, nevertheless, and
difficult to eradicate because of their traditional character.
It may be expected that the future will find extended specialization, together with coöperation among the agencies which
deal with the young, toward the end that functionally differentiated facilities will be applied in cases where experience has
shown their superiority. At that time fewer behavior problems will go into courts, more into agencies, clinics, and hospitals. The adolescent court will perform a more narrow and
specialized service in dealing correctionally only with cases
which have already proven serious enough to warrant court
attention by specific offenses or crimes and by their intractable response to prior agency efforts: It will be suggested
that selection for specialized treatment might best be effected
by a coördinated council of social agencies.

PRE-ADJUDICATION INVESTIGATION

Closely associated with the question of whether noncriminal
conduct and character should be used as criteria for adjudi-

cation is that concerning methods used in the adjudicative process. One of the central experimental features of the Wayward Minor Court is that of the pre-hearing investigation upon the basis of which the judgment of the Court, as well as the disposition of the case, is partially determined. Consent to this procedure is secured quite automatically in what must appear to the defendant as merely a part of the rapid formulary through which she must go. The securing of consent is necessary to justify the deprivation of her normal trial rights. Question may be raised as to the utility, efficiency, and justifiability of the device; and the issue is extremely important since this process of determining both guilt and treatment on the basis of social and character evidence is spreading to other courts. It may profoundly affect the future of the adolescent court movement.

The use of pre-adjudication investigation in the courts for children and adolescents differs from adult court procedure in a simple but significant way. In the traditional processing of the criminal, information on his social history, personality, and conduct may be sought by probation officers after trial and presented to the court to direct the disposition. Such material would be excluded as incompetent and irrelevant if presented at the trial itself, since it is derived from hearsay and usually does not bear significantly on the issue of guilt, the criterion upon which corrective action by the law is based. In the courts for the young, as suggested, however, inquiry into social background is made before the hearing and presented to the court as an important basis for adjudication as well as for treatment.

Assuming the value of the device in itself, it must be vigorously maintained that as a prerequisite to its application the following conditions (absent in the Court for Wayward Minors) are necessary or highly desirable:

There should be an attorney for the defense in the Court

at all times to give legal guidance and advice to the girl. This is the minimal requirement for fair adjudication. If, through this technique, the defendant is to be deprived of a large section of her traditional rights of due process by permitting communication to the judge of the information and misinformation gleaned from gossip, community opinion, unthoughtful and often unfriendly neighbors and relatives, there must be an opportunity for an attorney representing the defendant to bring into the open the source and nature of the evidence so that where the source of the testimony is of inferior credibility little weight will be attached ot it. The defense attorney should be, not only legally trained, but experienced in the problems of dealing with the adolescent girl. He should conceive his function to be that of aiding the defendant legally and socially; in many cases an important service would be to induce the girl to tell her story, since under present circumstances she is inclined to stand mute at the bar, confused and afraid. Too, he should aid the Court in its attempt to understand and assist the defendant. His role then would be constructive, not obstructive to the purposes of the tribunal. A representative from the Legal Aid Bureau regularly assigned to the Court over an extended period of time would seem to be the optimum choice for fulfilling the function.[13]

In a tribunal such as the Wayward Minor Court, where there is no jury to be deflected by incompetent testimony, much of the historical justification for the rules of exclusion is lacking. However, the question still remains as to the validity of evidence obtained from probation reports to prove waywardness even if a defense attorney is present to test its

[13] One of the judges has requested that an attorney be assigned from the Legal Aid Bureau. That agency was said to have no presently available defender for regular assignment to the Court, but it could at times assign one upon special request.

strength.[14] Unless probation investigations have decided value
in producing relevant facts from credible sources, one of two
results is likely to ensue: injustice, in the absence of a skilled
attorney for the defendant, or nullification of court action
through the attorney's deserved attacks upon the reports
submitted. Under present circumstances it is believed, from
careful study of the records and extended court observation,
that the reports are rarely adequate to evidence the moral
depravity and disobedience which the statute requires and
which adjudication should require in practice.[15] Under present staff handicaps it would be impossible to bring in the sort
of report needed for adjudicative purposes and still perform
the supervisory function which is the chief constructive contribution of probation. A staff of officers skilled in social and
psychological investigation would be required. Whether such
a staff, adequate in numbers, could be procured is an open
question, but it is extremely dubious. However, until the reports are convincing as to impartiality and fullness of information in a majority of cases, it should be simpler, cheaper,
and more effective to require the witnesses themselves to be
in court, obviating the need for pre-hearing investigations.
Under a statute clearly defining the proscribed offenses, this

[14] But see the argument of Chief Justice Cobb of the Domestic Relations
Court, against the evasion of the competent evidence rule in Children's
Court, "Social and Legal Aspects of the Children's Court," pp. 22, 24.
Therein he says, "It is understandable that the social case work mind
does not relish having the future of the child depend on a relatively narrow issue of fact, but prefers to evaluate the whole personality of the
child through social investigation and the application of 'social evidence'
on the hearing by means of a pre-trial investigation. The social worker
wishes no such bar as a legalistic adjudication depending on forms of
law and legal evidence, even though the whole field of social diagnosis and
treatment opens up once the adjudication is secured." See Pauline Young,
op. cit., p. 194.

[15] See Young, *op. cit.*, pp. 105 ff., where she indicates that in the reading
of hundreds of probation records, she found the majority to contain only
very meager information. This has been the writer's experience, too, in
his considerably less extensive review of probation reports.

should be no more difficult here than it is in other tribunals.

Assuming provision for a defense attorney and for adequate probation reports to be delivered to the Court before adjudication, there is a further basic need for the statutory establishment of definite offenses or courses of conduct before pre-hearing investigation reports should be allowed in evidence. The course-of-conduct concept has been analyzed above; here let it merely be reiterated that if a system of conduct can be determined to justify preventive adjudication, it should be defined with sufficient clarity to limit and direct court handling. This is especially important in the procedure under consideration, for loose, vague statutory definition of the area of court power has permitted loose, vague probationary investigations to lead to adjudication. And, once again, to allow general character evaluations formulated by nonspecialists to establish the foundations upon which judgment and extended commitment may occur is a dangerous procedure. Even though an attorney be present to represent defendants in the Court, if he is confronted by a statute excessively vague and general, he may well prove helpless to protect his charges from its expansive tentacles. He alone could not prevent adjudications under a loose statute.

The defendant should be fully and not formalistically informed of the court procedures and her rights under them in order that she may be encouraged to meet the issue squarely at her hearing. She should know what the Court is attempting to do and how it does it. The friendly guidance and advice of some such person as a representative of the Juvenile Aid Bureau, in addition to her legal representative, could be very helpful. This qualification is not so basic as the three previously enumerated, to be sure, but it is important.

Even though the above preconditions to adjudication based upon probation reports should be achieved, the question still remains as to the relative value of the device compared to the more traditional procedure, with fuller preservation of the defendant's trial rights. Justification for the modified procedure must rest upon improved adjudicative accuracy and/or efficiency without unduly increasing the hazards to the defendants or the costs to the state. Theoretically, investigation before trial might result in getting at more of the facts upon which adjudication should be denied or imposed: in administrative tribunals it is believed that fact-finding methods result frequently in eliciting more of the needed information. It may well be that in this tribunal, too, greater accuracy could be attained by the investigative method than by ordinary trial evidence if a sufficient number of trained investigators were used. Yet the two stubborn difficulties challenge this procedure again. If it becomes a choice, as it must under present circumstances, between the intensive, individualized, rehabilitative work of probation supervision—utterly essential to the constructive function of the Court—and investigation of all cases before trial, it appears clear that the officer's time can be used more profitably in supervision. Even if the probation staff could be greatly increased in size to assure better performance of both functions, it is a nice question whether a sufficiently greater accuracy in adjudication would result to warrant the use of the method. And, secondly, character and conduct evidence from probation reports—even if they be more accurate and complete factually—is of dubious probative value in showing the danger of future criminality, under present limitations of knowledge in the field of criminogenesis.

Another defect of the current procedure arises out of the fact that during the adjournment for investigation the defendant is frequently confined on remand. As a result, the person who under more favorable circumstances would often yield the most important clues to the problems of the case is made least accessible to the psychological rapport which is essential to effective probation. Interviewing a confined defendant is most unsatisfactory, since the atmosphere precludes free discussion and increases tension.[16] Too, the officers of the Wayward Minor Court are apparently inclined to give less careful attention to interviewing remanded offenders than to interviewing those on parole who are found at home with their families during investigation.

Certainly the value of the pre-hearing investigation has not been proven in this court up to the present time, though the Court has operated under some adverse circumstances, to be sure. This conclusion is inescapable; under present circumstances of staff and statute and the limited protections surrounding the defendant, pre-adjudication investigations are not warranted. For the future, it would need to prove its value after the preconditions stated had been established. This would involve, not only experience and research, but changes in legislation, budget, personnel, and institutional procedures. Until more nearly adequate protections to the defendant are developed, the Court would perform a far richer service if it confined investigations to offenders adjudicated by testimony of witnesses in court and extended its supervisory work. This would permit both more probationary dispositions and more careful work in supervision.

The opposed point of view is expressed by Brill and Payne:

However, it is the point of view of most enlightened criminologists that our courts, if they are to be effective in reducing juvenile delinquency and adolescent crime, must be social clinics. Since a clinical diagnosis is made after a careful study of the individual and his problem, and not before, the court, likewise acting as a clinic, must make a diagnosis based upon the facts contained in a preliminary investigation conducted by the agents of the court.[17]

[16] *Ibid.*, pp. 60, 63, 87.
[17] See Brill and Payne, *The Adolescent Court and Crime Prevention,* p. 190.

It is suggested that there are several sources of error in this view. There is no clear reason why investigation must precede adjudication as well as treatment; the "clinical diagnosis" idea itself clearly need not imply investigation before a hearing so long as it precedes the prescribing of treatment. Moreover, the notion of a social clinic with implicit comparison to medical clinics does not yet mean very much; the analogy is scarcely merited, what with present limitations of information in the fields of sociology and psychology. For purposes of prescribing treatment the court should and must rely upon data gathered by court officers, whatever their adequacy, in the absence of any superior methods. But to forsake the methods of guilt determination on the basis of a weak clinical analogy, seeking to determine the applicability of court weapons through the interpretation of social data (often derived from hurried investigations of social history), will not advance the status of juvenile and adolescent courts as crime-preventive and reformative agencies. If, by the assumption of a social clinical role, the courts are to continue attempting to solve large varieties of social problems, adjudicating young people for that purpose, they may indeed themselves become the generators of more crime, for it is probable that court contact and penalties are themselves factors in the genesis of criminal careers.

Justice Cobb, in his criticism of this device of pre-trial investigation in our Children's Court, points up some of its weaknesses:

It is not fair to a fair minded judge to place at his elbow a "pre-trial investigation," least of all to permit a probation officer who has made the investigation to make statements or to give evidence which would be incompetent or inadmissible from the mouth of any other witness. The tendency of a probation officer whether sworn or not when allowed to take part in a hearing is inevitably to wander into the field of hearsay or opinion.

No matter how competently and carefully an investigation may be conducted and reported, it filters through the probation officer who presents it. To a large extent it can be none other than hearsay and the fact that it comes from an official of the court gives it no quality of admissibility.

. . . There is nothing anywhere in the law to warrant the belief that anything other than an orderly hearing held with promptness and based on competent evidence is contemplated. Nothing in P. 83 of the Domestic Relations Court Act or P. 931 of the Code of Criminal Procedure as to investigation before adjudication alters this principle. . . . Otherwise, the words in P. 83 "proceed to hear and determine the case," and "if satisfied by competent evidence may adjudicate the child to be delinquent or neglected . . ." would have little meaning. Nor does the use of the word "may" mean that the court may do something contrary to the intent so disclosed of reaching both hearing and decision.

A probation officer who is assigned to investigate, has a better start when the facts relevant to the petition have been established before he begins his investigation. He has something solid on which to build.

There is another side to "pre-trial investigations." If the court does not know whether the child is delinquent what is it going to do with the child during the period of postponement? If the child is innocent, it should not be unnecessarily locked up however grave the charge but should receive dismissal.[18]

Clinical objectives are served by considerations of personality and character; careful diagnosis, prognosis, and prescription are highly desirable in the process of treatment determination. However, if this clinical idea is used to establish adjudication upon issues of character, then the subjection of individuals to the criminal system may be based upon frequently equivocal, sometimes irrelevant, and insufficiently substantiated covert traits of personality rather than overt acts of misconduct. Broad laws may be set up and adminis-

[18] Cobb, *op. cit.*, pp. 18–19, 20. See also Judge E. F. Waite, "How Far Can Court Procedure Be Socialized without Impairing Individual Rights?" *Journal of Criminal Law and Criminology*, XII (Nov., 1921), 339–47.

tered—like the Wayward Minor Act—which permit the processing of many defendants whose conduct was legally innocuous in itself and unlikely to produce legally undesirable results. In essence, the menace is that this procedural technique will subject to essentially criminal adjudication those who are suspected of personal problems needing therapy. Enrico Ferri, the Italian positivist, has well stated the issue of adjudicating on the basis merely of character diagnosis:

Although the data furnished by criminal anthropology and criminal psychology are not yet complete, it may yet be affirmed that the dangerousness or anti-sociability of a man can be argued from the character of his personality in connection with his social behavior, even before he commits, or attempts to commit, an offense. But if this probable dangerousness may call for some measures of personal and social prevention (e. g., the selection for instruction and training of the morally deficient, "candidates for delinquency"), it evidently is not sufficient for the calling forth of judicial repressive measures. Just as for segregation in a lunatic asylum there is at least necessary the concrete fact of a morbid manifestation on the part of the patient, so for a repressive sanction there is at least necessary the attempt to commit an offense.[19]

Judge E. F. Waite may be quoted on the related question of the degree and kind of "liberalization" in procedure which may be appropriate to juvenile proceedings:

Rules of ancient origin, approved or at least tolerated by the community for generations, encountered by the citizen whenever he resorts to other legal forums to assert, or defend his rights, should be not lightly set aside in juvenile courts. The only safe practice is to observe them. If hearsay, for example, has not been found justly admissible in civil disputes and criminal trials, it is no better in juvenile court proceedings. Exceptions should be made when appropriate, and informal short cuts will often be found agreeable to all concerned; but the exception should always be recognized as an exception. No judge on any bench has need to be

[19] For the point of view expressed here, see Ferri, *Report and Preliminary Project for an Italian Penal Code* (Betts trans.), p. 405.

more thoroughly grounded in the principles of evidence and more constantly mindful of them than the judge of a juvenile court. The boy against whom it is supposed to make an official record of misconduct, involving possible curtailment of his freedom at the behest of strangers, has the right to be found delinquent only according to law. . . . The greater the conceded discretion of the judge, the freer he is from the vigilance of lawyers, the less likely he is to have his mistakes corrected on appeal, so much the more careful should he be to base every judicial conclusion on evidence proper to be received in any court of justice. Otherwise, the State's parental power which he embodies is prostituted; the interpreter of the law degenerates into the oriental *kadi,* and the juvenile court falls into suspicion and disrepute.[20]

CASES PROCESSED BY THE COURT

The procedures of the Wayward Minor Court and the varied succession of problems which confront it may be seen in a series of briefly summarized cases which were brought to the intake officer in the course of one day:

Case 1: H. T., age eighteen, was the daughter of Polish parents who had brought her to the United States when she was a young child. Her parents were divorced when she was seven years old, and the mother sent her back to Poland to be boarded with friends. She remained there until the age of sixteen; at that time the mother remarried, and H. T. returned here to live with her. She was unhappy in the home, disliked by her stepfather, and resisted the unaccustomed parental authority. Falling in love with a married man, she went to live with him. After arraignment in court upon complaint of her mother, H. T. was remanded for a week to Florence Crittenton League for shelter and while there was found to have no venereal disease. Magistrate X. adjudged her to be a wayward minor and placed her on probation. Within three months she was brought back to court under a warrant issued for violation of probation when she returned to live with the man. Judge S. committed her directly to Westfield State Farm.

[20] Waite, "How Far Can Court Procedure Be Socialized without Impairing Individual Rights?" *Journal of Criminal Law and Criminology,* XII (Nov., 1921), 339–47.

Case 2: E. K., sixteen years of age, was the daughter of a minister living in New Jersey. Five weeks prior to the complaint she came to live with a sister in Brooklyn. She left this home, however, and was picked up a few days later in a house on 53d Street where she had been living with several men. She resisted violently upon arrest. When E. K. was brought into Women's Court on a prostitution charge, the judge referred the case to Wayward Minor Court. Her father complained that she had behaved badly for seven years, and he asked that she be adjudged. The girl refused in court to return home with her father. However, Magistrate M., who heard the complaint and testimony, dismissed the case for lack of jurisdiction because the parent's residence was outside the state. (This is customary, though not universal, practice in this court, apparently based on the idea that the parent's foreign residence renders the daughter's depravity and disobedience an issue beyond the Court's jurisdiction.)

Case 3: T. H. was the eighteen-year-old daughter of Greek-born parents who believed in the tradition of strict discipline and filial obedience. The girl asserted her love for a dark-skinned Puerto Rican whom her parents considered unsuitable. She resisted parental authority, claiming that they frequently humiliated her deliberately before her friends. Upon the mother's assertion that the defendant was "mentally backward," T. H. was remanded first to Bellevue Hospital for observation and then to Florence Crittenton for custody. Bellevue's psychiatrist, finding her of normal mentality, recommended that the girl live and board away from home to avoid the domestic conflict. To this the parents objected, saying that she should be "put away" where she could not see the boy of whom they disapproved. The girl was confined for three weeks at Crittenton on remand. The Court then further adjourned the case for eight months during which time T. H. was paroled to the Crittenton League, which had obtained a housework position for her in New Rochelle. When she did poorly on this job she was returned to the Court and again remanded in the custody of Crittenton until such time as her father should move his family to a new home, thereby removing the danger of her further association with the Puerto Rican. When the family moved, their daughter was placed on official probation, being adjudicated by the Court a year after the original complaint. A few months later the case was dismissed because the defendant had married another boy. She was considered no longer to be under the jurisdiction of the Court, since after marriage she did not owe the statutory filial obedience. (This participation by the Court in issues of nationality, racial, and cultural preference is a not uncommon but extremely questionable practice.)

Case 4: E. G. was the daughter of an apparently paranoid Italian mother who had requested the help of the mayor in controlling her family. Nineteen years of age, E. G. was accused of staying out after eleven o'clock at night, sometimes as late as three in the morning. The case was brought into the Wayward Minor Court by the chief of probation to whom it had been referred by the chief magistrate after the latter's receipt of the communication from the mayor. Though the mother was suspicious that her daughter engaged in sexual activity, there was no evidence of it, and E. G. maintained that she did not; her Board of Health report was negative. The defendant asserted that she slept in a garage out of fear of her mother's habits of biting, scratching, and striking her. On these facts the girl was arraigned and docketed. Adjournments were declared by the Court for a period of more than a year. She was first remanded to Villa Loretto, the House of the Good Shepherd at Peekskill, and after a physical examination and report, was returned there for a period of three months by Magistrate S. Thereafter she was returned home under parole, subject to the unofficial supervision of a representative of the Italian Center of Queens. The mother was outspoken in her objection to the ending of her daughter's incarceration, complaining at the increased cost in her home. The case was dismissed as adjusted after a little more than a year.

Case 5: A. L. was a Negress, aged seventeen, brought by her mother to Women's Court because of her promiscuous behavior and pregnant condition. After referral to the Wayward Minor Court, the mother made a complaint and then withdrew it, asking to be referred to an agency which might help. She was directed to the Department of Public Welfare, Out of Wedlock Division; thus the case did not then go into court but was kept at the intake level. A baby was born to A. L. shortly thereafter in Harlem Hospital. A month later A. L.'s mother signed a recurrent complaint against her daughter, based on her continued promiscuity and the lack of sufficient supervision in her home. The daughter planned to marry the putative father of her child, a Puerto Rican, but since it was found upon examination that he had syphilis, no license could be issued. This defendant was committed to Westfield, upon a hearing, by Magistrate T. (No report of a probation investigation appeared in the records of this case.)

Case 6: D. A. was also a Negress, aged seventeen. The mother complained in Women's Court that her daughter had left home and refused to return. A warrant was issued from Women's Court, returnable in the court for girls. The defendant claimed that, upon discovering she was pregnant, she left home fearing to have her mother learn of her condition. The boy who was responsible expressed his willingness to marry her, and his mother wrote a statement of consent. Although D. A. was not diseased or promiscuous and was pregnant, Magistrate S. committed her without adjournment to Westfield, the baby to be born during incarceration. In referring to the father of the child the probation officer reported: "Due to his age [seventeen] and the fact that he was being supported by his mother, it was deemed wise to send D. where she would receive care, and by the time the baby is born he might have a job and be able to assume responsibilities."

Case 7: W. C. was the sixteen-year-old daughter born illegitimately to a mother who had twice married thereafter and then died, leaving the girl to be raised by her maternal grandmother in Georgia. Her half brother complained to the Court that she had run away from his mother's home in Syracuse two years before to live with an uncle in New York City and was now missing. W. C. was picked up on a warrant and found to be pregnant. She was placed in Women's House of Detention on remand during investigation and, little being learned about her, she was committed to Westfield after a hearing on the return date.

Several cases may serve to indicate other aspects of the Court's problems and dispositions:

Case 1: C. D., aged eighteen, was a student at Brooklyn College, with an I.Q. of 128. A legally adopted child, she left home without her foster parents' consent and was living with a blood relative at the time of the complaint. She was remanded to Bellevue Hospital and the Brooklyn House of the Good Shepherd during adjournments lasting for two and one-half months; she was then paroled to her adoptive parents for three months. In this case the girl was arraigned originally by Magistrate T.; the case was later adjourned by Magistrate M., and finally dismissed by Magistrate S.

Case 2: R. F., a Negress, aged sixteen, was pregnant but without venereal disease. During her stay at Crittenton on remand she was so well liked that, upon a hearing, the League indicated its willingness to keep her until the girl's mother could move into a new neighborhood. In this case the baby was born at St. Vincent's Hospital, from the shelter. The probation officer assisted R. F.'s mother in securing inexpensive housing and an allotment from the Board of Child Welfare.

Case 3: M. N., aged seventeen, was accused of being beyond parental control for three years, staying out often until three in the morning, and having fits of temper in which she struck and bruised her mother. According to the probation officer's report, the mother, "though reared a Catholic, was married by the City Clerk," there was no "mother-daughter relationship," and the "mother was more interested in the boarder than in the welfare of her husband and children." The case against the girl was dismissed for insufficient evidence.

Case 4: In the case of A. C., brought to court by the father's complaint for truancy and staying out late with a boy of whom he disapproved, it was learned that the mother and father were separated, each living in a meretricious relationship with a paramour. Arrangements were made by the Court for the girl to attend a school in New Jersey, the case against her being dismissed. When the father objected to the tuition expenditures for his disobedient daughter, the probation officer wrote: "You are to bring her dress-suit case that you have, in order to send her off to school. Judge S. has demanded that this girl go to school, therefore there is nothing left for you to do but to follow out the magistrate's orders." The girl was later dismissed from the school because of her misbehavior and paroled to her mother. When she absconded a warrant was issued for her arrest, but she evaded the jurisdiction of the Court by marrying.

Case 5: In the case of L. G., brought to court by her father for disobedience, the girl made a better impression upon the Court than did her father. The probation officer arranged for the girl to receive training in baby nursing at the Salvation Army nursery and hospital, and the case against her was dismissed. The probation officer wrote in her report: "Her mother is acquainted with the fact that she is in her present position, but her father, who is absolutely antagonistic to her, has not been informed. He will not be informed if there is any way of keeping it from him. If he knew of her whereabouts he would without doubt jeopardize her outlook."

Case 6: M. G., seventeen, had been raped by a soldier, according to her testimony. Her mother harassed her so frequently about the sex experience thereafter that she ran away from home three times. After remands to Bellevue Hospital and the House of the Good Shepherd, her mother (in the words of the probation officer), "came to court, prepared to take M. home with her after two months' time, during which she proposed to sell her business and move to a different neighborhood. Miss D. offered to ask Mother G. at the Peekskill House of the Good Shepherd to take her back again upon M.'s promise of good behavior, but upon this suggestion M. flew into a temper tantrum in court, shouting that she hated her mother, and Judge A. thereupon committed her to Westfield State Farm."

From this series of cases there may be drawn several observations which study of a large number of records tends to confirm:

1. The cases which come to the Court do involve a large variety of nonlegal social problems with which a judicial and correctional system is not equipped effectively to deal. Yet referral to outside agencies for more specialized aid is not sufficiently frequent. The seriousness of this problem is enhanced by the lack of coöperation of such agencies with the Court.

2. The treatment techniques established by the statute are not sufficiently varied for optimum individualization. Often probation may appear unwise, yet the indeterminate sentence which generally extends for a period of a year or more is excessively severe. One result of this situation has been a high rate of extended commitments. Another has been the development of a series of informal expedients to avoid the methods sanctioned in the statute. The long remand has thus become a common device and, with some judges, has been almost au-

tomatically applied. In numerous instances the remand has appeared to be in effect a constructive compromise. However, the fact of its unofficial and extralegal character, associated with the simple method of securing the defendant's consent, facilitates a frequent use and abuse of the technique that too easily escapes criticism and correction.

3. The dependence for jurisdiction upon parental complaint and testimony, often in cases where the parent himself is in greater need of correction, has limited the effectiveness of the Court. The wayward minor has come to warrant the definition, "a girl whose mother is willing to talk." It appears from the cases that the judicial and correctional system should not be used as a mere extension of familial control, but must operate as a secondary group sanction of a different order after primary group control has failed. In their nature, the judge, court, and reformatory are not normal projections of father, home, and domestic discipline; nor should the former be additional weapons in the hands of parents to be used at their pleasure when they have failed in their child-rearing.

4. The unfortunate consequences of taking the defendant before a diversity of judges are apparent in the records. Conflicts of purpose, multiplication of effort, and confusion of the girl are thereby accentuated.

5. The operation of biases among the motives of court personnel is apparent again and again in the cases, attesting the importance of private and personal attitudes which may function within the adjudicative process, especially in a court whose defendants are usually sex offenders.

6. The plight of minorities for whom no sufficient special provision is made becomes clear in the cases.

6

A Cross-sectional View

DATA HAVE BEEN GATHERED from the intensive analysis of a
continuous series of 150 case records from 1938 and 150 from
1942, with reports from social agencies, hospitals, psychiatrists, custodial institutions, etc. Procedures in the Court
have also been observed over an extended period of time.
The following analysis attempts to give a rather complete
view of the procedures used in 1938 and 1942, and in 1945
in so far as the records and observation have revealed them.
More might have been learned, to be sure, if the records of
testimony were available for study. It must be repeated that
the materials set down here do not attempt to present a ka-
leidoscopic view of the entire eight years of court operation.

Referrals.—Since the Wayward Minor Court is both relatively young and unusual in its kind, the public is not well
informed concerning its activities; indeed, the nature, jurisdiction, and policy of the Court have apparently not been
well known even to some of the specialized social agencies of
the city. Partly, this results from the fact that the Court has
neither desired nor sought publicity for its work, what with
the limitations of its facilities; partly, it reflects the failure
to build that close coöperation with agency and institution
upon which the most effective work with adolescents depends.
The mutual misunderstanding and antagonism which commonly mark the relations of private social agencies and
public probation have affected the operational efficiency of
the Wayward Minor Court. The situation is revealed, to some
extent, in the following figures taken from the intake sheets
of the Court:

TABLE 1

Source of Complainants' Referrals to the Court

	1938	1942
Police	52	40
Social agency	31	62
Another court	25	20
Unknown	42	28
Total	150	150

These data reveal several changes which occurred during the period from 1938 to 1942. The drop in referrals by police, despite the aging of the Court and increased familiarity with it, is attributable largely to the termination of much of the work of the Juvenile Aid Bureau which had carried on extensive work with this adolescent group and coöperated closely with the Court.[1] The growth in referrals from social agencies, for the most part family and welfare agencies, shows their increasing dependence upon the Court as a "last resort" for their cases. It may be surprising that so small a group comes to the Court from other courts; the fact is that a few judges in other magistrates' courts, aware of, and sympathetic with, what the Wayward Minor Court is attempting to do, are inclined to refer young and presumably corrigible girls to the specialized court for the application of its more concentrated facilities; some, indeed, reduce a charge from a

[1] In the summer of 1941, with the cut in Works Project Administration personnel, the work of the Juvenile Aid Bureau was reduced from 60 to 75 percent. See New York *Times* for June 29, 1941, p. 30, column 2. In 1942 the Juvenile Aid Bureau was dropped from the budget by the Mayor, "its work to be performed by welfare agencies of the precincts." See the New York *Times* for April 2, 1942, and for April 18, 1942. The protest of the social agencies of the city was strong but ineffectual (New York *Times,* April 23, 1942). The bureau is being revitalized and expanded. It has real potentialities for meeting the serious problem of delinquency in New York City by assuming a more active role than it has taken during the past few years. The Wayward Minor Court, however, has learned to prefer to do the work (with different methods and consequences, necessarily) through its own probation officers.

misdemeanor to an offense so that they may refer the case to the Wayward Minor Court. Many judges do not approve, however, of what they consider the excessive leniency or sentimentality involved in this procedure; others consider it unnecessary or even illegal. It is anticipated that with the apparent increase in the amount of adolescent sex delinquency [2] and the developing public consciousness of the existence of the Court, referrals here will be more common. An increase has already occurred on a substantial scale, making it advisable to extend court sittings to a three-day week beginning in April, 1944.

Complainants.—The data on the source of complaints in the Court is suggestive in the light it throws on the operation and limitations of that tribunal. No changes of great statistical significance occurred between 1938 and 1942. It is believed that throughout the history of the Court the proportions of the various types of complainants have not changed appreciably.

[2] According to the Federal Bureau of Investigation report for the first half of 1943, the arrests of girls under twenty-one for "crimes against common decency" were 89.5 percent higher than during the same period of the previous year. All arrests for girls under twenty-one increased 64.7 percent, nineteen and eighteen being the predominating ages for arrests of females. Rapes increased 10.5 percent for the first half of 1942 and 28.4 percent for the first half of 1943 in comparison to a similar period for the prior year in each case. See New York *Times* for September 17, 1943, and October 7, 1943. According to the Office of War Information juvenile delinquency among young girls increased 38 percent from 1940 through 1942 with an especially great spread of venereal disease; see New York *Times* for October 10, 1943. The increase in infectious syphilis in New York City has been estimated at 132 percent in the age group from fifteen to nineteen during 1943 as compared to 1941. According to Katherine Lenroot the figures gathered by the Children's Bureau, indicate an 18 percent increase in cases of girl delinquents in New York City (New York *Times* for April 12, 1944). See the Quarterly Reports of the Federal Bureau of Investigation. It may well be, of course, that these increases reflect, at least in part, the greater publicity and attention given to delinquency: the data represent enforcement, not violation. From 1939 to 1945 arrests of girls under eighteen in the United States had increased 198 percent; see New York *Times* for December 11, 1945.

TABLE 2

Source of Complaints

	1938	1942
Parent	132	122
Guardian	1	5
Kin	12	10
Agency representative	2	8
Police officer	3	5
Total	150	150

The most striking fact which the figures reveal is the great preponderance of parental complaints. This is a result of the limitation by the Court of its operation to those cases coming under Section 913-a (5) of the Code of Criminal Procedure, defined as those in which there is "willful disobedience to parent or guardian." Such allegation must generally come from the parent. As indicated above, this leads to an excessive dependence upon a parental decision as to court action and disposition. The Court is disinclined, if it can be avoided, to rely upon the complaint and/or testimony merely of an agency representative or police officer for its jurisdiction, some judges doubting the validity of adjudication under the act unless the parent is willing to sign a complaint and testify to the misbehavior alleged therein. Others believe that so long as the social purposes of the Court are served, the questions of formal legality in complaint and testimony are not so important. The restriction of the Court's jurisdiction has been apparent in instances where, in pursuance of the drive on the "bobby socks Victory girls" of Times Square,[3] the police have picked up teen-age girls but found it impossible to secure

[3] See "Police Drive on 'Bobby Socks' Girls Will Curb Teen-Age Night Owls," New York *Times,* February 15, 1944; "Midtown Round-up of Teen-Age Boys, Girls Now Totals 51," New York *Times,* February 26, 1944.

complaints from the parents against their daughters. Moreover, cases of "runaway girls" have gone unprosecuted in the absence of a parental complaint. The legislation passed in 1945 will bring such cases under the jurisdiction of the Court by specific provision.

Intake.—An intake officer is on duty at 100 Centre Street daily to conduct preliminary interviews with complainants. Such an interview is generally held prior to the signing of any complaint and, in some cases, referrals have already been made to other agencies outside the Court in order to effect an adjustment without formal and official action here. One former judge of the Court has described this as a "farming-out process which resulted in removing the responsibility from the Probation Department, where, under the law, it belonged." [4] However, as will appear below, practice has varied in this respect, and some officials of the Court believe that success in individualizing treatment can best be achieved by full utilization of supervisory assistance from family, recreational, and other social agencies of the city. One rather recent development promised to be of considerable value: social agency representatives were assigned to the Court and at intake might suggest referrals in place of adjudication. Thus many girls could be spared exposure to court. This agency liaison did not persist for long, however. At intake an effort is made to obtain a standardized body of information concerning the family background and the educational, religious, vocational, and personal history of the defendant.

The Court clears all cases through the Social Service Exchange in order to gain whatever information may be available concerning the prior contacts of the family with social agencies, institutions, and courts. Useful, time-saving sum-

[4] Kross, *Procedures for Dealing with Wayward Minors in New York City*, pp. 15–16.

maries from earlier investigations are frequently obtained from the agencies.

TABLE 3

Disposition at Intake

	1938	1942
Referred elsewhere	36	3
Intake only	12	17
Case docketed	102	130
Total	150	150

The information available on intake indicates that until 1942 referrals to agencies for supervision of cases were quite frequent. (The process of referral from the intake officer is roughly analogous to the refusal of a complaint clerk in an ordinary magistrate's court to issue a complaint. In the procedure of the girls' court, however, the referral is more constructive than rejection of the case, being based on the attempt to procure service for the girl or her family. In 1939, out of 300 cases, thirty-seven were thus referred, and in 1940, out of 330 cases, sixty-six were referred to agencies.[5] There is no doubt but that in many instances the practice resulted from the lack of adequate probation staff to carry on investigation and supervision for all the cases brought into the Court. Frequently, however, it was based on the realization that an agency contact would be less damaging and that a court hearing was unnecessary. In the majority of instances in which the girl was turned over to an agency neither her offense nor her character appear to have warranted court action. It will be observed that in 1942, however, the Court itself handled virtually all cases, as it has continued to do since that time. This represents a partial drying-up of supervisory assistance from the agencies—particularly the grave loss from the

[5] Wayward Minor Court, *An Evaluative Review of Procedures and Purposes;* computed from data on p. 51.

budgetary mutilation of the Juvenile Aid Bureau,[6] which at one time did invaluable work with delinquents through the age of adolescence. Partly, it reflects the opinion of some of the judges that all cases should come before them. One judge insists that the girl should be brought before him rather than disposed of by unofficial means at the discretion of a probation officer.

Among officials of courts, who are well conditioned to the atmosphere of criminal justice, there is little understanding of the traumatic response which exposure to the court may arouse in the adolescent. A small proportion of cases brought to intake was neither referred to an agency nor sent to court, chiefly when the intake officer felt that the problem represented by the case needed neither official action nor the supervisory assistance of an agency. In some instances the girls were handled unofficially by probation officers without any court appearance, thus adopting the procedure which has become common in the Children's Court; in others, the complainant was simply told that there was no case for action by the Court. It is apparent, however, that for the most part the Court takes and dockets virtually all who come, considering each case as a social problem to be solved by the socialized court. This is especially true since the practice of "farming out" cases has declined. Nearly all cases, whether or not they were ultimately adjudicated, were at least brought before the Court and investigated.

Complaints, summonses, and warrants.—After a complaint has been signed (or, under some circumstances, prior to a complaint), the girl's appearance in court is sought. In so far as possible, it is preferred that she come before the judge voluntarily without official process of the Court. The means by which her appearance was induced in the 300 cases of 1938 and 1942 appear in the following table:

6 See footnote 1. The Bureau was expanded again in 1946.

TABLE 4

Defendants' Pre-arraignment Appearance

	1938	1942
Voluntary	92	78
Summons	12	27
Warrant	19	33
Summons and warrant	1	10
No appearance	26	2
Total	150	150

It may be seen that a majority of the girls came voluntarily to the Court in response, generally, to a letter from the intake officer. The cases revealed too that more were brought in on warrants than by summonses alone; this was partly because of the number of girls who had run away from home and whom the parents believed they could not find or induce to come to court. A small group failed to respond to a summons and required a warrant. Though the Code of Criminal Procedure provides for a $25 fine for contempt on refusal to obey a summons,[7] this penalty is not imposed in practice, and the girls sometimes display a surprising sophistication in refusing to honor the summons. There are relatively few instances, however, in which both processes have been used.[8] In comparing the two years we find that a significant difference is the virtual disappearance of cases eliminated without court contact; this is associated with the drastic reduction of referrals to agencies.

INTERIM PROCEDURE

In the words of Magistrate Kross, who developed what

---

[7] Code of Criminal Procedure, Sec. 150.

[8] The legislature has passed a bill that would permit the judge, within his discretion, to issue a warrant without first having issued a summons, when it would appear that the latter would be a useless act. Actually in the past the Court has followed this procedure, but there has been some questioning of its legality without further statutory authorization.

may be called the "interim device" in the Wayward Minor Court:

Upon the first appearance of the girl complete Intake information is presented to the presiding Magistrate. The summary of the Intake interview sets forth not only the immediate complaint but also the real problems involved, whether they be economic, vocational, family incompatibility or any other reason. This enables the Magistrate to determine whether the girl shall be returned home pending investigation or detained elsewhere; and also makes provision for physical and mental examinations.[9]

After intake information has been secured and a complaint signed, the girl is brought before the Court. On the basis of the information provided, the presiding magistrate may determine either that the girl should return home, or that she should be detained in a shelter. He sets an adjourned date and orders that an investigation by the probation department be made in the meantime. This is the pre-adjudication investigation to which reference has been made. It has become characteristic institutionalized procedure to secure a social case record before trial, and to parole or remand the defendant during the three or four weeks of the investigation.

Thus a most central, and perhaps the most unique, procedure of the Court, is the pre-hearing adjournment during which investigation is made by the probation officer; in some cases, a Board of Health examination is given, and a psychiatric or psychometric examination may also be ordered. During the years 1938 and 1942 interim procedures were used as indicated in Table 5.

The most significant item in Table 5 is the number of instances in which a custodial remand is used rather than parole. We find that in 1938, seventy-eight of the 150 girls were remanded to one or more institutions for periods ranging from a few days to several months. Checking these, it was found

[9] Kross, *op. cit.*, pp. 5-6.

TABLE 5

Interim Dispositions

	1938	1942
Parole	15	26
Remand	57	87
Parole and remand	21	22
No interim procedure used (withdrawal of complaint; lack of jurisdiction; inability to serve warrant; referred to agency directly)	46	12
Direct commitment (without interim disposition)	11	3
Total	150	150

that in thirty-two instances the case was ultimately dismissed without formal adjudication. In 1942, 109 cases were remanded, the larger number apparently reflecting again the reduction in referrals and the growing inclination to make institutional remands automatic. Of these, fifty-four were not adjudicated. The proportions here should be compared with the results of the interim practices used in the youthful offender division of the special and general sessions courts, where only 15 percent or 20 percent of the cases are remanded prior to sentence. The situation in the Wayward Minor Court reflects the influence of several factors. Where there is strong disagreement in the home, it is deemed therapeutically desirable to remove the girl from the arena of conflict for a time. If the complaint indicates venereal contact it is thought necessary, in the interest of social protection, to avoid the risk of spreading infection. Some of the officers believe that a short period of "cooling off" in institutional confinement may be beneficial in restraining future misconduct. Indeed, one of the most important uses of the interim device is to encourage the adjustment of the case, if possible, without either a formal adjudication or formal commitment. Moreover, it is held to be a helpful circumvention of the excessively limited statutory provisions for treatment, making it possible to confine the defendant for periods of a few weeks or months, and permitting treatment without necessarily resorting to adjudication.

Despite these arguments, the wisdom of the interim remands may be doubted in these instances: (1) where there is no indication of sex delinquency; (2) where, though there is a measure of domestic discord, more harm may easily be done by confinement in an institution (though it be called, euphemistically, a "shelter") than benefit from the separation; and (3) where the great variations in these institutions lead—as they often do—to gross inequality in treatment based, not on individual need, but upon such irrelevancies as religion and race. It may well be asked whether there is justification for sending the young adolescent girl of presumably corrigible character to that mecca of prostitutes, the House of Detention, in advance of trial when—in the view of the law—she will not be found "guilty" of an "offense" even if adjudicated, and, moreover, since more than 40 percent of the cases will not be adjudicated.

The attempt is made to justify fairly extended remands on the ground that not only are they socially beneficial, but also they are more lenient dispositions than the Court might impose. Legislation proposed by one judge of the Court has been adopted, whereby longer automatic remands are permitted without consent of the defendant than were formerly possible. As one officer of the Court has put it:

It is a matter of common experience in this court for a distraught parent to present herself at the court with her daughter and demand that she be "put away" forthwith. Frequently, too, defendants, incensed at their parents, flatly refuse to go home and state that they would rather go to jail than to return home. We have learned that after two or three weeks' separation, these antagonisms frequently disappear and the rejecting mother and protesting daughter can be, and generally are, reconciled. It is obvious that if the court were to proceed in the face of the emotional disturbances which present themselves upon first appearance, and were to exercise its full powers of forthwith hearing, adjudication, and commitment, many unfortunate situations would arise. This is particularly apparent when it is realized that the law provides that a commitment made by this court must be for an indeterminate period of time, not to exceed three years.[10]

To the writer, this attempt to solve such problems of domestic conflict "clinically" by means of detention in a custodial institution is rather like surgery with an axe; the apologist quoted above points out that the clinician had the power to use a blunter instrument. Significantly, the Court may also use probation facilities to promote understanding; it can often find and provide shelter, with relatives of the defendant or in a noncustodial home. Such substitutes would, of course, be more time- and energy-consuming in a department that is already overoccupied with pre-trial investigations.

Moreover, this method of circumventing the excessively narrow and rigid statutory provisions for treatment methods encourages customary resort to extralegal devices and their application in cases which the Court might otherwise leave to more appropriate social agency therapy. The association of interim remands with "unofficial treatment" encourages the trend in the Wayward Minor Court, as in so many of the contemporary tribunals for the young, to deal with more social and behavior problems which do not belong in court at all. In avoiding adjudication and formal treatment it has become easy to rationalize dealing with "minor problems" unofficially. This drive in our courts is a hazardous one; for the courts are still agencies of law, designed to deal with offenders, staffed with personnel whose methods and philosophy are punitive-rehabilitative (not preventive), using correctional facilities, and carrying an institutional stigma.

[10] Wayward Minor Court, "An Evaluative Review," p. 14.

A suggestion that this remand procedure protects the rights of the girl has been rationalized by terming it "remand by consent." Yet, as Magistrate Kross has indicated, the pre-arraignment procedures in the first years were based upon implied consent, and today the consent is still frequently left to implication or else coerced by the Court's offer to the girl of a choice between shelter at a sectarian institution and detention in the women's jail. The right of the Court to adjourn on remand is granted in the Code of Criminal Procedure,[11] but it was designed to be applied to defendants after conviction and before sentence, and allows for three-day periods only, permitting longer adjournments by consent. The methods of obtaining such consent in the Wayward Minor Court are effective, whatever else may be said of them. As in the other adolescent courts where "consent" is secured before the defendant may be investigated as a youthful offender, a fiction is established, in effect, to permit the Court to do indirectly what the statutes do not directly allow. To reiterate, there are serious dangers attending the rapid influx of consent procedures in our adolescent courts whereby legal rights of the defendant are surreptitiously denied. The threat, increased by the frequent proposals to avoid even the necessity of consent, has finally culminated in a law which abandons the requirement of consent for fifteen-day remands. One officer of the Court has said: "Actually no harm was done to any of the girls and all were glad to consent to such shelter— and, as a matter of fact, many, on the adjourned date, requested to be returned to the institution." The morbid psychological implications of this statement appear to have been lost to the speaker. The "gladness" of the girls is far more frequently expressed, more normally, in tears. The harm which may be done by remand institutions is apparently too intangible for judicial notice.

[11] Code of Criminal Procedure, Sec. 191.

Related to the purpose of remand by consent is the use of parole for extended periods during which the defendant's case is adjourned. This permits informal probationary supervision of the girl and may be used in place of adjudication, formal probation, or commitment. When there is conflict between the daughter and her parents parole to other relatives, an agency, or friends rather than interim commitment might be used more frequently. It would seem, at least in the case of many girls over eighteen against whom no very serious delinquency is charged, that the girl might be freed on her own recognizance to live at a girls' club or a place of her own choosing. Again, it may appear upon its face that parole with unofficial supervision and without adjudication is a least injurious technique of the Court, exposing the girl neither to the risks and stigma of an institution nor to the status of a wayward minor. Too, since no definite period of supervision need be established in advance, its duration can be adjusted to the requirements of the case. If the girl fails there is still the opportunity to adjudicate and make disposition accordingly.

Yet, to reiterate and emphasize the point, the device encourages the expansionist drives of the courts to treat extralegally all manner of situations where court processes and personnel are inappropriate. As the useful practice of referral to social agencies equipped to deal with general personality and social problems has declined, the Court comes to deal with a wider range of issues for which it is unfitted. These informal, unofficial, extralegal, and discretionary administrative procedures can and do entail abuses concealed from scrutiny or correction. Individualization of treatment should be carried on within the framework of proper limitations on the power of the Court and of correctional agencies. If adjudication be first required to help insure that only cases needing court handling are dealt with by court personnel, then short-duration parole, and, occasionally, remand prior to sentencing could still be used to avoid extended treatment under the act. Under the law recently enacted such post-adjudication remands may be established for a one-month period.[12]

Several other factors of importance are suggested by Table 5: the reduced frequency of sending the girl directly to an institution of final commitment without a period for investigation; indeed, the still occasional practice of committing at once upon arraignment is unfortunate in a court attempting to individualize treatment. It means that no adequate effort has been made to determine the existence of mitigating circumstances which might suggest probation. Such immediate disposition has been made upon the testimony of parents without even the substantiation of a probation officer's confirmation so far as the records reveal, although experience has shown the Court that parents are frequently glad to be rid of their children without just cause. The decline in the number of cases completed without court contact is a less fortunate trend; it implies that court contacts are being made in instances similar to those in which, in earlier years, the girls were spared the experience by referrals elsewhere.

In conclusion it should be stated that the writer's chief objections to extended remand do not result from the provision made thereby for social, psychological, and physical examination, but because the remand is made before and without adjudication. Remand or parole for fairly extended periods may be justified legally and socially when the defendant has had a full and fair hearing and has been found an offender. Indeed, these devices may be useful for informal

---

12 Legislation has been enacted providing for thirty-day remands after adjudication and before final sentencing. However, it is combined with numerous other features which fail to protect the defendant.

circumvention of an absurd statutory provision which established no type of treatment between probation and indeterminate commitment. The Court has in many instances worked out rather well its interim dispositions—within the limitations of the available facilities. The girl may be tried first on parole, if it appears that she will behave reasonably well, or she may be paroled after a short remand to Bellevue for diagnostic observation. It is then possible for the parent to call upon the Court if the conduct complained of continues, and the disposition may be changed. In some instances where the girl has been placed in a sectarian or private shelter her subsequent misbehavior may require that she be transferred to the House of Detention. It is thus possible to modify the treatment in the light of experience with the case, an important flexibility in a system which characteristically assumes to deal with criminals finally and in advance, regardless of the limitations of available diagnosis and the necessary hazards of prediction. Needless to say, this adaptability is equally possible after adjudication (when warranted by evidence) and during investigation or informal supervision, prior to final disposition of the case; in this way the girl innocent of proven wrong would not be subjected to what is, in fact, a partially punitive treatment. The logical improvement in interim methods awaits more adequate and individualized facilities.

Hearing and adjudication.—The Wayward Minor Act provides that at the hearing the defendant shall be advised of her legal rights, informed of the charge, and given an opportunity for an adjournment to secure the aid of counsel and to procure witnesses and friends. These matters are formally announced to the girl. The hearing generally occurs on the first adjourned date and is usually followed by adjudication unless the Court is attempting to handle the case by unofficial supervision, in which instance a final determination of the issue is postponed. At the hearing there is available an investigation report from the probation department and such other data as the Court may have ordered during the period of interim adjournment. In the evaluative review of procedures and policy the Court has described and attempted to justify the investigation report prior to adjudication in these words:

> When the case returns to court on the first adjourned date, after a period of investigation, *there is available for the Presiding Magistrate a complete Preliminary Investigation report made by the probation officer which contains pertinent data as to the social, educational and vocational background of the defendant* [italics not in original], and discusses in detail as well significant factors contributing to the immediate delinquency problem. Summaries of contacts with agencies which knew the girl or her family previously are also available in the folder and, frequently, representatives of these agencies appear in court for consultations with the Judge and the probation officer as to methods of attempted adjustment.[13] Generally, there is also available a psychological examination and a report of her physical condition. Thus the Presiding Magistrate is in a position to determine whether circumstances are such that the court must proceed forthwith for formal hearing. It will be seen that the responsibility of the probation officer is great and that *she is expected to have delved into various complicated and complicating factors regarding the problems surrounding the girl, her family, and her behavior difficulties.* [Italics not in the original.] Since the probation officer has done intensive work in this case, the Presiding Magistrate relies to a great extent on her recommendations.

The question has always arisen as to the extent to which the Magistrate may legally make use of this social data before he has proceeded formally to determine the competency of the actual Wayward Minor charge against the defendant. As indicated previously, our sanction for this preadjudication conference with the Magistrate is contained in Section 931 of the Code of Criminal

[13] During the writer's observation in the Court there was rarely a representative from a social agency available for consultation in the tribunal, although a representative from one or more of the detention institutions was frequently there.

Procedure with its phrase, "prior to or after adjudication," [14] relating to the type of material which a Magistrate may have available to him.

Regardless of the legal aspects, however, this procedure has more than justified itself socially. In many instances where emotional conflicts have been the basis of the Wayward Minor charge successful adjustments have been made and the cases have subsequently been dismissed without adjudication. It is necessary of course, to adjourn a case from time to time in order to carry out this attempted adjustment; and, during that period, the defendant is kept under the unofficial supervision of the probation officer and reports concerning progress are made to the court on each adjourned date. If the adjustment is successful, charges are dismissed at the request of the complainant or upon the recommendation of the probation officer, or the case-working agency cooperating. In this way, the stigma of adjudication is avoided in the vast majority of cases by this court.[15]

[14] The section of the Code of Criminal Procedure referred to provides: "Probation officers when directed by the court shall fully investigate and report to the court in writing on the circumstances of the offense, criminal record and social history of a defendant, and in the case of a child in children's court the circumstances responsible for the child's appearance in court and his social history. Whenever desirable and facilities exist therefore they shall also obtain a physical, mental and psychiatric examination of such defendant or such child and report thereon in like manner to the court prior to sentence or adjudication. Such investigations and reports shall be made promptly. The court shall have such information before it prior to sentence or adjudication. When an offender is committed or sentenced to a correctional institution for adults for a period longer than three months, or when a child is committed or placed in an institution either for delinquent or neglected children, a copy of the probation officer's investigation shall be sent by the court to the warden, superintendent or directors of the institution."

This section, if properly interpreted by the Wayward Minor Court in its procedure, is certainly of dubious constitutional validity. In a passage quoted from an address by Justice Cobb, *supra,* he maintains that this section of the code does not authorize the submission of hearsay evidence from probation reports to the judge in advance of a hearing or during a hearing. See Cobb, "Social and Legal Aspects of the Children's Court," pp. 18–19, 20.

[15] Reference to the statistics on dispositions from the Court will show that the stigma of adjudication is not avoided in the vast majority of cases handled by the Court.

The quotations in the text are taken from Wayward Minor Court, "An Evaluative Review of Procedures and Purposes," pp. 27–28.

Since these devices of pre-adjudication investigation and unofficial treatment have been criticized in some detail [16] the writer's argument need not be repeated at this point.

The adjudicative process itself is similar to that in the other magistrates' courts but for the following exceptional court-ways:

1. Usually the testimony of the complainant is the only evidence submitted which would, under the rules of evidence, be competent—and it is often of doubtful credibility.

2. The procedure is more informal, the defendant frequently being permitted to talk from her seat before the judge's desk.

3. The probation officer discusses the case with the magistrate before adjudication and submits her report to him. (One magistrate refuses to receive such information or report until after adjudication.)

4. The hearing is private.

5. The judge must act as prosecuting and defense attorney in so far as those functions are performed at all, since there is no prosecutor in the Court and almost never is there an attorney for the defendant.

6. There is always a liaison officer of the probation department in the Court, assisting in the integration of probation investigation and supervision with the Court's function of adjudication and disposition.

7. Sometimes there is a psychiatrist in the Court to aid in the selection of cases which may require more careful observation at Bellevue Hospital for possible abnormality.

8. Hearing, adjudication, and disposition generally occur at one sitting, the investigation having already been made. Further adjournments may be had, however, before the final disposition is made.

Final disposition.—A most important feature of the Court

[16] See *supra*, Chapter V.

is the disposition made by it upon adjudication. It is necessary to dispel at once and in advance the common illusion that the Wayard Minor Court has a small commitment rate, a fallacious notion generally entertained in the Court as well as by the public. The statute, to be sure, recommends the use of probation, but inspection of court data leads to the unquestionable conclusion that incarceration is by far the most common method of disposition. The findings for each set of 150 cases studied intensively are presented here:

TABLE 6

Final Dispositions

	1938	1942
Intake only	5	1
Referred elsewhere	36	3
Dismissed		
Adjusted (unofficial supervision)	10	11
Lost jurisdiction (nonresidence; warrant not served; defendant married)	10	21
Committed by Bellevue Hospital (psychosis or feeble-mindedness diagnosed)	4	11
Complaint unfounded (dismissed by the Court)	6	3
Complaint withdrawn (by complainant)	16	24
Probation		
Discharged as adjusted (probation "successes")	8	16
Revoked, and suspended sentence	6	
Revoked and defendant committed	9	9
Revoked, and defendant committed; revoked, and defendant recommitted	2	2
Commitment		
Direct commitment	36	46
Revoked and defendant recommitted	2	3
Total	150	150

These data contain much of interest to us. It will be observed, first, that a large proportion of the sample is not officially disposed by the Court: only in the probation and commitment cases has the tribunal exerted its ultimate powers of disposition. Thus in 1938, sixty-three cases only out of 150 were adjudicated, and in 1942, seventy-six out of 150. Comparing the percentage of discharges for other offenses with these figures, it might appear that a rather high proportion of cases against alleged wayward minors was dismissed by the Court. Thus, in the annual report of the magistrates' courts for the year 1938 the following data on the adjudication of female offenders appear:

TABLE 7

Dispositions of Female Offenders: 1938

	Disorderly Conduct		Prostitution (Sect. 887, subd. 4)		Wayward Minor	
	NUMBER	PERCENT	NUMBER	PERCENT	NUMBER	PERCENT
Discharged	1,659	40	1,231	36	165	51
Convicted	2,292	55	2,178	64	149	46
Transferred jurisdiction	186	5	4	..	7	3
Total	4,137	100	3,413	100	321	100

Although 51 percent of the cases are shown by the official data to be discharged in the Wayward Minor Court, it becomes apparent upon studying the detailed breakdown of 150 cases that, in striking contrast to the high proportion of acquittals characteristic for other offenses, there are extremely few actual acquittals in the Wayward Minor Court: six out of 150 in 1938, and three out of 150 in 1942. It is true that there were dismissals for other reasons, particularly the withdrawal of complaints by parents—sixteen in 1938 and twenty-four in 1942—yet these represent for the most part a "change of heart" by the parents as a result of which they decided not to prosecute their daughters.[17] Too, in 1938, a

---

[17] The result is frequently a waste of the facilities and the time of the Court. Sometimes, however, the court contact and remands are helpful in reëstablishing parental authority without the parents' pursuing the complaint further. In the 1938 sample, of the sixteen whose parents

considerable number of cases (thirty-five) was referred to other agencies; these cases were not official court dismissals on the merits, but largely dispositions at intake. As previously noted,[18] these referrals are comparable to a refusal to issue a complaint in other courts: cases which in such other courts would not appear in the records or on the dockets. Thus, though eighty-seven out of the 150 cases in 1938 were not adjudicated, only a small proportion was discharged on the merits of the individual case. In 1942 the situation was similar but was aggravated by the decline in referrals; the Court itself kept jurisdiction over these more corrigible cases and dismissed only a few. In these figures is the clearest substantiation of the belief that the Court, viewing itself as a social agency, attempts to diagnose and treat nearly all who come, without great regard to the legal merits of the case or to the limitations of its own social facilities. This follows out the expressed purpose of the magistrate who initiated the court procedures: ". . . the alleged delinquents between the ages of 16 and 21 should best be handled as a social rather than a criminal problem" [19] and "first offenders particularly, and others not yet hardened in the ways of crime, will then be transferred to this special tribunal to be treated initially as a social problem." [20] This attitude has been preserved, if not extended, in the Court, assisted by the vague generality of the statute; it is abundantly clear through the observation of processing in the Court and is tangible in the figures from the court records.

To carry a step further the comparison of dispositions of female offenders, it is worth while to observe the relative figures on disposition of cases:

---

withdrew their complaints six had already had one institutional remand; two had had remands to two institutions; and one had been remanded to three institutions.

[18] See *supra.*   [19] Kross, *op. cit.,* p. 35.
[20] *Ibid.,* p. 4.

TABLE 8

Dispositions of Female Convictions: 1938[a]

	Disorderly Conduct	Prostitution	Wayward Minor
Fined	458	...	...
Workhouse (definite sentence)	542	1,150	...
Reformatory	13	44	96
Sentence suspended	1,094	809	2
Probation	133	172	38
Hospital	52	3	13
Total	2,292	2,178	149

[a] Adapted from the Annual Report of the Magistrates' Courts, 1938.

Striking at once is the fact that the judges saw fit to mitigate the sentences for disorderly conduct and prostitution through suspending sentences in a large number of cases [21] (whether on the basis of extenuating circumstances, corrigibility of the defendants' characters, political pressure, fatalism as to offenders of these sorts, or because of other factors does not appear). At any rate, of those convicted, 47 percent received no penalty for disorderly conduct, and of those charged with that offense, two thirds received either a discharge or a suspended sentence. The comparable data for prostitution indicated that 36 percent received a suspended sentence while 60 percent of those charged received no penalty. In the sample of 300 cases used in this study, no suspended sentences were given to wayward minors except after a period of probation (and there were very few of these): all those convicted received treatment, either under probation or commitment. Suspended sentences were used generally after the defendant had married, thus escaping the Court's jurisdiction.

[21] The suspending of sentence is theoretically an unusual remedy, and its very frequent application for some offenses has been considerably criticized. See New York *Times,* April 16, 1938. Chief Magistrate Schurman requires that judges give a written explanation for their suspended sentences. *Ibid.,* June 18, 1938.

These disparities may be attributable largely to differences in the statutes covering the offenses as well as to differential approaches to the problems involved, of course. Thus, since the Wayward Minor Act in Section 913-c of the Code of Criminal Procedure has provided specifically for probation and commitment only, some judges believe this precludes application to the wayward minor of Section 2188 on suspended sentence in the general article 196 on "Sentence of the Penal Law." Other judges, however, have occasionally suspended sentence in this court. The legislation on the Court provides specifically for suspending of judgment.[22]

To take one further step in comparisons, a scrutiny of the sentences imposed for prostitution (the offense most closely analogous to that of the wayward minor) reveals that 27 percent of the workhouse sentences were suspended.[23] As a result, some 70 percent of the cases charged with prostitution received no penalty, and less than 2 percent received an indeterminate term in reformatory or workhouse. The remaining 28 percent received definite sentences of from one day to six months; approximately half of these were for ninety days or less. In contrast, if we exclude from our sample of 150 cases in 1938 those which did not come before the Court and those in which complaints were withdrawn (this would include a small percentage of the total who were treated unofficially by the probation department before discharge), we find that thirty-eight cases out of ninety-three, or 41 percent, were committed directly on indeterminate sentences up to three years, and forty-nine, or 53 percent, were eventually so committed. Moreover, parole in less than ten months or a year is not generally considered under an indeterminate sentence in the institutions used, the time limits being entirely out of the hands of the Court once it has made

22 See Appendix.
23 Annual Report of the Magistrates' Courts, 1938, p. 25.

its disposition. (Comparable percentages of indeterminate commitments in 1942 were: 41 percent committed at once from the Court and 50 percent eventually.) The data comparing dispositions for prostitution and for a sample of 150 wayward minors in 1938 may be summarized thus:

TABLE 9

Comparative Dispositions of Female Offenders: 1938

	Prostitution	Percent	Wayward Minor	Percent
Discharged	1,231	36	30	32
Sentence suspended	809	24	..	..
Execution suspended	310	9	..	..
Indeterminate sentence	44	2	38	41
Probation	172	5	25	27
Definite term	840	24	..	..
Total court appearances	3,406	100	93	100

It may be seen that only 31 percent of those charged in court with prostitution receive a penalty, whereas 68 percent of those who come before the Wayward Minor Court do; that among prostitutes only 2 percent receive indeterminate sentences, while 41 percent of the wayward minors are given that penalty at once. In sum, the "conviction" rate for wayward minors is high, and the treatment imposed, which *de facto* amounts to a penalty, is severe. This is the more striking in view of the purpose ascribed to the act and the character of the institutions available for commitment. To reiterate, these differences may be explained or rationalized, in part, by difficulties implicit in the Wayward Minor Statute. Yet the Court has generally not been narrowly constrained by the statute in practice. And the data attest a fact of peculiar interest: the Wayward Minor Court as a total institution in operation does subject a relatively large proportion of its defendants to punitive and semipunitive treatment, considering their age, character, and the charges made against them.

It appears that the raw data on discharges of wayward minors as they appear in the annual reports are not directly comparable to those from district courts of the system. This is because some of the cases at intake are not sent to the Court; also there is considerably more frequent withdrawal of complaints (by the parents) than is true in other courts. If the entire 150 cases be considered as defendants officially dealt with by the Court (though they were not), and the cases referred elsewhere and those withdrawn included (as in the official court reports) among cases discharged, the contrast is modified considerably, of course. Even then, however, the proportion actually punished or treated by the Court (42 percent) proves to be considerably greater than that for the prostitutes (31 percent), and the proportion incarcerated for periods of over six months (25 percent) is more than twelve times as great; and it must be recalled that the practice of referral to other agencies, reflected in the 1938 data, no longer prevailed to any great extent in 1942.

A tabulation comparable to the above for 1942 alone shows dispositions from the Wayward Minor Court. Data from the Women's Court are not broken down in the annual report for this year, but the dispositions are believed to have been similar to those of 1938.

TABLE 10

Original Dispositions of Wayward Minors: 1942

	Number	Percent
Discharged	46	37
Sentence suspended	..	..
Execution suspended	..	..
Indeterminate sentence	49	41
Probation	27	22
Definite term	..	..
Total court appearance	122	100

Here, because of the drop in referrals and the official court handling of those cases, the proportion penalized by the

Court increased. Thus, if the entire sample of 1942 cases (150) be taken as the base, 51 percent were given treatment of some sort (cf. 31 percent for prostitutes in 1938), and 33 percent of all cases were given an indeterminate sentence. When one then adds to the group of forty-nine the eleven cases in which the original probation was revoked and commitment imposed (see Table 6) 40 percent of the 150 cases were eventually exposed to the indeterminate sentence in an institution. If, to test the Court's operation as such, one excludes the cases in which the defendant was never brought before the Court proper, the proportion of the remaining 122 defendants who were eventually exposed to the indeterminate sentence becomes 50 percent.

That these proportions are not misleadingly high for the Court is indicated by checking them against the raw figures for 1939 and 1940 printed in a summary report of the Wayward Minor Court: [24]

TABLE 11

Dispositions of Wayward Minors: 1939 and 1940

	1939	*1940*
Committed	75	69
Dismissed: no adjudication	92	123
Official probation	30	27
Total	197	219

(Other cases pending at the time of tabulation are omitted from this table, although they appear in the annual report.)

According to these data (again, they need detailed correction on "dismissals"), 38 percent of all cases completed were committed, and 15 percent were placed on probation in 1939. In 1940, 31 percent were committed and 12 percent put on probation. Contrast with these data the percentages and penalties in the Women's Court for prostitution (Table 9), in the Brooklyn Adolescent Court for serious offenses (Table 12), and in special and general sessions youth courts for mis-

[24] Wayward Minor Court, "An Evaluative Review," p. 51.

demeanors and felonies (about 85 percent of these cases are
placed on probation).

Probation.—As indicated in the tabulation of dispositions
for 1938 (Table 9), 27 percent of these cases coming before
the Court were placed on probation, while there were 22 percent in 1942 (Table 10). Considering that it is the explicit,
enunciated policy of the act that probation should be used
wherever possible, the proportion of cases so disposed appears decidedly low in comparison with commitments and discharges. True, there is at least some contact with the probation department in all cases, and where unofficial or official
supervision is used this contact may be considerable. However, unofficial handling has declined greatly since 1937, and
so the proportion of all cases treated by probation was distinctly small. It is striking to note, in contrast, that in the
1938 data of the Brooklyn Adolescent Court,[25] 53 percent of
the boys were placed on probation, 23 percent dismissed or
sentence suspended, and only 13 percent committed, held for
more serious court procedure, or lost to the courts' jurisdiction—and this, even though the Brooklyn court handles primarily more serious violations against the law. Both courts
are specialized to deal with adolescents.

TABLE 12

Dispositions from the Brooklyn Adolescent Court: 1938

	Number	Percent
Probation	264	52.6
Returned home (out-of-town cases)	13	2.6
Dismissed and sentence suspended	118	23.5
Held for the Grand Jury	12	2.3
Held for special sessions	21	4.2
Committed	29	5.8
Absconders	5	1.0
Pending	40	8.0
Total	502	100.0

[25] Annual Report, Brooklyn Adolescent Court, 1938, Table VIII.

It is also interesting to note the subsequent treatment of probation cases. Of the twenty-five cases which were studied among the wayward minors in 1938, only eight were discharged as adjusted or improved, while the number rose in 1942 to sixteen out of twenty-seven. Probation was revoked in the remainder of probation cases and generally followed by commitment, in the samples studied.

Westfield State Reformatory commitments.—A further breakdown of cases has been made to determine the extent to which Westfield is used for the wayward minors. The attempt is made by the Court, within the limitations of the institutional facilities available, to keep at a minimum the number of commitments to that institution because the possible deleterious effect of association with older and habitual offenders there is recognized. By the express policy of the act, where probation is not used offenders are sent whenever possible to an institution of their religious faith. Aside from the statute, it is obvious that an institution which largely accommodates confirmed prostitutes, shoplifters, and petty thieves as well as more serious offenders is likely to be of little reformative value for an adolescent girl. The lack of needed institutions thus presents a serious problem of policy. But the solution reached has been not so much the extension of probation nor the dismissal of cases, but an excessive use of Westfield by the Court. Thus in 1938, of thirty-six direct commitments, seventeen were to that institution, and of forty-nine ultimately committed, twenty-seven were sent there. In 1942, out of forty-six, nineteen were committed directly to Westfield, and of sixty ultimately incarcerated thirty went to Westfield State Reformatory.

Even more troubling than these general figures, however, is the picture that is presented by a more detailed analysis of commitments in terms of race. The extent to which the irrelevant factor of color affects the disposition of cases from the

Court is significant both statistically and socially. The almost utter lack of institutional facilities for the Negro offenders results in a continuous inequality of treatment in the Court and an inability to deal effectively with these girls, however much the Court may wish to do so. Virtually the only available facilities for Negro girls are the House of Detention for remand (sometimes Florence Crittenton), and Westfield for commitment. The Court's recognition of, and response to, this situation shows in the statistics. The proportion of Negro girls committed to institutions (one sixth), is markedly smaller than that of white girls (one fourth). This difference cannot be regarded as reflecting any feeling that the Negro girls are more corrigible or better probation risks. The general social environment is certainly not more favorable to Negro probation cases. Until recently the Court lacked any Negro probation officers, although in most years some 30 percent of the cases are Negresses. Meanwhile, of the white girls committed, fewer than one third go to Westfield, whereas from 90 percent to 100 percent of the Negro girls are sent there. The contrast is shown in these figures, drawn from the 1938 and 1942 samples:

TABLE 13

Direct Commitments to Westfield, by Color

	1938		1942	
	Direct Commitment	*Commitment to Westfield*	*Direct Commitment*	*Commitment to Westfield*
White	24	7	33	8
Negro	10	10	12	11
Puerto Rican	2	1	2	..
Total	36	18	47	19

One important reason for the disparity is the fact that the Houses of the Good Shepherd in Brooklyn and Peekskill take the great majority of Roman Catholic girls (eleven out of seventeen in the 1938 sample), so that few of this faith see Westfield. Though the girls of those faiths are equally a community concern and responsibility, no comparable facilities are available for many of the Protestants and Jews, particularly for the Protestant Negro. The fact is significant in its bearing upon the successes and failures in our treatment of delinquent Negro girls. It is equally significant of the degree to which such a court as this depends in its operation and for its success on factors beyond its control in the surrounding community. And the fact reinforces the doubts expressed above on the wisdom of an intake policy which does not look toward full capitalization of the possibilities of referral to other available agencies.

The relation of sex behavior to dispositions.—The Wayward Minor Court has come to be considered a tribunal almost exclusively for the adjudication of corrigible sex offenders. Its traditional association with the Women's Court, its statutory emphasis upon "moral depravity," and its verbalized purpose combine thus to define the nature of its function. Although in the founding of the Court its presiding magistrate expressed the hope that eventually all offenses of adolescents, male and female, should come to be tried there,[26] its official policy would seem to restrict its province rather narrowly. It is interesting, then, to look at the complaints in which the offenses are described, to observe the cases, and to study the probation records for information on venereal conduct and disease. In 1938, of the 150 complaints in the sample, only ninety alleged sexual intercourse on the part of the defendant. Thirty-seven of these cases were found prior to adjudication to have a venereal disease; eight were unmarried mothers; and seventeen were pregnant. In 1942, 104 out of the 150 were accused of sexual delinquency; 36 were found to be diseased; 7 were unmarried mothers; and 19 were pregnant.

26 Kross, *op. cit.*, p. 3.

In Women's Court, where Board of Health examinations are made on all defendants, the results of the tests are not before the judge until after trial.[27] In the Wayward Minor Court, however, and in keeping with the generalized attitude of tolerance toward legally prejudicial evidence, such information on venereal disease has generally been available to the Court prior to adjudication. The majority of diseased offenders have been committed at once, usually to Westfield. Board of Health examinations are not usually given in this court when no sex offense is alleged; indeed, sometimes the Court fails to order an examination where there is a charge of such conduct. Twenty-two such cases appeared in the 1938 sample.

On a careful reading of the records it is found that, although a majority of the defendants are alleged to have indulged in sexual behavior, a large proportion has not even been accused of this, and in a vast preponderance of cases no sufficient and competent proof has been made of such conduct even where it has been alleged. There is a remarkable number of defendants whose depraved conduct has not been proven and many cases in which no single instance of depravity has even been alleged, yet the case has been docketed, the girl arraigned, remanded often to an institution during one or more adjournments, and in some instances adjudicated. There are cases recorded of institutional commitment where no sexual delinquency, no venereal disease, indeed (in this observer's view) no offense against the law has been properly alleged

---

[27] Article 17b of the Public Health Law, providing for the venereal examination of those suspected of menacing public health, was passed as a war measure in 1917; it was not applied in the Women's Court until January, 1936. Until that time tests were not given until after conviction, so that those determined to be not guilty were released without knowing whether or not they were infected. The law is poorly drawn, so that the Board of Health has preferred not to attempt to extend its scope of application lest it lose the power now exerted by adverse appellate decision. New legislation of an effective sort is difficult to procure in this field.

and proven. To be sure, only the presiding magistrate need be convinced of the adequacy of testimony to evidence an offense. And the fact of conviction does indicate that magistrates were convinced. As previously asserted, the nonspecificity of offense and of court purposing extends the range of judicial discretion to an absurd and dangerous degree, particularly where—as in this court—the methods of processing virtually nullify the right of review.

The relation of alleged sexual conduct and venereal dis-

TABLE 14

Dispositions and Frequency of Sex Problems: 1938

	Number of Cases	Sex Offense Alleged	No Sex Offense Alleged	Venereal Disease	Unmarried Mother	Pregnant
Intake only	5	2	3	1	..	..
Referred elsewhere	36	14	22	4	1	2
Dismissed						
Adjusted	10	5	5	1	1	2
Lost jurisdiction	10	9	1	5	2	..
Committed by Bellevue	4	3	1	..	..	..
Complaint unfounded	6	3	3	..	..	..
Complaint withdrawn	16	7	9	2	..	..
Probation						
Discharged as adjusted	8	6	2	3	..	..
Revoked, sentence suspended	6	3	3	..	..	..
Revoked, committed	9	6	3	1	1	2
Revoked, committed and recommitted	2	2	..	1	..	..
Commitment						
Direct commitment	36	29	7	17	3	8
Commitment, revoked, and recommitted	2	1	1	..	..	..
Total	150	90	60	35	8	14

ease to court disposition may be sought in a breakdown of the
table of dispositions for the 1938 and 1942 samples (Table 6).

TABLE 15

Dispositions and Frequency of Sex Problems: 1942

	Number of Cases	Sex Offense Alleged	No Sex Offense Alleged	Venereal Disease	Unmarried Mother	Pregnant
Intake only	1	1	..	..	..	..
Referred elsewhere	3	..	3	..	..	..
Dismissed						
Adjusted	11	10	1	..	..	1
Lost jurisdiction	21	15	6	4	1	2
Committed by Bellevue	11	8	3	4	2	3
Complaint unfounded	3	..	3	..	..	..
Complaint withdrawn	24	11	13	1	..	..
Probation						
Discharged as adjusted	16	11	5	5	1	1
Revoked, suspended sentence	..	..	..	..	..	..
Revoked, committed	9	4	5	2	..	1
Revoked, committed, and recommitted	2	2	..	2	..	..
Commitment						
Direct commitment	46	40	6	17	3	9
Commitment revoked and recommitted	3	2	1	1	..	2
Total	150	104	46	36	7	19

One observation is clear from the tabulation: there is no
attempt to confine adjudication or commitment to cases where
sexual conduct by the defendant is charged or where venereal
disease is found. The data for 1938 indicate that while 60
percent of the complaints involved girls who were alleged to
have had sex contact, 70 percent of those placed on probation

and 80 percent of those with a single direct commitment were so charged. Also, whereas 25 percent of the cases were shown to be venerally diseased, only 20 percent of those put on probation were infected as against 47 percent of those committed. The proportions for 1942 were rather similar. It is apparent too that a person alleged to be sexually delinquent or found to have a venereal disease may be disposed by the Court in any of the ways indicated in the tabulations (except that in these samples no complaint was dismissed as unfounded if the Board of Health report showed a positive reaction for gonorrhea or syphilis; though the sample of unfounded complaints is small, this may well reflect the practice of making the health report available before adjudication).

A large proportion of the cases which were treated on unofficial probation and discharged as adjusted involved sex complaints (50 percent in 1938 and 91 percent in 1942, though the samples were small). The Court either lost or refused to take jurisdiction in numerous similar cases, and parents were permitted to withdraw complaints in spite of their own allegations about the sexual misconduct of their daughters. It will also be seen that neither the fact of unmarried motherhood nor pregnancy is determinative of disposition; there is, however, a definite tendency to commit the pregnant girl; this raises important questions of social policy in a court which assumes to operate socially. These girls are rarely encouraged to marry, and they are sometimes actively dissuaded when marriage is possible.[28] Public institutional delivery and illegitimacy are the most common consequences of these cases. It is not known whether the Court's inclination in numerous instances to discourage marriage (and even continued association with boys where a nonconsummated affectional relationship has been involved) results from its loss of jurisdiction to control when the girl marries. One magistrate appears to

[28] See *supra*, Cases 3 and 6, Chapter V.

view marriage of the defendant as a frequently desirable outcome in his cases, often superior to artificial methods of treatment. Other judges strongly oppose the marriages as circumventions of the Court's authority.

In studying the complaints brought before the Court, a
remarkable diversity of charges is found upon which court
action has been based. Among the most common are truancy,
resistance to authority, keeping late hours, running away
from home, or staying away over night—the sort of charge
upon which delinquency is commonly found by the Children's
Court. Less frequent, but numerous, are allegations of drink-
ing, bad temper, associating with companions (usually male)
of whom the parent disapproves, and refusal to contribute to
the support of the family as much as the parents believe
proper. Rarely, girls are brought in by detectives or by parents or through referrals from other courts on charges of
shoplifting or other petty larceny, smoking marijuana,
breaking and entering, and other more serious crimes. In general, the defendants may be classified as the least serious and
most corrigible of offenders taken through our criminal court
system. As previously stated, many girls who should not be
exposed to a criminal or quasi-criminal court at all are
brought here, docketed, adjudicated, and punitively treated.

As to treatment, though the aim of the Court is individualization, only probation and the indeterminate sentence are
established by the act, most cases being disposed of in one or
both of those ways. Whereas the offenses charged are not
very serious, the available facilities make for protracted and
sometimes rather severe treatment (in commitments to Westfield, especially). The consequent disparity between offense
and treatment is acute, dangerous, and—as has been shown—
invidiously discriminatory in its social consequences. The
excesses which might result from unrestrained use of these
punitive weapons have been mitigated in a measure by deal-

ing with a small proportion of cases unofficially, but the discouragement of referrals and extrajudicial handling, resulting in materially increasing the number of inappropriate cases thrown into the Court, has brought about an increase both in probation and in commitment. This is true in spite of the fact that in our samples there is shown to be among the candidates for intake in the later year no significant increase in venereally diseased, unmarried mothers nor in pregnant defendants.

In searching for the reason for this disparity between conduct and disposition, one is led to two general conclusions about the handling of wayward minors: In the work of the Court, in general, sex behavior on the part of an unmarried adolescent or pre-adult girl looms as an offense of great gravity, which can lead to exaggerated punitive treatment. The standard here is largely one of religion and of personal morality. It is observable that those officers attached to the Court who have a strong religious bias or moralistic tone stress the "falling from grace" and the need for extended religious training. More important, perhaps, is the product of attempting by a reformative or curative philosophy to amalgamate a formal judicial structure with a humanitarian "social work approach." There are fundamental conflicts in the thought-ways and operative techniques of judge and social worker. On the issue of adjudication, the judicial inclination is to consider primarily, if not solely, the facts of the particular offense and their proof. He may consider the mitigating circumstances only later for the determination of treatment. To the social worker the significant thing is not the offense per se, but the behavior problem of the person. Any misconduct alleged is a symptom or culmination of environmental and behavior factors. This is sound, and these must be sought out in attempting to understand the genesis of the problem, and an appropriate treatment must cope with them. Both views are apparently valid, each so far as it goes: the former, because in subjecting an individual to treatment by the criminal court system, it should be necessary to prove a concrete, legally cognizable offense or course of conduct; the latter, since it is footless to formulate treatment (for adolescents certainly) without reference both to the antecedent circumstances and to the individual requirements of the offender. Not only are both these thought-ways valid, they both have a proper place in the system of criminal law: the former in adjudication, the latter in disposition.

In dealing with the child and adolescent there has developed a peculiar perversion from the contact and conflict of the points of view of traditional law and applied sociology. As in some other courts, the Wayward Minor Court was conceived and dedicated to the principle of humanitarian social work. As a result each case is considered a problem, and the emphasis from the start is on determining etiology and applying treatment, with little or no consideration to the actuality and proof of a specific conduct proscribed by statute or to the essentials of the defendant's legal and social rights. The result has been the confusion and deflection of the processes of adjudication and disposition to which we have referred. The result is unjustified, not only legally, but socially when there has been no conduct proven which would justify the Court in taking hold: when there has not been sufficient objective evidence to prove that behavior is creating a high risk of future delinquency and when the procedure has lacked the basic elements of a fair trial. For it utilizes criminal court facilities (which have limited general social value and material social risk) in cases not properly selected for disciplinary treatment by any social criterion clearly indicating the appositeness of the treatment.

It must be remembered that exposure to the Court and/or its treatment facilities may do more damage than benefit to mild and corrigible offenders. There is a real lack of justification under our political system for subjecting any person to actually punitive processes without a fair trial on an objectively defined standard of conduct, and there is a lack of social justification for differential punitive treatment based on irrelevant factors such as race. Yet a vested inertia in the established methods, sustained in part by an occupational philosophy, has developed in the Court to the point that sporadic attempts by individual judges (denominated "legalistic") to legalize the procedures and still retain the potential social achievements of the tribunal are met by the feeling that that judge should be moved or the Court abolished. There is here, as so often, an "all-or-nothing" reaction on the part of those with a social cause to pursue.[29]

Magistrates.—There is a great diversity among the judges who have sat in this court and in the results which have flowed from their work. Differences observed between some of these judges are summarized here to advance our understanding of the processing in the Court:

Judge A.: A humanitarian judge with a definite inclination to the "social work approach," this magistrate's tendency to circumvent "unimportant" formal legal matters has directed the growth of the Court into the procedures of "implied consent," remands before hearing, probation reports before adjudication, and treatment of the case as a "problem" rather than in terms of specific conduct. Well motivated by intention, the accomplishments of the judge in promoting a philosophy and method for this court as a socialized tribunal were narrowed and deflected by the poorly implemented character of the institutional machinery at hand. The plans were too ambitious for the proper detailed consideration, within such a court, of their varied implications. On the other hand, it must be remembered that in its formative stages the court processes were naturally shaped and limited by the devices earlier established in the children's courts and by the restricted facilities available to it. Too, the Court obviously could not spring full

29 See *supra,* Chapter II.

grown, well implemented, maturely shaped in philosophy and method from its diffused origins. Judge A.'s creative effort to supplant unspecialized criminal court handling by an experimental and individualized approach in this court was a great step forward. Weaknesses in the Court today are very largely traceable to the failure of succeeding magistrates to reformulate method and philosophy creatively to meet the needs of the tribunal and its defendants.

Judge B.: This magistrate was considerably concerned with legalizing the procedures of the Court. In his administration he was noteworthy for his inclination to discharge cases where there was insufficient evidence for adjudication, to exclude hearsay, and to instruct defendants carefully in their rights under the law. He also attempted to legitimatize court methods by recommending supplementary legislation. He tended to avoid both remands and institutional commitments wherever possible, and especially where a long prior history of confinement led him to believe that further incarceration would serve no useful purpose. His approach was essentially one of realism, with a strict legal conscience and a nonmoralistic point of view. His courtroom personality was not so piquant as that of certain others; for he was abrupt and brief in discussion with the offenders, seeming often to conceal a real warmness of sympathy for the defendant's problem. His decisions were said to be unpredictable, but this resulted from his applying legal standards rather rigorously, not purely social ones. He was inclined not to rely too heavily upon the advices of the court officers where the response of his own common sense and legal training differed from the proposals for social and psychological therapy. Some probation officers were disposed to ask for adjournments to other, "more coöperative" judges.

Judge C.: This judge felt that the problem of the wayward minor was primarily a moral and religious one, requiring reformation, moralization, and training in religious precepts. He disapproved of the clinical approach in the Court. Nor did he accept the "legalistic" principles of conformity to the rules of criminal procedure in dealing with adolescents, apparently accepting the principle that since the Court is there to help, it should not be hampered by the limitations inherent in preserving to the defendant her basic procedural rights. His role is close to that of father confessor, one of stern conscience and strong moral evaluations.

Indicative of his value-system was his threat of adjudication to prevent a mature and intelligent white girl from marrying a Negro.

Judge C., nevertheless, had a remarkably fine talent for establishing rapport with the defendant in the Court, for reasoning and moralizing effectively with her. He established rapport, too, with most of the officers of the Court—who tended, consequently, to bring their cases to him; there thus resulted a bulking of cases with this judge. He tended, generally, to accept the recommendations of probation officers unless he felt that his authority as disposing judge was being challenged. He believed in prevention by moral and spiritual education, and treatment by the same devices. His emphasis upon religious observance was expressed in the continually reiterated query as to the church attendance of defendants and his admonitions that they conform to their religious training. No other judge of the Court, within the writer's knowledge, has put so strong an emphasis upon religious treatment methods, though it is the predominant approach of several of the probation officers. (It has been striking to observe the number of defendants who claim to be "religiously observant" in their responses to court inquiry!) The commitment rate of this judge is very high, being approximately twice as great as that of Judge B. in the sample studied; the large difference reflects partially the inclination of probation officers to hold for him the cases they want committed.

Judge D.: Although this magistrate was characterized mainly by speed and impersonality in disposition of his cases, he would occasionally go to great pains to aid a defendant who was regarded as especially amenable because of her social class and family connections. A seasoned judge, he was more interested in efficiency than in the individual case. Since he sat for some time as the only judge assigned to this court, his cases were not confused by the handling of a succession of magistrates, and greater system was possible as a result. Judge D. remanded automatically, and he consistently required Board of Health examinations of the defendants. He used the facilities of psychiatric diagnosis more fully than did his predecessors and tended to follow clinical and social advice. He appears to have conceived of the Court's functions as largely clinical and deterrent. During his administration, however, the Court cut to a minimum the referrals to social agencies and also became habituated to the handling of all cases with little regard to the merits of the charge and the evidence to sustain it. The Court became, in effect, a "social clinic," but one using the judicial, custodial, and correctional features attached to the criminal court system rather than nonstigmatic social ones.

In the development of the Wayward Minor Court there has been a lack of sustained and thoughtful analysis of what the Court should do and can do, and how it may best do it. This failure may be attributed somewhat to the practice in the magistrates' system of the circulation of autonomous judges. Generally, a single judge does not sit long enough in the Court to evolve a workable legal and social procedure and philosophy. He tends to take the Court as he finds it, i.e., with a continuity established chiefly through the probation officers and their social work objectives. He then functions as best he may within these briefly established traditions. He is not encouraged to innovate and he generally varies from his fellow judges chiefly in the moral, economic, educational, religious, or clinical biases that may come to expression in his dispositions from time to time. Since he spends the larger part of his time in other courts, his opposition either to prevailing methods in the girls' court or to efforts to change them tends to be weak. This difficulty is exaggerated by the fact that the rotation of the judges is frequent (every two or four weeks usually), so that a given magistrate cannot follow through on his cases and a defendant may be adjourned to three or four different magistrates.[30] The efforts at consistency among the probation officers are, in turn, thwarted by the need for frequent readaptations to different judges. Either a systematic procedure and philosophy or the sustained development of a sound one by trial and experience is difficult if not impossible to attain under such circumstances. The natural result has been cross-purposing and conflict of varied

[30] Since this was written, it has become the practice for the magistrate to adjourn his cases generally to a time when he will again be sitting in the Court.

means and ends. Again, confusion is encouraged by the nearly unlimited discretion permissible to the magistrate in this court. Under the guise of humanitarian and individualized purposes, treatment out of all proportion to conduct is not only possible, but common.

Also the very autonomy of the magistrate, together with that of the probation workers and the officers of correctional institutions, has proved a fatal preventive to system. Each jealous unit operates so far as possible in insulation and isolation. Without conference of magistrates, without a systematizing through case supervision of probation, without general staff meetings by which the stratified hierarchies of the Court might meet together in discussion of their common problems, it is impossible to build that coöperative teamwork by which intelligent, planned, and systematic procedures and philosophy might be evolved. It is a happenstance if all the varied and semi-independent agencies touching successively upon a wayward minor have functioned toward a common and fruitful objective in her development. If she is very fortunate, the defendant may encounter during her processing one individual who will exert a decisive and constructive influence.

To reiterate, the agencies and institutions which impinge upon the wayward minor are inevitably a continuum, concatenated and interdependent in their influence, determining in their total combined effect a profit or loss in the girl's experience; but in practice there is little organization or harmony in their impact. The stratification of functions and the independence of functionaries have until recently left the process haphazard and confused.

Recent conferences of the three magistrates currently assigned to the Court, and their attempt to work out a procedure both legally and socially sound, are among the most hopeful developments in the history of the Court. Since these magistrates differ markedly one from the other, however, the

situation is still pregnant with the dangers of complete disagreement on purpose and method; it may lead to an utterly
impossible impasse, followed by a return to the normal and
traditional "isolationism." Under the new statute it is believed that their differences in viewpoint may be accentuated
by the extended range of discretion which it permits. More
completely than ever the allegedly wayward girl is at the
mercy of the widely varying normative values of the magistrates who man this bench.

7

Determinants of Disposition

OUR SYSTEM OF CRIMINAL LAW has long since abandoned the doctrine of equating penalties precisely to crimes. The fault of another (preclassical) age in permitting an excessive and abused judicial latitude in fixing punishments gave way—largely during the eighteenth century—to the establishment under Beccarian classical theory of definite and mandatory sentences proportioned to the gravity of social offense. The modern movement back toward discretionary determination of treatment has been guided by conceptions of degrees of responsibility for behavior or freedom of the will, associated chiefly with a punitive-retributive criminological philosophy that would punish according to the degree of moral blame. More recently, under the philosophy of the contemporary clinical school, deterministic ideas of social causation and psychological motivation have extended the idea of discretion in disposition; here, however, the movement has been associated with criminological drives toward prevention, reformation, and rehabilitation. The result today is found in the familiar statutory provisions for wide ranges of sentence, a restoration to the judge of considerable discretion in his dispositive powers. The largely indefinite penalty provisions have become particularly common in the statutes applied by courts to the young. Usually, too, these courts are permitted to impose indeterminate sentences, the commitment institution to decide within statutory prescribed limits the time of release. Such is the situation in the Wayward Minor Court under its indeterminate sentence provision for commitment.

However, with this drive toward a criminal justice based

upon the personal requirements of the individual case, the extended discretion of the Court and its agencies has not been supplemented by legislative criteria to instruct the judge in determining treatment. Whereas the law has provided generally in sufficient detail for the procedures and standards by which guilt should be determined in the criminal court, the equally important and certainly no less difficult question of adjusting sentence to the offender has been relegated to the area of common sense and informal practice. As a consequence, the discretionary abuses of an earlier day have again become possible, although in fact they are less frequent. Experience has exposed the extent to which a judiciary unlearned or self-tutored in the field of treatment has varied among its members in disposition tendencies, struggling as they have without guidance from established and relevant standards.

Frequent criticism has resulted from this situation, and some recent efforts looking to the establishment of more "scientific" treatment tribunals to take over the function of determining disposition. Yet, with opposition from the bench to a release of its prerogative, and inertia or distrust in the legislature, little has been done thus far to make sentencing practices more sound or more uniform. One major difficulty has been that the advocates of change have proposed little more than the replacement of judicial common sense by the common sense of other experts, theoretically more informed in the mysteries of deviant human behavior.[1] Some compromise of practice has, in fact, been made by the increase of probation

[1] The recommendation to Governor Thomas E. Dewey by his Interdepartmental committee on Delinquency that a classification center be established for all male offenders, aged sixteen to twenty-one, at Elmira and that girls under sixteen be treated through the State Department of Social Welfare is the sort of proposal which looks to an individualization based on a needed uniformity of standards to adjust treatment to the personality. The effectuation of this policy through adequate personnel would remove many of the dangers which come from ignorance, invidious discrimination, or abused discretion in the courts. See Chapter IX.

investigations and the willingness of some courts to consider the social findings of their officers. However, for the most part, neither general standards nor specific principles have come from the specialists in conduct or in law. Courts have continued to determine penalties on the basis of those extenuating circumstances brought to the attention of the judge which have appealed to his preferences; age, sex, offense, mental condition, and other factors relevant or impertinent, rational or sentimental, known or guessed, may chance to move the court.

The Wayward Minor Court has shared in this universal problem of methodology in determining dispositions. Indeed, the problem is more acute in an experimental court of this kind where the effort is distinctly to break away from traditional retaliatory considerations and to work out treatment techniques in accordance with individual requirements. The difficulty is further accentuated by the development of those procedural methods in the Court which permit of adjudication on the same imprecise social standards which fix treatment there. Thus, as previously noted in some detail, social, personality, and conduct data—in so far as they may be secured and for what they may be worth—are brought in, both to justify the Court in taking hold and to direct its decisions on treatment. Yet, since there is no standard and accepted relation of datum to disposition, the magistrate must in each instance decide the relevance of a fact to the action of the Court and its persuasive weight toward guilt and treatment. The problem is difficult, therefore. However, there are several factors, relevant and irrelevant, which steady or homogenize disposition-tendency in this tribunal, controlling or limiting variation between the magistrates; other factors make for continuity in the practice of any given judge from day to day and from case to case. Outside the range of these discretion-limiting incidents there remains a large degree of freedom for the exercise of judgment; herein special circumstances of the case may lead toward dismissal or commitment.

One factor which, however sociologically irrelevant, is of great practical significance in affecting dispositions from the Court is that of the available facilities; the circumscribed treatment possibilities emanating from restricted provisions for commitment, probation, and agency contacts do clearly restrain the magistrate's freedom to prescribe appropriate treatment. The limited extent of existing coöperation among the organizations, due to the personnel attitudes and rivalries, constitutes an important part of their availability to the tribunal, of course. More specifically, the following limitations appear:

1. Custodial and correctional institutions.—The adequacy, variety, and quality of the institutional facilities, together with their personnel and policy, are of prime importance since they limit the types of treatment under remand or commitment. The limited custodial flexibility of the Court is one of the handicaps to the achievement of more effective results.

2. Probation staff.—The limits in size, training, philosophy, and general quality of staff affect the amount and kind of social investigation, official probation, and unofficial supervision which can be performed. Both the effectiveness and the methods of the Court may be further constricted by the attempt to handle so many cases that superficial treatment results rather than to handle a few adequately and to select for probation work the cases which legally and socially best merit investigation and treatment. Apparently the magistrate's decision on disposition is somewhat limited, though it is not necessarily directed by his conception of adequate probation work.

3. Social agencies.—Public and private social agencies deal with the social, economic, medical, psychological, and other problems which confront the Court. The limits both in variety and in quality of these agencies affect the extrajudicial and extracorrectional treatment which may be applied. The utilization of those facilities which are available depends in large measure upon the preconceptions extant among both correctional and noncorrectional workers, upon their mutual understanding and coöperation, or lack of them.

The provision in the Wayward Minor Act only for probation and indeterminate sentence has tended further to narrow the operation of judicial choice, eliminating fines and definite sentences. These statutory boundaries are somewhat extended by the elastic interim procedures developed informally by the Court itself; they are limited in other respects, however, by established dispositional habits, such as the Court's general avoidance of the suspended sentence, of the suspended execution of sentence, and of indeterminate probation, and by the trends in court practice toward nonreferral to agencies and toward automatic remands. Thus we find the Court provided by statute, habit, and facilities with a rather small variety of types of treatment for its selection; this limited freedom of disposition may be contrasted with the relatively wide freedom of decision on whether or not to adjudicate.

Among other factors which limit in some measure the extent of free judicial discretion are the restraints upon jurisdiction of the Court which have been established. There has been the basic—but in this court only very general—definition of norms in the statute itself, providing a rather wide province of power in determining the wayward minor status. As previously indicated, the statutory provisions have been cut down by court interpretation and practice so that only the most general and nonrestrictive section of the law (subsection 5) is applied, basing adjudication on filial disobedience and the danger of moral depravity. The jurisdictional area has been restricted more precisely and effectively by interpretations requiring complaints to be made by parent or relative, excluding married girls and girls whose parents live outside the city. The parent's refusal to sign a complaint, or withdrawal of the complaint after signing it, and noncoöperation have frequently frustrated the Court's intentions, limiting its exercise of control. This narrowing of jurisdiction is to be contrasted with pervasive drives within the agency toward its extension, particularly through the trend toward nonlegalistic adjudication, the drive to act correctionally in a socialized court, and the attempt to solve general family problems.

There are certain other influences which restrain and steady the individual magistrates in their practices, factors which operate quite differently among the judges. The magistrate's fears of reversal on appeal undoubtedly have some effect on his decisions, but since the defendant is rarely represented by an attorney and since appeals are almost never taken from the Court, this factor seems seldom to be persuasive. However, the knowledge of the extralegality of the Court's procedures is a subject of concern to the judges and, although they still operate in extralegal ways, there is little doubt but that the pangs of legal conscience operate among them in some restraint against excesses. One of the strongest directives to the individual judge in this young court, with its experimental growth through methods developed informally by autonomous judges, is the past practice of the particular magistrate—his own precedents for court action and disposition —the bench habits which have become a part of his own rules of procedure and decision.

The individual judge will be swayed too by motives which lie within his personality, by his idiosyncrasies of attitude and behavior, which, however irrelevant they may be in fact to the issues in the Court, are often determinative in his decisions. Of special importance are his preconceptions about the types of offense that come before him, about the purposes and methods of treatment of the offenders, the extent of his willingness to stretch or defy traditional legal procedures in adolescent cases and of his willingness to follow the counsel of probation officers and psychiatric, psychological, and medical advice. His general tendency in disposition, whether harsh or lenient, socially motivated or legalistic and conservative, is also of apparent importance. His class, race, and sex biases and the extent to which his emotions may be aroused and expressed in his verdicts are of significant influence. The reactions of the magistrate to the particular types of conduct or offense and their related social situations may set the pattern for his dispositions. Similarly, the importance which he attaches to the courtroom behavior of the defendant and complainant may bear strongly on his decision.

There are, in addition to these limiting and steadying situations, a series of factors which drive definitely toward dismissal or commitment. Though it is clear from the data that no one of these is conclusive upon court decision, some are heavily weighted, and in combinations they point strongly to release or confinement. Some of these motivating influences are soundly relevant to the objectives of the Court; others, in varying degrees, deflect it from its ends. Of special importance are the defendant and the situation which surrounds her, especially the seriousness and emotion-provoking power of her offense. Thus whether there be involved promiscuity or a single offense, normal heterosexuality or Lesbian and other deviant patterns, enjoyment and acceptance of sexual expression or feelings of guilt and contamination, or an offense nonsexual in character may be extremely important in determining her disposition.

Of considerable importance too is the personality of the defendant, her character and personal history as evaluated by the officers of the Court. Her condition at the time of the hearing—whether she be venereally infected, pregnant, in need of physical or psychiatric treatment—and the Court's knowledge of such facts may be very significant. Their known presence makes strongly for adjudication, though the particular type of treatment may depend upon some of the other varied limiting factors. More generally, her need for educational, occupational, religious, or other training—in the view of the Court—may determine her adjudication and treatment. Finally, her behavior and appearance during court hearings may be extremely important determinants of adjudication. Thus whether she be docile or aggressive, repentant and respectful or defiant and noncoöperative, attractive or repulsive, may be enough to sway a decision toward release or adjudication. In some instances where the girl has "blown up" in court, a prior plan to release her or to put her on probation has been altered at the last instant and incarceration imposed instead.

It is clear that the Wayward Minor Court can and does act much more freely than do other courts in determining whether or not to adjudicate. Statute, habit, and purposing of the Court encourage the wide latitude which is exercised by the magistrates, without the need here—as there is elsewhere—to establish proof of an offense, nor, indeed, to establish convincing proof of a specific course of conduct if an adjustment problem is shown. Within its freedom of discretion, then, the strong drive in the Court to correct the problem girl weighs heavily toward court adjudication. After attributing the wayward minor status, however, the tribunal is rather circumscribed in its efforts to individualize treatment. Here statute and habit have narrowed the choice of methods; inadequacy of probation facilities has led toward commitments; and severity of indeterminate commitment has encouraged interim institutional remands. The consequences are apparent in the data: a high frequency of adjudication, of remand, and of commitment.

8

Inclusive Needs for Change

THE PURPOSES OF THIS STUDY may be restated at this point. First let it be emphasized that the writer has not attempted to establish policy or set a norm as to what adolescent conduct should be prohibited in the law. Rather he has essayed to determine what the standards of normation are, how they have become what they are, and to evaluate their soundness and efficacy in practice. It has been shown that the Court's purposing, as it now operates, has developed from its institutional antecedents in the Women's Court (whence a vague moralistic norm of sex conduct has come to prevail) and in the Children's Court (which has induced a broad, expanding effort at prevention and rehabilitation of the delinquent). The product is a conservative, moralistic-retributive striving wedded strangely to a liberal, reformative-preventative drive, this union begetting diverse conflicting aims of punishment, rehabilitation, and deterrence.

As the Court has developed it has tended increasingly to take on the characteristic philosophy and methodology of juvenile courts, though preserving in its statute, procedure, and philosophy a strong leaven of religio-moralistic retribution for the sex offender. It is our thesis, then, that a definite substantive norm of conduct requires to be stated by the legislature in order to inform and channelize court action. Thus we may avoid the injustice, unevenness, and invidiousness of a relatively uncontrolled administrative justice with its application of varying personal and emotional standards under an omnibus statute. Moreover, as to procedural methods, we attack the developing ideology of a wholesale "liberalization" of court methods in the effort to diagnose potential delinquency or depravity by loose standards of personality and conduct and to found the adjudicative process thereon. We recognize that diagnosis and treatment based on a noncriminal course of conduct may be somewhat feasible and justifiable—if not, indeed, essential—in social agencies where little opprobrium attaches to the processing and where the facilities for applying the available social-scientific knowledge are greater. But we maintain that the same approach in a court situation spells the taint of a quasi-criminal status induced by inadequate and unobjective diagnosis and followed by generally unbeneficial and frequently injurious treatment experience.

The inadequacies inherent in the Court, it has been shown, result in excessive adjudication and incarceration and in unnecessary demoralization of defendants. A very real issue is raised thereon: Is there any sufficient justification to maintain a specialized court with the mixture of goals and the grossly inadequate instrumentation found here? It is felt that the advantage of a tribunal designed and serviced particularly for the adolescent girl should not be abandoned. In such a court the state might attempt to control promiscuous and commercialized sex conduct with a statutory specification of standards. It remains dubious, however, whether a court can be effective in remedying or dealing with such cases; certainly the experience of the Women's Court in New York City and of morals courts elsewhere teaches little optimism.

Finally, it will be suggested that a differing but legitimate and promising province of such a specialized court could be based upon the principle of adjudicating to a wayward minor or offender status those individuals whose acts would be crimes if they were committed by adults. But such adjudication should result only from procedures wherein the basic trial rights of due process and fair hearing have been preserved.

The variety of law violations covered by this principle of adjudication in the Brooklyn Adolescent Court is revealed in the Table of Appendix B. Note that these boys were rarely adjudicated for mild conduct or personality problems.

One great advantage of the Court is that it brings together in one specialized tribunal a diversity of means and methods to treat the peculiar problems of the adolescent girl, thereby mitigating to some extent the almost haphazard consequences of dealing with such types through a profusion of uncoördinated courts, judges, probation officers, and social agencies. The Wayward Minor Court provides a potential for specialization and individualization which is impossible in more general courts. Indeed, as the most specialized court in New York City—and very probably in the whole country—it could epitomize the ideals of coördinated and effective service to guide the growth of other adolescent courts. It has the advantage, too, of relatively good personnel: probation facilities superior to those in the courts of more general jurisdiction and to those in some of the specialized courts ; magistrates who are clearly interested in the problems with which they deal and who, through the limited rotation system, are increasingly experienced in a practical way with methods of treating them ; and psychiatric and medical aid which is somewhat more frequently available and more often applied than in the other courts.

Certain other assets of the Court should be noted: The use of the status concept avoids the establishment of criminal records for young offenders, thus permitting a measure of preventive action. Moreover, the general ideological emphasis of the tribunal upon reformative and rehabilitative effort is socially constructive. In meeting its goals it has developed a flexibility in the right direction of individualization which, in some of the methods used, widens the excessively narrow statutory provisions of disposition. The Court retains some of its early experimental attitude, too, in attempting to improve the effectiveness of its methods. Specifically, the Court and other interested groups, though disagreeing in many particulars, are conscious of the need for new shelters, new personnel, and more integration and planning of the Court's services.

On the other side there are certain conditions, where improvement may be desired, which have persisted in the Court. Apparently the Court has not yet determined upon a well-defined goal for its efforts, displaying some contradiction on the level of theory but still more in practice; variety and conflict in purposing thwart its potential effectiveness. Some of its procedures, particularly that of pre-hearing investigation and report with adjudication based on social data, are unjustified and fail sufficiently to protect the defendant in the present stage of evolution in statute, personnel, and other facilities. The associated excess of adjudications and incarcerations impedes the realization of the agency's constructive functions. These high rates reveal, in part, its attempt to perform in unsuitable situations. The inadequacy of facilities, personnel, and organization is a serious limitation upon the Court's performance. Particularly disadvantageous are the failure of the public to assume its responsibility for construction and supervision of the treatment facilities and the poor relationship of agencies, public and private, with the Court. Finally, the Wayward Minor Statute itself is fundamentally at fault in its failure to set up an adequate and specific substantive norm and to provide for sufficiently varied and appropriate rehabilitative treatment techniques.

In the following pages the writer will set down what appear to him to be the most important inclusive changes required in and for the Wayward Minor Court to make it a considerably more useful and effective instrument of justice. The reader will observe that several quite basic innovations are suggested as desirable in a long-time court telesis: substantive and jurisdictional, procedural and administrative, for adjudication and for disposition. These recommendations, then, are goals toward which to strive. Although in the aggregate they are ideal ones, by accretions of institutional improvement they may gradually come to be attained. Lest the scope of the criticisms and suggestions contained herein appear to counsel an unreasonable and impossible perfectionism, lest they be employed in general attack to abandon a much-needed specialization of court facilities for the adolescent girl, the writer will follow up these general and inclusive recommendations with a summary of some of the immediate stopgap modifications which could be initiated rather quickly without statutory or other formal alterations in the present court in order to increase its effectuality.

At the very core of the ensuing recommendations is the assumption that in adjudicating a status the Court should base its action upon either an offense or a course of conduct. In either case, to accomplish its purpose of aiding an offender, the Court must be interested in two matters, in the order indicated: (1) the defendant's guilt or innocence and the circumstances of the offense, if any; and (2) the reasons, motivations, or genetic factors in the social history (if determinable) upon which rehabilitative treatment may be predicated. It has been urged that, under present circumstances of knowledge concerning the etiology of delinquent behavior and the limitations of court facilities, the adjudication of status should be based upon convincing proof of specific, socially undesirable conduct, not upon general social data gathered in reports of probation investigations.[1]

It has been the trend, deemed extremely unfortunate by this writer, for progressive courts, as they take up the dif-

[1] In the *Report on Prosecution* by the National Commission on Law Observance and Enforcement, it was recommended that: "In the processes of trying and passing upon the issue of guilt or innocence and hearing and passing upon the disposition of the offender, the segregation of the

ficult and important problems of dealing more effectively with
adolescent delinquency, to adopt methods which virtually
assume *a priori* the guilt of the defendant or postpone its
determination and proceed at once to an investigation of social background. Such "consent" as the defendant may give
to this transposition of procedure depends, commonly, on his
ignorance or on coercion which the court may apply. As a
consequence, the information derived from a probation investigation into his history is available and may become the
chief evidence presented at the hearing to determine guilt.
Considering the limitations of personnel and available time
and the necessarily cursory nature of the judge's review of
the record of investigation, the information is most apt to be
poor social evidence, as well as poor legal evidence, of the defendant's guilt of the offense implied in the charge. It is suggested that the reaction of the judge and/or probation officer
to the defendant and his parent—their personalities, moral
views, and behavior during the traumatic and nontypical epi-
sode of court contact—readily becomes an excessively important determinant of the decisions both as to guilt and to
treatment. This is especially true when the statutory definition of the offense or conduct is vague and when the emphasis
of the court is almost wholly on the problem of treatment.
This is a danger in the other adolescent courts which operate
under a system of consent to social investigation in advance
of hearing as well as in the Wayward Minor Court. The same

---

presentation and hearing of those facts which bear on the guilt issue
from the presentation and hearing of those which bear on the disposition
issue, thus removing from the trial of the guilt issue the confusions
resulting from the introduction, at that stage, of those facts and considerations not logically relevant to the guilt issue but which are appropriate to the disposition issue; and the formulation and development of
procedures appropriate to each of these issues, particularly procedures
appropriate to the disposition." See "Conclusions and Recommendations," pp. 179–82.

problem has also developed in other jurisdictions out of the administration of courts for children and adolescents.

Again let it be asserted that unless an offense be specific and serious enough to warrant its proof by competent evidence, it is not sufficiently serious to merit the adjudication of a condemnatory status and the common remand or commitment to an institution, nor even the annoyances of probationary supervision. Despite the restrictions that liberty and civil rights may impose on the simplified administration of criminal law, they have proven too precious to be lightly abandoned by "consent" in a procedure wherein the facts of an offense are assumed or treated as virtually irrelevant, and treatment automatically applied on the basis of personality and social background. That treatment is frequently much needed by a defendant and his family is not questioned; that it can be or should be applied by criminal court probation officers and so applied without a soundly guarded determination of a ground for it is denied.[2]

SUBSTANTIVE NORMS

In place of the present broad "omnibus" statute with its vague connotations and all too easy adjudication on unsub-

[2] This issue is well analyzed in Michael and Wechsler, "A Rationale of the Law of Homicide," *Columbia Law Review*, XXXVII (1937), 731–32, note 128: "To warrant subjecting any one to the extraordinary measures of the criminal law, there must be some reason for selecting him rather than his neighbor. The reason must be that it is substantially more likely that he will engage in undesirable behavior. Since the measures involved may be seriously inconvenient or distasteful to the individual, such behavior must be undesirable to some fairly serious degree. Four variables are involved: (1) the degree of probability that the individual will engage in undesirable behavior; (2) the degree of undesirability of the behavior; (3) the degree of inconvenience and unpleasantness of the treatment and (4) the degree of probability that the power to employ the treatment may be abused by the officials to whom it is given. Where the lines should be drawn in a particular society at a particular time is a political question of the gravest character."

stantial evidence, a new law defining the status of the adolescent offender should be enacted. The allegations of "willful disobedience to the reasonable commands of the parent" and "danger of becoming morally depraved" are too indefinite. Though experience has brought some specific content to these amorphous stereotypes, their continued use is unjustified. The present law fails to set down, for the judge or officers of the Court, standards indicating with any objective clarity the types of behavior that are sought to be proscribed. Neither does the statute make clear that the avowed purposes of the Court are to aid and rehabilitate the offender; rather the act seems to imply, in fact, that the primary aim is to aid the parent against the recalcitrant offspring. This latter influence, implied in the statute and preserved from the tradition of the earlier incorrigibility statutes, continues side-by-side but in devastating conflict with the other implicit purpose of helping the adolescent. This is painfully apparent in the numerous cases where investigation has revealed the source of the complaint to be founded actually in the omissions or commissions of the complaining parent, and in no "fault" of the child. Yet adjudication of the status is still possible and common under such circumstances, facilitated by a statutory definition so broad that "the facts" as elicited from the parent (and sometimes "coached" by the probation officer) can easily be stretched to fit the elastic rule.

Least defensible, perhaps, is the concept of "moral depravity" to which little more than a feeling-content can be attached. To be sure, sex conduct of the unmarried girl has come to be considered a part thereof, yet the data show judgments without sexual involvement and sex contact without adjudication. At different times or with different personnel almost anything may be implied thereby; the very term brings to bear personal moral judgments of the officers in a field of great divergence in our society. In issues of morality it is difficult even for a court to be nonmoralistic and objective; yet the specification of concrete standards, generally and rigorously applied, may go far to remove the elements of personal bias and excessive emotion from the functioning of judicial discretion. Vague, generic moralism should be avoided.

Raymond Fosdick, in his book *American Police Systems*, has pointed to the futility in the American inclination to attempt to regulate morality by formal and official methods:

> Nowhere in the world is there so great an anxiety to place the moral regulation of social affairs in the hands of the police, and nowhere are the police so incapable of carrying out such regulation.
>
> From this condition arises one of the most embarrassing phases of the whole question of law enforcement. Mayors, administrations, and police forces are more often and more successfully attacked from this point than from any other, and the consequences are corrupted policemen and shuffling executives who give the best excuse they can think of at the moment for failing to do the impossible, but are able to add nothing to the situation but a sense of their own perplexity. Of all the cities visited by the writer there was scarcely one that did not bear evidence of demoralization arising from attempts to enforce laws which, instead of representing the will of the community, represented hardly anybody's will.[3]

Our analysis and criticism of the consent procedure have been concerned primarily with issues of its social validity. Yet it should not be forgotten that legal and constitutional questions too are involved and must be an important practical consideration in court action and reform. Adjudication without an offense or specific course of conduct, the consent of an adolescent to deprivation of fundamental rights of due process, the allowance of untested hearsay communicated from probation reports—these are all practices of highly dubious legal validity. Here, as in many other areas of "legal technicality," the long-sanctioned traditional procedures of the law reveal a central core of social merit and sound good sense

[3] Pp. 48–49.

which should be modified only through the application of similarly careful thought and adequate substitutes.

The principle asserted in *People* v. *Lewis* [4] should be as applicable in the Wayward Minor Court as in the Children's Court, where it is said that "a proceeding in a juvenile delinquency case must be based on a reasonably definite charge." It has been held that running away from home does not establish moral depravity in a girl of sixteen, within the meaning of the Wayward Minor Statute. [5] On the other hand, in *People* v. *Brewster* [6] "waywardness" was defined as "not a crime, but a moral delinquency to be corrected in the interest of the minor and state." Beyond this, however, the courts of appeal have not gone in construing the conduct proscribed by the act.

The basic need remains, therefore, to establish a substantive norm which may appropriately and feasibly be applied by the processes of law. It is recommended that a new statute be enacted, containing in an introduction thereto a clear statement of its principles and purposes, the social objectives which it seeks to accomplish. It should then enumerate in specific terms the offenses or conduct it would proscribe, offenses defined by objective behavior criteria rather than by moral culpability alone. If the adjudication of a "status" should remain the aim of such a statute, it is nevertheless true that such a status can justifiably attach only to an offense or course of conduct defined with enough precision to lead to reasonably similar results in similar cases.

It may be difficult, as suggested previously, to determine a standard of conduct which the law should impose. It is quite possible that no more should be attempted in the field of sex conduct, among girls over eighteen at any rate, than to pre-

[4] 260 N.Y. 171, 183 N.E. 353., 1932.
[5] *People* v. *Palmer,* 244 N.Y.S. 727. App. Div., 1930.
[6] 248 N.Y.S. 599. App. Div., 1931.

vent the spread of venereal disease and to protect them from
"third-party interests"—the pimps and panderers by whom
they may be exploited. The first of these functions, which is
primarily a preventive and public health measure, is large
enough to occupy the full attention of a court or clinic during this period of liberalized sex behavior. The argument
appears sound, however, that this problem might be better
solved by diagnostic and clinical agencies outside the judicial
framework and of a noncorrectional nature. This would frequently require referral from the judicial to the clinical agencies. Indeed, one of the most important functions of the Court
should be that of making agency referrals.

It is clear in any event, that the function of protecting the
adolescent girl is not efficiently served under the statutes and
their administration either by this court or by other courts
of the city. The courts neither reach an adequate proportion
of the girls who need treatment, nor accomplish adequate results with those they do reach. By the emergence of more
definite standards, at least careful and exact evidence sifting
will be required before a minor is adjudicated to a status
which, however helpful to her may be its intent, carries a
stigma and a series of treatment-experiences which have serious import. Less tangible but not less hopeful is a result on
the positive side, of getting the legal issue more clearly focused
at the point of whether the Court can and shall take hold. A
normal though not inevitable effect of such focusing is to
concentrate treatment-thinking on the treatment side, with a
materially greater chance of more sustained and careful probation supervision of the promising cases.

A further and wholly different advantage may accrue from
reformulating the statute so that jurisdiction of the case
need not depend upon the defendant's parent or husband. It is
a strange consequence of the administration of the present
law that the married girl may be permitted her "moral de-

pravities," although they are similar to those punished in the unmarried, and that a minor is not "wayward" unless her parents say she is. The clause now used (913-a, 5) frequently results in loss of court jurisdiction or ineffective court action by refusal of the parent to make a complaint or to agree to remand, probation, or commitment. Entrusting to the parent any considerable voice in determining whether the girl is to be adjudicated or how she is to be dealt with after submission to the Court's jurisdiction is unbeneficial when her presence in the Court is due, in great part, to the proven failure of the parent in maintaining control over her. If in a more adequate statute provision be included to cover the disobedient adolescent, considerable emphasis should be laid on other sections under which parental complaint or consent would be unnecessary. To be effective, the Court should have jurisdiction regardless of the parents' desire or complaint. The Court should be available at their need without resting exclusively upon their demand or coöperation, nor should the existence of a husband foreclose the tribunal from action where the girl's conduct warrants judicial intervention. Decisions in New York cases dealing with children and adolescents have asserted this principle as to parents, though the Wayward Minor Statute does not recognize it. Thus it has been affirmed that children are to be protected from their parents when the latter exceed reasonable bounds in correcting them.[7] Although the adolescent requires similar protection in this court, it cannot be adequately assured by informal and extralegal circumventions since the Court lacks jurisdiction over the parent and, at least under its interpretation, complaint by parent or guardian is required. Too, the weight of authority in the United States is that though an infant be married, that fact does not deprive the juvenile court of its jurisdiction.[8] A

---

[7] *In re Carl,* 22 N.Y.S. 2d 782, 174 Misc. 985. Dom. Rel. Court, 1940.
[8] See *American Law Reports,* XIX, 616 and *American Law Reports,* XLIX, 402.

similar rule should be applied to a court for adolescents. Finally, there is no convincing argument in justification of a court's abandoning control over a defendant who marries to escape its jurisdiction, though this result also follows from the Court's interpretation of the statutory emphasis upon "willful disobedience to parent or guardian."

Considering more specifically the norms which the Court should apply, it is certain that in the present stage of limited knowledge of crime-causation and our inadequate facilities for treatment the Court is not now and will not in the clearly foreseeable future be prepared to act in prevention of delinquency on a course-of-conduct principle. It would appear to be only sound and sensible policy, therefore, for the tribunal to perform the function (which it apparently can) of adjudicating those who have committed real and specific offenses against the law. Yet, considering the past history of the Court and the pressure-group influences which will continue to influence the legislature, it is improbable that the sex-moralization and delinquency-prevention purposes which are now central in statute and court will be eschewed entirely.

Perhaps the most that may be hoped for, then, is that the Court may come to shift its emphasis toward two more definite objectives: (1) to adjudicate to an adolescent offender status those who have committed acts which if committed by an adult would be crimes (a principle applied under the juvenile delinquency and youthful offender acts and under the Wayward Minor Statute as well in other courts) ; and (2) to adjudicate and treat therapeutically those girls whose conduct has been promiscuous, commercial, and indicative of moral depravity, and who have failed to respond to the efforts of other social agencies. Under a statute thus designed the purpose would be neither retributive nor preventive, but reformative and rehabilitative; these goals alone would call for great expansion of skilled effort, both extensive and intensive, for fairly effective therapy. Emphasis would be upon probation for constructive guidance and for the enlisting of supplementary expert aid from hospitals, psychiatrists, mental hygienists, occupational specialists, and others. Mere conduct problem cases would be referred to specialized, noncourt agencies.

It would seem that this extension of the Court's jurisdiction to wider ranges of nonsexual offenses is highly desirable. More frequently the adjustment of the adolescent girl to the community should be possible if in the future she is dealt with in this court for the several reasons which have appeared in this study: The judges sitting here become more familiar with the special problems, methods, and goals in treating the adolescent. The various facilities for dealing with the girl, psychological, probationary, medical, and institutional, are needed for other offenders as well as for sexually delinquent girls, and they can be used more consistently and intensively through a single specialized court. The sound reformative principle of treating the offender as an individual is violated by running adolescent girls, frequently first offenders, through any one of a large variety of courts, depending on the time, place, and circumstances of the girl's act. As a result, the duration and associations of her detention, the form of hearing provided her, and the ultimate treatment prescribed may encourage rather than dissuade her from future crime. The fact that the adolescent courts of Brooklyn and Queens have used their facilities successfully for a large variety of crimes, reducing the charge for corrigible cases, is a precedent which points to the provision of a similar right to the girls of New York City at large.

PROCEDURAL STANDARDS

It is not believed that technicalities and forms should be preserved for their own sake. The test of their value lies in the degree to which they serve to implement and assure the objectives sought in the substantive norms of the law. If the rule of law is vague and formless, no amount of formal procedure will insure predictable or desirable social consequences. But, conversely, though the rule be ascertainable and clear, if the procedure be loose, the results will be unpredictable. The virtue of procedural form is not in its technicality, but in the nicety, precision, and uniformity with which it accomplishes the social results desired in applying the established norms.[9]

[9] An excellent analysis of the need for legal regularities as a supplement to, and control of, pure authority appears in Llewellyn, "The Normative, the Legal, and the Law-Jobs; the Problem of Juristic Method," *Yale Law Journal*, XLIX (1940), 1368–70, and the further need, beyond authority and regularity, of making "the Law As Is *become* the Law That Should Be, the merely 'legal' become the rightly Legal," (1372). In his "Horse-Trade and Merchant's Market in Sales," *Harvard Law Review*, LII (1939), 1876–77, he illustrates the difficulties where "facts are in a welter from case to case," without repetitive pattern: "Until the case-results get themselves a prophet and a suitable doctrine, there is unpredictability, high, wide, and handsome."

Dession in his article "The Role of Penalties in Criminal Law," *Yale Law Journal*, XXXVII (1928), 1048–69, very aptly stresses the danger in the application of vague general statutes and frequent indeterminate sentences—with their high levels of ideal theory—when the public is unwilling to assume the necessary obligations to implement them. He points out as conditions precedent to the use of the indeterminate sentence, good diagnostic facilities, good resources for rehabilitation, and public enlightenment. Without adequate implementation, he predicts, we risk the scrapping of our precious, if imperfect, guarantees of individual liberty.

In Arnold's, "Law Enforcement; an Attempt at Social Dissection," *Yale Law Journal*, XLII (1932), 1–24, is expressed a contrasting point of view, with a somewhat cynic emphasis upon the symbolic value of laws. He suggests that, "most unenforced criminal laws survive in order to satisfy moral objections to established modes of conduct. They are unenforced because we want to continue our conduct, and unrepealed because we want to preserve our morals"—an interpretation which may be peculiarly applicable to such legislation as the Wayward Minor Act. He proceeds to suggest that we need not fear for an excess of laws, since their function—and especially, by implication, that of broad statutes—is to insure sufficient coverage so that the vicious or criminal types may be convicted. This is an unusual variation of the theory of fitting the law to the offender rather than the offense. There is not in his theory the stress upon prevention and rehabilitation with which Dession was primarily concerned. Arnold's principle is undoubtedly applicable in

Intake.—The work of the intake officer is one of the most central and vital functions of the Court. In her discretion, the complainant may be informed that there is no basis for court action or she may be discouraged from using the facilities of the Court. Potentially, the most significant service of the officer is referral to social agencies for supervision. As the data from the Court show, this method has been virtually abandoned. While it should be restored to the fullest possible use of nonpunitive community resources, a rounded handling of intake is a task calling for peculiar and many-sided expertness. Because of its importance the writer believes that intake should be carried on by a social worker well trained and experienced in individual case work and thoroughly familiar with the available social facilities of the city. She could infer from an original and separate interview with the adolescent girl and with her parents, or other complainant, whether the alleged conduct merited official action by the Court or should be handled informally by an agency. If no statutory violation were alleged or if no sufficient evidence were available to prove an offense, but if treatment appeared nevertheless to be desirable, agency referral should be made. Thus if careful family case work should be the primary need or if other social, economic, or psychological problems be urgently involved, referrals to outside agencies should patently be made. It is clear that the intake officer needs to know as precisely as possible

---

some degree to the serious habitual criminal for whom the prosecutor desires easy conviction and punitive treatment under a broad statute. However, this writer feels that even in the case of incorrigible criminals it should be possible and necessary to prove a specifically defined overt offense before criminal adjudication is permitted by law. What Arnold suggests is subject to grave abuse in practice through invidious discriminations, crusades of legal prosecution, irresponsible administration of law through lack of proper limiting control and direction. Too much is sacrificed for the sake of incapacitation alone. Certainly, in so far as wayward minors are concerned, it would be difficult to justify the broad statute on the basis of a need to simplify the rounding up and incapacitative treatment of minor sex offenders.

the jurisdiction of the Court and should also be able to discriminate among social and psychological problems those which can legitimately and most effectively be solved by official court action. A competent psychiatric social worker could be obtained for intake from the Department of Hospitals, it is believed, as has been done at Westfield and other institutions, thus relieving a probation worker for the more extended program of informal supervision and official probation.

Service of process.—A common abuse of the authority and dignity of the Court has been encouraged by the issuance to the complaining parent of a summons which may be used in advance of adjudication as a club to coerce the daughter. It may be a threat to insure obedience to parental commands, however unreasonable, or a symbol of parental rejection as the daughter is hailed into court. No ex parte procedure is ever desirable; its use in law is a creature of necessity and requires strict limitation to cases of necessity. Where parents and daughter are at odds no such necessity appears for this type of action by a court designed to protect and cure the daughter. It is proposed, therefore, that the adolescent should be protected against any misuse of the summons by parents. It would be a legitimate and extremely helpful function if a member of the Juvenile Aid Bureau were enabled to serve and explain the summons to the girl in every instance where she failed to respond to a simple letter from the intake officer. Such a practice would result in less frequent need for warrants from the Court and in an atmosphere materially more favorable, both to accurate determination of facts and to successful treatment.

Representation by counsel.—Though fully in accord with the reaction of a "socialized court" to the common run of criminal lawyers, the writer believes, nevertheless, that courts dealing with adolescents will better stand the tests of legality and "sociality" if they provide fully for the right of counsel.

For the court which assumes to operate in rehabilitating the offender it seems especially important that her civil and legal rights be assured, and it is paradoxical to require only that the judge may protect them. When a court retains the contentious philosophy and procedure, it is inevitable that the alleged offender will often need the counsel of an advocate who is present to represent her interests solely. Moreover, as a practical matter, the court will risk less danger of attack if legal advice is freely available to the defendant. On the other hand, the too common lawyer-attributes of technicality and contentiousness are out of place in such a court. But the choice is not limited to "no lawyer" or "a nonunderstanding lawyer." It is entirely feasible to develop a type of lawyer who fits into the procedure of the Court and yet adds the performance of a needed function.

It would be desirable, therefore, to have a representative of the Legal Aid Society in the Wayward Minor Court, to advise and protect defendants who are more innocent in their knowledge of their legal rights than are the defendants of any other criminal court in New York City. He may be especially helpful in eliciting from the girl her own story, so easily neglected when she is not represented. He may assist in determining whether, in fact, the girl was guilty of an offense warranting adjudication, thereby frequently saving time and preventing error in the Court. He may assist in the procuring of witnesses for the girl when the allegation against her may thereby be rebutted. Finally, he may aid considerably in a psychological sense, being felt as her friend in the Court during a normally bitter experience of apparent parental rejection.

It is not meant to be implied that the Court affirmatively forbids to the defendant her legal right to counsel and witnesses. But it is suggested that the mere rapid formulary exposition of those rights leaves the adolescent unaware of either the nature of the right or the means to exert it. The

mere right to counsel, moreover, remains rather meaningless
when the defendant has no means to secure one and none is
ever assigned. And it is most unfortunate if the idea is explicitly or implicitly maintained that attorneys have no standing in the Court.

Arraignment and adjudication.—It is strongly recommended that a hearing of the issue as to the defendant's
behavior be held at the earliest possible date after the complaint is drawn, allowing, however, sufficient time for the pro-
curement of witnesses. This is especially important for several reasons: institutional confinement, even at a so-called
"shelter," must inevitably be stereotyped as a penalty so long
as it is associated with the correctional system. It is symptomatic that even the records occasionally speak of remand
as "incarceration." Not only is a stigma attached to detention, but institutions for that purpose do actually operate
under punitive assumptions; of the girls received, enough are
so recalcitrant as to make this almost inevitable. In total
effect, it is inconceivable that any currently available remand
institution, save a hospital, can be both justifiable and beneficial to the defendant awaiting a hearing in any case in which
the girl will be found innocent of serious wrongdoing.

While the Court may rightly be pleased that the adolescent
need no longer be confined with hardened older criminals, yet
the young respond easily to the suggestion and social pressure of their own age group, and contamination during institutional detention is still a fact of common observation.
This is a sound reason for not detaining long a defendant
against whom no case has yet been made on competent evidence. A basic tenet of our criminal law provides the right to
a hearing without unnecessary delay, that the innocent may
be quickly freed. It is a right to be denied the adolescent less
lightly than to any other person. No more specious argument
for its abandonment could be made than that frequently ad-

vanced: its prior disappearance in the juvenile court. For it is particularly at the childhood and adolescent levels that the innocent must be preserved from the dangers of corrupting associations. Only by clear proof that the individual or society will profit more from its abrogation should the right be qualified, and then not surreptitiously by extralegal methods. Here again is observed a fallacy, brought about by the infiltration of certain inapplicable ideals from applied sociology: the assumption of an identity of function and effect between a court and a social agency or clinic and between a detention institution or shelter (in the context of criminal or quasi-criminal procedure) and a foster home.

To drive home a major contention of this study: In the development of its methodology a juristically interesting phenomenon has occurred in the Wayward Minor Court as the dual functions of the Court have collapsed into one. In the traditional judicial system the decision as to guilt, or adjudicative process, and the imposition of penalties or other dispositional process have been strictly bifurcated. In this court the technique has been to combine the two. After arraignment of the girl an adjournment is called for social investigation; at the adjourned date, upon the "evidence" gathered and put before the Court, both adjudication and disposition are announced at once. Generally, as indicated by the data given above,[10] either the girl is found to be a wayward minor and subjected to probation or confinement or, if the probation officer and parent indicate the offenses to be minor or her character corrigible, the case is further adjourned to permit unofficial interim supervision.

The important point is this: The techniques of adjudication under the criminal law have been refined and limited by methods wrought through tradition and experience for the selection and protection of the innocent. The rights of due

[10] See *supra*, Chapter VI.

process have been vested in the defendant by constitution and statute. In marked contrast, however, the methods of disposition have been evolved informally and administratively, for the most part without the guide of established rules. As the range of discretion permitted the courts in aggravation and mitigation of penalties has increased, there has been little coördinated effort to guide the procedural means used by courts in expressing their expanded powers of disposition. Legislative efforts to direct the discretion have been few, and, though personnel and methods through which punishment is meted out have been frequently criticized, little attempt has been made either to analyze empirically the consequences of existing procedures, or to evolve new ones more nicely adjusted to the ends sought.[11] As a result there is a remarkable variety of methods employed by courts, counsel, and defendants to influence disposition, with little or no attention to questions of credibility, competence, relevance, any communicable or perceptible standards of action of a legal nature, or even good sense. One of the greatest contemporary needs in improvement of the judicial process is the modification of methods by which disposition is determined; for it is apparent that the judicial ordering of penalties may be at least as important as adjudication itself.

It becomes clear, therefore, that when these two processes are drawn together, with the informality of dispositional methods incorporated into the adjudicative process as well, then the whole body of basic protections to the defendant is lost or relegated to the vagaries of discretion. This discretion is no less administrative for being exercised by a judge,

---

[11] See Llewellyn, "On the Good, the True, and the Beautiful, in Law," *University of Chicago Law Review*, IX (1942), 259, in which he stresses the need for improving the machinery by which rights are made real: ". . . to take rules of law and goals of law and ideals of law out of the realm of *mere* doctrine, *mere* paper, *mere* words, *mere* dreams, and body them forth among law's people in vibrant realization."

and has not behind it, to semiregularize it, even the expertness in the particular area of a skilled and specialized administration or the unspoken but powerful lines of traditional guidance and restraint which go with judicial work under familiar judicial conditions and established judicial forms, or with judicial work within a college of judges. Incompetent and irrelevant testimony becomes determinative, not only of treatment, but of guilt as well. Even in the informality of administrative procedure the fundamental judicial requirements of a fair hearing are retained, e. g., the right to be heard, a definite charge, confrontation by opposing witnesses, advice of counsel. Yet in the Wayward Minor Court, through the peculiarities of its procedure, the accused frequently may not even know the nature of the evidence by which she is adjudged, much of which is contained only in the records of the probation officer, often read by the judge or whispered by the officer. The data in the records, gathered after the alleged conduct, untested for their bias or incompleteness, are not the evidence upon which adjudication in a court of criminal law is warranted.

It is the writer's contention that the court hearing should not be preceded by a probation investigation into the social history. The arguments of efficiency, practicability, adjudicative accuracy, justice to the defendant, and ignorance of pre-criminal behavior sequences have been advanced to stress the point that, under present circumstances at least, the Court should proceed at once to determine on the basis of tested evidence whether the defendant's conduct justifies adjudication. The decisions of our courts in cases of children and adolescents, moreover, support this right of the alleged wayward minor to full and fair trial of a concrete issue; for it has been held that a girl of fifteen is entitled to the presumption of innocence and the benefit of every reasonable doubt.[12]

[12] *People* v. *Fowling*, 148 N.Y.S. 741. Bronx County Court, 1914.

In a later case the Children's Court said:

> To serve the social purpose for which the Children's Court was created, provision is made in the state for wide investigation before, during, and after the hearing. But that investigation is clinical in its nature. Its results are not to be used as legal evidence where there is an issue to be tried. When it is said that even in cases of lawbreaking delinquency constitutional safeguards and the technical procedure of the criminal law may be disregarded, there is no implication that a purely socialized trial of a specific issue may properly or legally be had. The contrary is true. There must be a reasonably definite charge. The customary rules of evidence shown by long experience as essential to getting at the truth with reasonable certainty in civil trials must be adhered to. The finding of fact must rest on the preponderance of evidence adduced under those rules. Hearsay, opinion, gossip, bias, prejudice, trends of hostile neighborhood feeling, the hopes and fears of social workers, are all sources of error and have no more place in Children's Courts than in any other court.[13]

In *People* v. *Harris* [14] the principle is again asserted that one charged with being a wayward minor "is entitled to all the safeguards surrounding ordinary trials, especially since conviction may result in incarceration in a reformatory."

For the future, if there emerges sufficiently convincing indication that certain specific courses of conduct are associated significantly and genetically with criminal behavior, and if provision be established for the protection of the defendant by an attorney against charges made under these specific statutory norms, there is no very convincing argument against the abandonment of some of the traditional due process rights, particularly the rules on exclusion. However, the issue would still remain as to the relative efficiency and accuracy, in a court of this kind, of the consent-procedure technique as against the traditional procedures of guilt determination.

Where, during the adjudicative process, the fault appears

13 *People* v. *Lewis,* 260 N.Y. 171. 1932.
14 *People* v. *Harris,* 230 N.Y.S. 767. Court of Spec. Sess., App. Pt., 1928.

to be that of the parents, it is highly impractical and unjust
to find against the girl in the hope that the Court may thereby
affect the parent indirectly. The damage done to the girl by
an unwarranted adjudication and her feeling of injustice are
not balanced by a positive gain to the family when the Court
lacks both jurisdiction over the parents and the family case
work facilities which are required for the adjustment of domestic discord. Unfortunate "tinkering" is the result. Such
cases should be referred to a domestic relations court, if sufficiently serious, otherwise to a case work agency. The practice of "taking jurisdiction" by adjudication and remanding
in order to "help the girl" in an unfortunate family situation
is not sound. It is undeniably true that when the family is
taut with conflict, much may be gained by a brief separation
brought about through the ministration of an agency. This
procedure should not be indulged and rationalized by a court,
however, when the only available "placement" usually implies
an institution defined in the minds of the girl and the public
as punitive. This is patent where good family therapy is impossible in any event.

It may frequently happen that without the guidance of a
probation officer's report before trial it will be impossible to
find facts upon which to base an adjudication. If the facts of
wrongful conduct do exist, it is an unfortunate limitation
upon effective legal action that they cannot always be educed
in relevant and competent testimony. It is better to accept
this qualification of prosecution than to supply the needed
evidence through social diagnosis which, however relevant to
treatment, does not bear significantly upon the question of
guilty conduct. It is believed that if the Court accepts the
proposition that wrongful conduct must first be proven, there
will be a better selection of cases which warrant court treatment, and justice will more frequently be done. Naturally,
then, humanized or clinical treatment may follow upon social

and personality diagnosis after adjudication. The investigative and supervisory work of the probation officer should become more effective through the proper legal selection of cases for social treatment.

The following secondary suggestions are made for possible ultimate improvement of the adjudicative process:

1. The presence of a psychiatrist or, if that is not feasible, of a psychiatric social worker, in the Court at all arraignments would make for increased efficiency and fairness. This is clear in cases where the mental subnormality or other abnormality of the defendant could be apprehended at an early stage and proper disposition made by Bellevue Hospital without formal adjudication. The not uncommon incompetence of the parental complainant might be recognized and his credibility attacked at a stage where the Court can act, at least in this limited way, in reference to the parent. In the frequent psychological issues raised in the Court, the advisory guidance of a person with good psychiatric training could be extremely helpful: What is the "willful disobedience" of a moronic or emotionally distorted child? What are the "reasonable commands" of an unstable parent? What are the chances of successful adjustment of a moron, a neurotic, a "psychopathic personality," under probationary supervision or in the available institutions?

2. Wherever possible the testimony against the girl should come from someone other than her parents. Officers acquainted with the cases believe that usually other witnesses might be brought before the Court to testify. The accusations of the mother before her child as to the latter's existent or imminent moral depravity are psychologically undesirable in most cases. The mother and home must be depended upon for the ultimate regeneration of the girl in the vast majority of instances. The frequently brutal experience of the mother's official and semipublic repudiation of her child in the Court may

complicate the difficulties of improving the amenability of the girl in her home situation. The commonly rebellious reaction of the girl in court, harmful as it is in effect, is a natural response to the peculiar situation in which the mother is called upon to disavow responsibility for her daughter.

3. Bearing upon the entire question of the preservation to the girl of her legal rights in a quasi-criminal proceeding is the need for clear and careful exposition to her of those rights rather than their concealment. A representative of the Juvenile Aid Bureau or from the Legal Aid Society might well perform this function. It is necessary, in dealing with the young girl during the confusing experiences of the Court, that the meaning of the proceedings be made clear along with her rights and duties. As the Court said in reversing a conviction in *People* v. *Brewster:* "In many instances, the charge is made by the parent or other guardian or custodian of the minor. She may be confused or overawed or the procedure be unintelligible to her. She would in many cases have no one to advise with." [15] The girl should be better informed before coming into court; the posting of an informative notice in the detention pen of the Court could be very helpful. Such a notice would be difficult enough to phrase in the simple but clear and instructive form that would be required, but how much more effectively and certainly the job could thus be done! The right of the girl to explain her side of the case deserves emphasis; her tendency under the combined pressure of judicial and parental authority and the utterly strange and threatening environment and procedure is to be silently convinced of the futility of self-defense. Much might be gained in the way of intelligent handling of cases if the judge made a definite effort to encourage the girl to discuss her conduct.

In addition to advice as to her legal rights, the girl clearly needs a *Beistand* in the court to act as friend, guide, and ad-

15 *People* v. *Brewster.* 248 N.Y.S. 599. App. Div., 1931.

viser during this difficult period. The probation officers sometimes perform this function very well, but in many cases, and with certain officers, the defendant must feel abandoned and alone. If an officer does not act as her friend in court, a member of the Juvenile Aid Bureau could do so ably.

4. Cases should be continued and ultimately disposed by the judge with whom they originate. A greater economy in time and effectiveness in adjudication and disposition could result from this practice than where two or three judges must at different times be apprised of the circumstances of the case. Failure of a judge newly sitting on a case to inform himself sufficiently may lead to very inapposite disposition. Moreover, the meeting of a new judge throws into the discard for the defendant a needed sense of continuity and of nonarbitrariness.

Since the quality of the work of the Court depends so largely upon its personnel, there is need, not only that the judges assigned be especially interested in dealing with adolescent problems, but that they be experienced. Since the experience must usually come from work in the Court itself, it is important that the judges assigned and proven capable remain there over extended periods of time. Moreover, in the light of the sexual offenses involved in this tribunal, it is desirable that the judge's reaction-system be objective. Here, if anywhere, realism, good sense, and emotional balance are needed for the difficult task of adjudication in the field of sex deviation.

Judges and probation officers should be made thoroughly familiar with the institutions and agencies which may be used in treatment. The independence of sectarian facilities and their power to reject cases and to use widely varying discretion in the duration and methods of treatment they impose, constitute some of the serious handicaps to effective consummation of adolescent court efforts—as they do also in the

Children's Court. However, institutional visits by the justices are required by the Children's Court Act, and a Committee on Institutions (founded in 1936) provides information on the program, facilities, and life at the institutions most frequently used. Such "inspection and investigation of private institutions" has been strongly resisted by the heads of the Protestant, Jewish, and Catholic agencies of the city. Indeed, the Roman Catholic diocese in Brooklyn has refused to permit the staff of the Court's committee to visit its institution.[16] Clearly, visitation and investigation of, and publicity for, the institutions for detention and commitment, both public and private, are needed. Partially, at least, they could be provided for by statute. Ideally, public standards and supervision should be established if the courts are to use these facilities. That frequency and duration of institutional confinement should vary radically with one's religious faith in the Wayward Minor Court (as in the Children's Court) is a strange and senseless anomaly. Apparently, court personnel require enlightenment in these matters.

As a matter of motivation, it is suggested that improved conduct is an improbable result if a judge expresses to the girl his grave doubts as to the wisdom of his action in freeing her, and his feeling that she will continue to misbehave. Though differing personalities require differing appeals or stimulants to reformation, such a prediction would rarely be accepted as a challenge by those who pass through this court. More commonly it would provide an easy rationalization for continued misconduct, the defendant accepting her wayward minor role as officially defined. Would it not be more effective for the judge, even though he may be skeptical, to display confidence in the girl's ability to achieve the standard that he attempts to establish for her? Fatalism in the Court, certainty that "we'll see her later in Women's Court," though

[16] See Polier, *Everyone's Children, Nobody's Child*, pp. 228–31.

it may have the virtue of realism in the judge's silent recognition of probabilities, is not constructive in effect when revealed to the girl.

5. Where evidence educed at the arraignment is sufficient to make out a *prima facie* case of sexual misconduct, there ought always to be a remand for physical diagnosis to determine the venereal condition of the defendant rather than waiting, in some instances, until after disposition to determine the fact.[17] If a case on which the health report shows the presence of disease has been dismissed, the public health can and should be protected by public health laws providing for treatment without criminal conviction.

Interim disposition.—When, after a hearing, the facts elicited by the Court warrant adjudication rather than dismissal, the wayward minor may properly be held for investigation pending final disposition. Where sex misconduct has been shown, or where serious strain in the family relationship is indicated, generally the girl should not be returned to her home during the period of probation investigation. It is more beneficial to her and to the community, her guilt of a sex offense being proved, to hospitalize or quarantine her for physical attention. If there is considerable domestic discord, she may usually be paroled to relatives or friends, to a residence club or to an open shelter, or discharged on her own recognizance to stay at a private residence and thus continue to go to work or to school. It should be necessary in only a small proportion of cases, it is believed, to remand the girl to a custodial institution; there is certainly no justification for making it a nearly automatic process. Again to iterate a point previously emphasized, where a girl is remanded without prior adjudication, she is convinced only of injustice. Even

[17] Though the practice is standard in the Women's Court, some of the judges are wary about ordering the Board of Health examination for fear of being overruled.

if she be guilty, she is conscious of a sense of unfairness in being "put away" without a hearing, a sense which vigorously militates against successful rehabilitation. When to this is added the damage which may be done through institutional associations, it is clear that the risks of remand prior to adjudication are excessive. The Court should not continue to expose to the ineradicable experience and associations of detention girls whom they concede to be blameless.

Improved detention facilities are among the most serious needs of the Court. The possible therapeutic effect of a short detention away from home in a favorable environment is unquestionable in some instances. When the provision of such facilities is left to the unplanned, uncoördinated, irresponsible caprice of wavering philanthropic and religious attention, however, the results are inevitably unequal and unjust. Under existing circumstances, open shelters which will care for all racial and religious groups, with clinical facilities for physical and mental examinations, are especially needed. The second greatest need is probably for an expansion of hospital facilities to permit observation and diagnosis of a larger proportion of court cases, thereby encouraging better informed dispositions.

More uniformity of interim procedure appears desirable, and the following steps are suggested:

1. A psychiatrist or psychiatric social worker with official status in the Court (assigned by the Department of Hospitals) should determine with reference to all adjudicated offenders whether they need to be remanded to Bellevue Hospital for more complete psychiatric and/or medical diagnosis or for a short period in the ward for observation and therapy.

2. Where sexual experience is indicated, a quarantine for venereal diagnosis and the beginning of treatment should be prescribed.

3. Where no sex offense is indicated, no psychopathic con-

dition observed, and no very serious offense has been committed, the girl should be paroled to her family unless the relationship is already too strained. In that case, some other individual should receive her as parolee if possible. If not, open-door shelter facilities should be available to her.

4. Where the offense proven was serious or parole for other reasons is impossible or unwise, the girl should be sent to a detention institution pending the probation report. In general, the period of adjournment before final disposition should be as brief as possible. A virtue of the procedure of the Wayward Minor Court should be the short period intervening between intake and arraignment and disposition—a brevity which is not possible in the higher courts for adolescents.

To carry the girl on unofficial supervision or institutional remand for extended periods before a court hearing has been provided, with the rationalization that she may thereby be saved from the stigma of adjudication and formal treatment, is in reality a hazardous procedure, for it further encourages the handling of cases that are not truly delinquent or recalcitrant. Social and mild behavior problems should be dealt with by social agencies. Only the offender who requires judicial and rehabilitative-correctional treatment should be exposed to the facilities of the Court. "Unofficial treatment," borrowed from the Children's Court, is a bastard spawn of court and case work, evasive of the law, inappropriate as therapy, expansive of jurisdiction. The liberal, experimental court for the young is typically understaffed, overtaxed, confronted with a great and growing body of real delinquents. For it to attempt to do a strictly preventive, social work job on the nonrecalcitrant is folly. The length of sentence established by the Wayward Minor Statute is excessive, to be sure. The remedy lies, however, in modification of the statute rather than in its circumvention by techniques which are inapposite, both to the Court and to its defendants. Prior to statutory change the Court could now, as suggested above, apply short-term treatment during a period between adjudication and later suspended sentence.

Probation investigation.—The chief recommendation as to procedure of probation—that investigation follow upon adjudication—has already been made in detail. The point need not be labored further. The next greatest need is for expansion of personnel in order that fuller attention may be given both to the cases and to case recording than is possible with a staff now too small. The officers of the Court are deeply interested in their work with wayward minors and generally devote as much care as is possible within the budgetary and institutional limitations imposed. It is extremely unfortunate that two of the most important functions of the Court—investigation and supervision—must be performed inadequately because of the niggardly allotment of funds. It is a profoundly naïve error of political and budgetary administration to set up a court elegant in its physical structure and then to promote its inevitable failures through lack of the personnel and institutional facilities necessary in the implementing of a constructive program. It is a dearly expensive error.

Final disposition.—It is at this stage of court proceedings that the clinical features of the Wayward Minor Court may be utilized most effectively. Assuming the probation officer's careful report of the social investigation to be available and the psychiatrist to be in the Court, a considerate, unhurried conference should be held to determine what treatment might best be applied in the light of the girl's history and character. (The judge, psychiatrist, and probation officer, together with the attorney for the defendant and perhaps the representative from Juvenile Aid, can constitute an objective disposition tribunal, guided by past experience of the Court and familiar with its problems through staff conferences.)

The discussion of the offender should occur, it is believed, before she is brought into the courtroom for disposition. Much of the content of probation and psychiatric reports, which under present procedure are delivered rapidly in whispered and partially audible terms, should not be brought out in the presence of the girl because of its highly personal nature; nor should secret information be imparted in her presence. It is clear that where mental inferiority or emotional instability is discovered, the fact should not be revealed to her in open court. To be described by a court officer as "obviously mental" or "not very bright" may easily be damaging to her psychological, emotional, and social adjustments. It is highly probable too that the shock of learning of her pregnancy or that she is suffering from venereal disease could be better sustained if the information were communicated to her outside of court by a member of the Juvenile Aid Bureau or by a probation officer; hence the suggestion that disposition be discussed after adjudication and interim disposition but before the girl is brought in to receive the Court's determination. It is believed that this procedure has greater legal and psychological validity than the process presently used; it also furthers the integration of experience among the various personnel.

It is assumed, the existing statutory policy being sound, that probation should be used in final disposition unless there are strong contraindications from the social or psychological history. More careful plans for supervision, more nicely adjusted to the needs of the individual case, should be drawn up and administered by an expanded department. Under current conditions there is such pressure for investigations that the real probation work of supervision must often be neglected. Also, where intensive work would otherwise be required there is an inclination to adopt the easier expedient of sending the girl to an institution. More uniform methods of investigation, supervision, and recording can be established so that in each case the relevant and useful information can be gathered and recorded and the irrelevancies which fill some of the records can be excluded. Such uniformities will not be produced, of course, unless the officers get together to share experience and method. Many useful ideas might thus be put into practice. One such fruitful thought contributed by a probation officer should be used frequently in the Court: an officer should be able to bring her probationer before the judge for counsel or reprimand instead of waiting, as at present, for a formal violation of probation, to be followed by commitment. Frequently, it would seem, more might be accomplished with the girls by an affirmatively helpful and sympathetic rapport than by the negative techniques of threat, coercion, and moralization which are so commonly used.

Where commitment appears to be necessary, the institutional disposition should be made, of course, according to the girl's character and her needs, psychological, medical, and social. Here again, the lack of adequate facilities has resulted, in large part, from the public's evasion of its responsibilities for equal provision for all classes of defendants. The establishment of institutional facilities has been entrusted to private sectarian and philanthropic enterprises, uncoördinated and, for the most part, unsupervised, though largely contributed to by city funds. One result, among many unfortunate ones, is the number of cases wherein no proper disposition can be made and misplacement results.

The most serious lacks are in facilities to care for the protestant Negro girl, the dull-normal or borderline child, the neurotic and the unstable nonpsychotic, the mentally superior, and the girl who needs little supervision or discipline but who cannot be returned to her home or relatives. A better coördination of facilities, with responsibility definitely vested in the city, where it belongs, could greatly expand and improve the treatment of offenders at little additional cost. The community should be made aware of what the existing provisions are and the needs. More specifically, of course, the parents of wayward minors should know the sort of institution to which their daughters are sent and the meaning of an "indeterminate sentence." Many parents have fondly thought they were giving their daughters a short "cooling-off" period at an institution, only to find later, upon inquiry, that their children were out of the control of both themselves and the Court for a period extending up to three years. An important change is needed in the commitment provisions so that the Court may permit indeterminate confinement for any period up to three years. However, present minima are set, quite inappropriately, by the institutions themselves, and it will therefore require an extension of control over them to make confinement reasonably short where it is needed at all.

Finally, where it is believed that neither probation nor institutionalization is suitable, the suspended sentence could be experimented with more generously with defendants of the type that this court processes. With the social investigation following the adjudication, it might be found desirable to suspend sentence in numerous cases where the girl's history was favorable.

9

Administrative Reorganization

ONE OF THE MOST BASIC NEEDS in the field of social administration in New York City is a fuller integration of the public and private facilities to the end of their more ordered and effective application to community problems. More numerous coördinating councils, composed of representatives of court and noncourt social agencies, could be an instrument of such integration.[1] Such councils have developed numerously and successfully to fill an apparent need in California and other states. A series of well-organized, fully coöperating councils could perform yeoman's service in the field of delinquency in New York as well.

More particularly, the council system could fulfill a significant function in directing those cases which do not require judicial and correctional attention away from courts and into the more appropriate specialized agencies. In the important service of drawing together information on the existing social facilities, such councils would point up the lacks which have resulted from unplanned, haphazard accretions of benevolence and could direct the trends of future agency development. It should produce acquaintance and understanding and a much-needed coöperative interrelationship of the now often opposed, competitive, and overlapping agencies. Ignorance of the existence of related community services is a familiar but unnecessary phenomenon blocking the efficiency of social agencies. The delinquent, and through him the community, suffers from these conditions of ignorance, competition, agency deficiency, and costly duplication. Economy to the

[1] See Pauline Young, *op. cit.*, Chapter 26.

agency and the community, and most certainly to the youthful offender and pre-delinquent, could result from coördination. The community-minded plan of the coördinating council rather than the agency-minded approach might be temporarily less satisfying to vested, autonomous agency interests, to those whom Justin Miller has called the prima donnas of social work. But integration should promote ultimately a broader satisfaction through the more effective implementation of social goals. Elsewhere, the adjustment committee of the coördinating council has been used as the agency of referral to appropriate treatment facilities for problem youth. A chief result has been the channeling of cases away from court and into nonstigmatic agencies, with a correlated emphasis upon prevention and reconstruction rather than correction. New York lacks adequate mechanics of referral with democratic and uniform policy. Each agency, institution, and court sets its own diverse course as to coverage, philosophy, method, and duration of treatment. The child is caught in the middle, or remains undiscovered until his rehabilitation is exceedingly difficult.

Specifically, the courts for the young, with their expansive inclination, attempt treatment for all manner of familial and psychological problems with which they are not equipped adequately to deal, essaying a preventive function impossible to them. They allege the lack of other resources to meet the need and claim that they themselves fill the gap so far as is possible. The result can be worse than useless; it may be disastrous in many individual cases. Coördinating councils could reveal the existence of appropriate agencies, allocating responsibility through referral of cases and encouraging the establishment of needed standards. Wherever the lacks might be, they would be more obvious and could, in time, come to be filled by suitable facilities.

It is the author's contention that a great part, if not the

vast majority, of the cases which today are dealt with in
some fashion by the Wayward Minor Court could be serviced
more exactly and appropriately by other agencies of the city,
leaving to that tribunal and its probation staff the sufficiently
challenging task of dealing reformatively with truly delinquent adolescents. Selective referrals could be made most ad-
vantageously by coördinating councils rather than in the
fashion of unplanned, spasmodic, fortuitous happenstance
which now prevails.

Kenyon Scudder has reviewed some of the main advantages
of the coördinating council plan as it operates in Los Angeles
County:

Through frequent contacts between agencies, as made possible
by the coördinating councils, officials and social leaders are rapidly
drawing together with a new understanding of the problems of
children. It is this new confidence between the Juvenile Court and
the social agencies that has resulted in a marked decrease in the
number of petitions filed in the Probation Department. The community is now first exhausting its own resources and using the
Court only as a last resort. Communities which formerly dumped
their cases into the Juvenile Court now take pride in trying first
to adjust them locally, knowing full well that the Court will back
them if help is needed. The simple practice of sitting around the
table together and becoming better acquainted with the other
fellow's problems has helped to make the community a better
place for children.

What can we expect to accomplish in a local community if there
is adequate coördination in the work of local officials, social
workers, character-building agencies, and civic groups? This is
what actually happens:

1. Individual children who are in need of some special service
in order to overcome behavior problems receive this service from
the agency that is best equipped to meet the child's need.

2. Present facilities that have hitherto been used chiefly for the
privileged children are made available for the underprivileged and
neglected.

3. Present programs are enlarged, extended, or changed in order to render service to groups or areas hitherto overlooked.

4. A change takes place in the attitude of officials, school teachers, social workers, character-building executives, and civic leaders toward these children with problems.

5. Workers from many departments and agencies form the habit of coöperating with others whom they have learned to know at the coördinating-council meetings.

6. The community is educated to feel a new sense of responsibility for those problems that had before been left entirely to the police.

7. The environment is improved through community action. Constructive influences are strengthened and destructive influences are eliminated. Citizens are aroused to clean up their own community and make it a more desirable place for their children.

It is the primary object of the Coördinating Council Plan not only to reduce delinquency, but to make the community a better place in which to live.[2]

In New York City the council scheme of integration and coöperation is most closely approximated by the police precinct councils and some of the developing youth centers, such as those in Washington Heights, Inwood, Harlem, and the lower West Side, where the community facilities are focused on the problems of youth. This drawing together of agency and citizenry to cope with delinquency is relatively new in New York City. For the most part it has not yet broken down the barriers of agency autonomy and public apathy, which thwart effective prevention and rehabilitation. The efforts toward integration, however, clearly look in the right direction of a combined, community approach.

NEW PROCEDURES OF DISPOSITION

The problem of objectifying the disposition process, of adapting it to the therapeutic requirements of individual

[2] Glueck and Glueck (eds.), *Preventing Crime*, pp. 44–45.

cases and categories of delinquents, may be raised at this point. Within the scope of this work it is impossible to consider the matter in any detail. However, the issue of legally and sociologically loose sentencing practices has been illustrated in the determinants of dispositions which appear to operate in the Wayward Minor Court.[3] Extreme judicial variability has been noted in other studies of court practices.[4] These critical analyses have resulted in recommendations for more scientific and better standardized procedures. Three rather markedly varying views on renovated procedures of disposition may be differentiated:

1. The existing procedure of preserving to the judge his ultimate power of sentence is widely cherished by the bench. The discretion of the judge under this system may be directed, in a measure, by recommendations from probation officers who have delved into the defendant's background history. Yet in the courts where such recommendations are permitted, the judge is not officially constrained to follow them in any measure and may function quite capriciously if he choose. In any event, there is no general uniformity among the probation officers in their philosophy and methods to assure consistent patterns of advice to the bench. Chiefly, then, the judges are limited today by statutory provisions on the treatment which may be applied for the given offense. Under some of the existing indefinite-sentence laws, however, much of the power to determine length of confinement has been transferred from the judge to the institution of commitment. Thus it has been seen that in the Wayward Minor Court, when the judge gives an indeterminate sentence, the institution to which he commits will decide the time of discharge. Practices

[3] See Chapter VII.
[4] See Gaudet, Harris, and St. John, "Individual Differences in the Sentencing Tendencies of Judges," *Journal of Criminal Law and Criminology*, XXIII (1933), 811–18; United States Attorney General, *Survey of Release Procedures*, Vol. II, pp. 412 ff.

and philosophy on discharge appear to vary among institutions as radically as do the sentencing practices of judges.[5] In the present procedure, then, we see the inherent weaknesses of tremendous variability among autonomous judges, probation officers, and institutions.

2. The idea of a pre-sentence clinic has been widely proposed and advocated by sociologists, liberal lawyers, and political leaders. It is chiefly the strong opposition of the vested interests of bench and probation which has prevented wider adoption of the scheme. The most thoroughgoing proposal of this order has come from the American Law Institute in its Youth Correction Authority Act, widely discussed in recent years. The act would set up specialized and professionally manned tribunals (Youth Correction Authorities) to which the courts could sentence young offenders, aged sixteen to twenty-one, indeterminately. The Authority would then order investigations to be conducted and would make dispositions according to the requirements of the case. Under such procedure there should be less caprice and more partially scientific standardization and classification through the accumulated experience of behavior specialists. Too, the Authority would follow the development of treatment in its cases, holding or discharging the offender or modifying the disposition according to the offender's progress.

The dispositions tribunal idea has been attacked chiefly as an unnecessarily costly duplication of present facilities.[6]

[5] See Polier, *Everyone's Children, Nobody's Child*, p. 229: "—in the three outstanding private institutions receiving delinquent boys, the percentage of boys detained over two years was ten, twenty-two, and ninety, respectively."

[6] Official draft, "Youth Correction Authority Act," *American Law Institute*, 1940. See *Probation and Parole Progress, National Probation Association Yearbook*, 1941, several articles: "The Youth-Correction Authority Act," "Analyzing the YCA Act," "The YCA Act—Is It Practical and Needed?" pp. 227 ff. See also Chute, "The Youth Correction Authority in Theory and Practice," in *Law and Contemporary Problems*, Autumn, 1942, pp. 721–31.

However, in appraising the principles involved, several points invite consideration. It would not deprive judges of the function for which they are most suitably trained, the determination of guilt or innocence. Nor would it deprive probation of its most constructive function, that of reformative supervision; indeed, it could relieve probation of the onerous burden of investigation and would undoubtedly expand its supervisory function in discouraging institutional commitment. It would standardize the function of disposition in the hands of specialized personnel and would look to the improvement and diversification of treatment facilities.[7] Above all, however, the success of such a venture as a dispositions tribunal would depend upon the appointment of well-trained, skilled personnel and the appropriation of sufficient funds to do the needed work adequately. In the long run, the use of such a system, if properly implemented, should save the taxpayer money through reduced institutional costs and the abatement of recidivism. If the program were financially starved or staffed with political incompetents, it would be worse than useless. In California, the only state which has adopted such a law, the Authorities have struggled under insufficient budgets. We must await empirical proof of the efficacy of the device there. Bills have been recommended to the New York legislature on several occasions for a State Youth Correction Authority, but opposition has been too intense.[8] Several other states have considered similar bills.

3. Finally, there is a technique less radically innovative

[7] See Harrison and Grant, *Youth in the Toils,* and Harrison's pamphlets published by the Committee on Youth and Justice, Community Service Society: *Correctional Treatment of Youth Offenders; Chaos in Sentencing Youth Offenders,* and *Prisons Cost Too Much.*

[8] See New York *Times* for January 21, 1942, July 27, 1943, and March 13, 1944, for recommendations by Austin McCormick, the Community Service Society, and Senator Desmond for the Youth Correction Authority. The bill is supported by Parent-Teachers Associations, the Citizens Union, National Urban League, and other groups.

but comparable in function to the Youth Correction Authority. The offender may be sentenced to a classification institution whence he may be diverted to any of a variety of treatment facilities according to his particular requirements. The
best precedent for this procedure is the English Borstal system for adolescents and young adults, in which the versatility
of institutional facilities and careful selection in dispositions
appear to have achieved a considerable success in inducing
youthful readjustment.[9] Its effectiveness in England rests in
part upon the advantage of a large, compact, politically unified population, where quite varied institutional choices may
be provided. In the United States the Federal prison system
has also worked out a classification system with different
types of institution; for the most part, however, these are for
adult offenders and are based more largely on deterrent and
incapacitative purposes.

New York has now embarked on a program of classification of adolescent offenders by institutions, having provided
for the sentencing of boys to a classification center at Elmira
where study of the case by experts is to precede the determination of the institution to which the boy will be remanded,
and the type of treatment to be applied.[10] It is proposed that
delinquent girls below the age of sixteen be treated under a
general disposition to the Department of Public Welfare.
Obviously, the success of this program too must depend upon

[9] See Healy and Alper, *Criminal Youth and the Borstal System,* and East
The Criminal Adolescent.
[10] See New York *Times* for March 11, 1945, March 23, 1945, April 8,
1945, and April 30, 1945. On the basis of the report by Governor Dewey's
Interdepartmental Committee on Delinquency, a start has been made
toward coördinating facilities to deal with delinquents and to provide
state aid to local communities in addition to establishing the reception
center principle. Another new law provides for greater flexibility of
treatment of young offenders by permitting their transfer among the
institutions of the Department of Correction, Social Welfare, and Mental
Hygiene. Under this, mental defectives may be transferred from correctional to noncorrectional facilities.

its proper implementation in personnel and institutional facilities. However, it does look to more just, uniform, scien-
tifically predicated dispositions, and it should eventually
result in an improvement in the treatment facilities themselves. The adolescent girls' court should similarly be provided, ultimately, with a specialized mechanism for disposition, whether it be a state Youth Correction Authority or a
classification center.

A UNIFIED COURT WITH A PART FOR GIRLS

We have seen how the Wayward Minor Court has developed as a part of the inferior court system, first as a division
of the Women's Court and more recently as an independent,
city-wide magistrates' court. It has been impossible within
the scope of this work to do more than allude briefly to the
operation of other city tribunals handling adolescents. But
it is clear that there has been a strong movement in New
York to deal in specialized and experimental fashion with
youthful offenders during the past decade. Thus far it has
been characterized in large part by a series of independent
and partisan efforts to establish particular courts and procedures. Thus have developed the adolescent courts—at the
magistrates' level—in Brooklyn and Queens, covering in jurisdiction a fraction of the city's youths aged sixteen to nineteen
and, for the most part, serious violations of the law ; and the
Wayward Minor Court, with city-wide coverage of girls from
sixteen to twenty-one, which is limited by court interpretation to cases involving "moral depravity" and excluding
serious violations. Finally, in our county courts youths from
sixteen to nineteen years of age are covered by the adolescent
offender statute for felonious crimes when they are deemed
promising, reformable cases.[11] Other adolescents, not cov-

11 For the terms of the statute, see Appendix A.

ered by these courts, go through the traditional criminal courts with their customary procedures.

Though there is considerable similarity in procedure among these courts,[12] they have remained an uncoördinated series with considerable overlapping and actual competition among them; certain social agencies and other political interests advocate more extended growth in jurisdiction at the magistrates' court level, others foster the more recent development in the higher criminal courts.[13]

It is the writer's opinion that in comparison with the specialized magistrates' tribunals, the county youth courts suffer considerably in the greater delays in processing (which often mean jail confinement) and from the exposure to procedures (police line-up, arraignment in open court, indictment, and detention) and personnel of the criminal court, in addition to contacts with older, habitual criminals. Yet, more powerful political interests appear to support the county youth courts, and, since the adolescent courts have endured only by the sufferance of year-to-year permissive legislation, it seems rather likely that eventually their function may be absorbed by the tribunals at the higher level.

There is, in any event, a pressure toward coördination of judicial and correctional facilities for the young in New York. It has been marked by rather frequent recommendations for an integrated youth court system. The most recent and strongest directive of this character has come from Governor Thomas E. Dewey's Interdepartmental Committee on Delinquency which has proposed a permanent Youth Commission to combat delinquency by state financial aid to local communi-

---

12 See *Young People in the Courts of New York State,* Leg. Doc. No. 55, 1942.

13 For illustrations of the conflict of opinion see New York *Times* for March 1, 1941, in regard to the disagreement between Chief Magistrate Curran and Thomas E. Dewey and footnote below.

ties. It has recommended too a reception center in the Department of Correction to receive, study, and classify male offenders sixteen to twenty-one years of age, the specialized personnel of the center to make investigations, tests, and inquiries on the basis of which programs of treatment may be established.[14] The legislature has provided for this program of classification.

In the light of all this it appears probable that the future will see a more-or-less unified court system to deal with adolescent offenders. It may be that integration will be brought about by an extension of the children's courts of the Domestic Relations Court system, though this seems rather unlikely in the light of pressures both from within and outside these courts [15] against such a movement. Ideally, a unified system might be set up at the magistrates' level—an objective which has been urged by former Chief Magistrate Curran and various groups for several years.[16] A centralized court there should mean that the young defendants would be brought before a magistrate without unnecessary delays and could be spared arraignment and preliminary hearing in ordinary district courts, indictment, and extended detention. It now seems more likely, however, that the inclusive youth court, when it comes, will be at the county court level. If so, greater expedition of cases is desirable, together with avoidance of the police line-up, arraignment in open court, and indictment.

From whichever system of courts the centralized youth court may develop, it should contain a section devoted to the adolescent girl wherein her peculiar problems may be met and the needed specialized treatment facilities may be brought to

[14] New York *Times* March 11, 1945, and April 30, 1945.
[15] For arguments pro and con on the upward extension of the Children's Court age jurisdiction, see New York *Times* for January 25, 1942, and December 3, 1937, and Blanshard, *The Adolescents' Court Problem in New York City.*
[16] New York *Times,* September 17, 1941, and January 26, 1942.

her. In such a part, as the writer has maintained, the substantive jurisdiction requires to be modified and extended in nonmoralistic directions to include girls who have committed actual crimes,[17] and might include the young, commercialized, promiscuous sex offender. This would involve a much-needed drawing together into a single tribunal those cases which now may be processed through district magistrates' courts, Women's Court, special sessions, and county courts. Such a coördination of function should encourage too the expansion of institutional and, especially, noninstitutional facilities for dealing with the adolescent girl. It would lead to the application from experience of tried and tested methods according to the individualized and classified requirements of the case. Such a unified youth court with a specialized part for girls should be the ultimate objective of change in dealing judicially with youth. It may be coördinated very effectively (1) with the idea of a dispositions tribunal or reception centers for the study of offenders and their classification for treatment purposes, and (2) with the work of a coördinating council of social agencies, the selected referrals from which would sharpen and limit the area of intensive court work.

Certain it is that today adolescents rarely receive the sort of specialized attention from the judicial system of New York City that is needed to halt delinquency in its early stages. Of those whose inexperience and reformability merit special consideration it appears that an all too tiny trickle of adolescent cases receives youth court treatment. That deflecting factors frequently determine the instances in which the specialized facilities are applied does not commend the current practices; nor does the preliminary mishandling which commonly precedes adjudication in too many of the cases which do receive special consideration.

Finally, the futile multiplication of cross-purposed agen-

17 See *supra,* Chapter VIII.

cies—though each may make great display of political and judicial concern for the adolescent—results in waste, inefficiency, and unevenness. As each new court or agency is created with proper furore of publicity and finely fashioned official phrase, the public relaxes in complacent assurance that the problem is being solved at last. Then each emergent institution can, in turn, be forgotten and left to struggle on, inadequately staffed and budgeted, uncoördinated in any system with its predecessors and successors, finally becoming moribund as something impressively new and equally partial is duly launched with flagrant publicity. The public, of course, would be assured from time to time, with appropriately drawn statistics, that no problem of delinquency exists, while the problem of improvements in the older institutions is lost in the launching of new ones. Thus have gone into decay some very useful programs of the Crime Prevention Bureau, the Social Service Bureau, the Juvenile Aid Bureau, and, to a considerable degree, the adolescent courts of the city.

The observer looks in vain for a systematic method, a prevailing philosophy, a consistently ordered and reasonably applied treatment. He finds, instead, a rich proliferation of courts, agencies, methods, ideologies, and buildings—impressive, expensive, and thus far destined to inadequacy by the inertia of the public and the partial nature of thinking in the field. Some results of a socially constructive nature there are, and in these lies further hope: There is a public and political consciousness of the problem of the adolescent offender. There are developing, though assorted and uncoördinated, techniques in the experimental stages which look to the individualized and specialized functions of reformation. There is recognition by a political and judicial minority of the need for a unified and interlocking system of agency and institutional devices to handle all adolescent offenders—and pressure for the establishment of proper courts and institutions. The present stage appears to be one of temporary, transitional confusion. In that very fact, however, it becomes vitally important that the methods put into operation be critically examined before they become crystallized and then diffused. Where error lies, it may most easily be rooted out before the vesting of political and personal interests and the clutch of institutional inertia have made changes difficult or impossible.

IMMEDIATE STOPGAP MEASURES FOR IMPROVEMENT IN THE COURT

In the preceding pages an attempt has been made to depict with rather broad strokes the character of inclusive institutional changes needed in and for the Wayward Minor Court. This has been, of course, no prediction of what will occur. Indeed, probably there will be other and different developments than those suggested as desirable. Yet it is possible that some modifications will take place in the recommended directions. Several steps might even now be taken, requiring no profound alteration—either statutory or in over-all administrative mechanism—to make the Court a fairly effective instrument of control. Immediately to improve the functional value of the tribunal, these stopgap measures (which for the most part have already been pointed to in our discussion) may be found to possess significant constructive value for the court "as is." They will be summarized only briefly here to avoid an unnecessary redundancy. (Naturally, statutory redefinition and other formalized change in norm and procedure would tend to channelize, standardize, and perpetuate the needed changes more effectively than would merely informal administrative alteration. Informal may precede formal change, however, as it often does in court evolution.)

First and most important of all, under the present Wayward Minor Statute and in spite of its wording, the norms for decision should be changed, and they can be, even as they have already changed somewhat during the short life-history of the Court. Speaking negatively, such modification should rigorously avoid adjudications aimed merely at "helping the girl" or "solving a social and familial problem" where no good legal grounds for action exist. More affirmatively, the Court under the law as it stands can and should hear and adjudicate cases of girls who have committed crimes, reducing the charge to the wayward minor offense. This has been standard practice in the adolescent courts of Brooklyn and Queens for several years under the same statute as that used in the girls' court, though most girls of greater New York have no such protection. The Court should also deal with the young commercial and promiscuous offender who is now tried along with chronic prostitutes of all ages in the Women's Court. The normative aim of the Court would become, then, one of rehabilitation of the young and incipient female offender. In implementation of that goal, certain sharply altered procedures would be required for just and effective operation; these could be instituted without statutory change for the present. At a minimum these changes demand to be made:

1. Stop pre-adjudication investigation, holding social inquiry into the case history only after the offender has been convicted. Where no offense appears under the above-stated norms, no other action is warranted than referral to noncorrectional social resources of the community. And that should be done.

2. Stop frequent and extended remands before adjudication. There would, in fact, be little opportunity or excuse for them when pre-hearing investigations are abandoned. Possible contamination of the guiltless must be avoided.

3. Make the hearing a real trial of the issue of factual guilt of an alleged offense, with the requirement of convincing testimony by competent witnesses before adjudicating the

defendant. This should be necessary under the statute today, obviously. It should be no more difficult in practice than is trial of similar issues in the Women's Court and special sessions courts. In the specialized girls' court the desired informality can and must be combined with basic rights of due process.

4. Use remand adjournments after the girl is adjudicated, if she is, and before final disposition, but only when there is a clearly indicated need of short-duration confinement and when the indeterminate sentence—as it is now administered under the law—would be an unduly prolonged period. Much more frequently than at present parole should be applied after adjudication and before sentence to give the girl a limited but indefinite period of supervision—thus avoiding definite one- and two-year terms of probation sentence. The suspended sentence should be used much more generally after such parole or remand, avoiding formal probation and commitment whenever possible.

5. Use probation (as well as the informal supervision during parole adjournments mentioned in paragraph 4) much more frequently than at present, seeking to make supervision by the probation officers as creative and rehabilitative as possible. Here would be implied a greatly extended effort to enlist the aid of specialized community facilities to deal with particular problems of the case.

6. Stop commiting noncriminal girls to correctional institutions, and commit criminal adolescents only when necessary. In the rarest of cases where the careful exertion of maximum effort and ingenuity has shown no other method of disposition to be possible and satisfactory and only where public security demands it should the girl be incarcerated with other convicted offenders—whether the institutions used be sectarian or secular, private or public.

7. To insure the operation of the above principles, one or

more of three changes are clearly required: (*a*) an altered perspective as to purpose and method on the part of the personnel which mans the court; (*b*) the pressure of informed opinion by interested legal and lay groups; and (*c*) support of the program through attorneys in the Court to protect the interests of defendants by criticism, objection, appeal, and, if necessary, downright technical obstructionism.

8. Finally, the Court would do well at once to stimulate supporting and substitutive case work and shelter service in the community. The Court has recognized, and perhaps exaggerated, the lack of agencies to perform functions needed for adolescent girls in New York City, and has rationalized the extension of its control on that ground. The extension of precourt, preventive, and socializing facilities (such as those once offered by the Juvenile Aid Bureau on a broader scale) would release the energies of the Court for work exclusively in its appropriate sphere and might diminish somewhat the growing volume of work with fully matured delinquents. A consciousness of the need for expanded and improved social facilities for the young has been developing in recent months. This may well lead into more adequate provisions for individualization and, it is hoped, a re-searching of policy and method used by the agencies which deal with the adolescent.

THE SOCIOLEGAL APPROACH

It was suggested at the beginning of this work that the combined approaches of law and sociology might contribute to an understanding of legal institutions, their development and functional operation. The services of each may have become apparent in the foregoing exposition and analysis. It must be clear, however, that though court analysis is clarified by this interdisciplinary approach, it is impossible to segregate completely the influences of either discipline: legal thinking is blended with sociological, each leavening the other.

Thought is affected, directed, channelized by all phases of life experience and learning. It is not strictly compartmentalized. Hence the critical reactions of a student reflect a fusion of responses previously conditioned and may be enriched by the scope of his relevant prior observations.

Courts are social institutions of basic importance in individual and group control. Court process is social behavior of a most important kind, behavior molded by culturalized patterns, but preserving zones for significant individual variations. Therefore, it is a task of sociologists and psychologists to aid in the understanding and clarification of the mechanics of the courtroom. On the other hand, the court is a province wherein the specialized craft and instruments of the lawyer are employed. His skills and frames of reference are to a large extent unavoidably outside the layman's grasp. Subtleties and technical distinctions may elude or deceive those who are untrained in the law. Hence the social scientist's uninstructed censure of court-ways and legal traditions often hits wide of the mark. A combination of legal and social sense is needed to analyze, appraise, and guide the growth of institutions that are both legal and social.

This specialized, interdisciplinary approach (woefully underemphasized in the content and method of our graduate schools of legal and social science) is a prerequisite to sound, substantial development in jurisprudence. Especial and acute necessity for this framework is seen in the more obviously sociolegal areas of the children's and adolescents' tribunals, in methods of disposition, in probation and parole, in courts of domestic relations, and in the rapidly growing fields of administrative adjudication. The need is perhaps less obvious but no less real in more generalized fields of public and private law.

It is believed that in this study the understanding of the growth and function of legal institutions was increased by a combined and homogenized training in sociology and law. Yet it is true, as the writer has stated, that each of these fields has its own peculiar area of emphasis, conceptual tools, and ways of thinking—and each can contribute much to the other. Sociology emphasizes, for example, interpersonal and intergroup relations, the developments and relationships of institutions and processes, objectivity of thinking; it uses relativistic and analytical concepts, though all too frequently they are loose and imprecise. Juristic training, on the other hand, stresses the employment of the craft skills and techniques of the law, as, for example, the formulation of specific norms and definitions, the application of similar rules to similar situations, accuracy and precision of thinking with nicety in discrimination of differences, and fairness in protection of individual rights and interests. Court-ways of procedure are rather definite and traditional for the most part, craft-ways of judges and probation officers are moderately clear cut; the application of consistent, time-tested rules and methods is a fundamental part of legal technique, instructive to the sociologist in displaying a uniformity of institutional control greater than that found elsewhere in forms of social constraint. Anyone interested in the sociology of institutions will find legal institutions an especially fruitful source of data and understanding because in law the factors (norms, customs, procedures, personnel, methods, etc.) are more explicit and fixed than elsewhere. Too, the legal framework may be illuminated considerably by the institutional conceptualism of sociology, by an appreciation for the meaning of growth, change, and function.

It is believed that in this study the sociological approach has been particularly appropriate in tracing the evolution of the Court and its purposes, in understanding this social institution with its implicit limitations as an agency of control functioning through imperfect methods and personnel. The

Court is viewed as an interdependent totality, depending for its efficacy upon the relationship of all phases in the processing of the offender and upon the interaction of numerous officials with the defendant and with each other. Social scientific thinking has been especially relevant to the analysis of processes, methods, and philosophy of disposition of cases (so inadequately guided by the law): pointing up the need for improved individualization and classification in treatment; the dangers of unnecessary incarceration, of the invidious disparities in treatment which are possible and actual under the statutes; and the effects of gross variations among the personnel, especially the differences among judges and among probation officers.

Juristic thinking, on the other hand, points up numerous errors which have arisen in the adjudicative process due to the attempted over-all "liberalization" of the Court into a surrogate for social agencies. It reveals the dangers and injustice in depriving defendants of the trial protections generally assured under Anglo-American legal tradition, the error which may result from basing court adjudication on vague hearsay social data, the need for statutory substantive norms of conduct as a pre-condition of trial justice. Specifically, the ideas of preadjudication investigation and course-of-conduct adjudication have been attacked as unjustifiable products of loose thinking in applied sociology, incompatible with sound legal theory.

The author has essayed an objective, analytical, critical review of a rather unusual type of morals court, a legal tribunal struggling valiantly against tremendous odds, inherent and external, to meet profoundly difficult, rapidly increasing social and personal problems. It has been only a lesser, and more specific, purpose to set down here the inconsistency and implausibility of objectives, the inadequacy and inefficacy of means, revealed in careful observation of the Court. More broadly, the motive has been to carry on an impartial and intensive study of functioning adjudicative machinery: to determine why, how, and when its destination is set and its directing course established; to observe the fascinations of legal institutional development and process; to avoid both the invidious rancor and the interested favor which may arise in court studies by court personnel or by other agencies with a vested power at stake; to wed legal and lay sense at the bar, aspiring thereby to contribute something in an area that is both juridical and social; and finally and possibly, to aid in setting a pattern for badly needed court observation and research to the end of enhanced understanding, improved implementation, and perfected accomplishment in our judicial system.

Appendixes

A: STATUTES

LAWS OF 1882, CHAP. 410, SEC. 1466

Whenever any female between the ages of 14 and 21 years shall be brought by the police, or shall voluntarily appear before a committing magistrate in the city of New York, charged with being a prostitute, or admitting herself to be such, and professing a desire to reform, and it shall appear that such female has never been an inmate of the penitentiary, such magistrate shall make an order, that in lieu of being committed to the work-house or penitentiary, the said female shall be removed to and detained in one of the following institutions, viz: The Protestant Episcopal House of Mercy, New York, the Roman Catholic House of Good Shepherd, foot of 89th Street, or the Magdalen Female Benevolent Asylum and Home of Fallen Women, provided that the magistrate shall designate in such order as the place of detention such one of the institutions above named as may be selected by the person so committed, unless notice shall have been received from such institution that there is not room for the reception of further inmates.

LAWS OF 1886, CHAP. 353, SEC. 1466, SUBD. 1

Whenever any female over the age of 12 years shall be brought by the police or shall voluntarily come before a committing magistrate in the city of New York, and it shall be proved to the satisfaction of such magistrate by the confession of such female, or by competent testimony, that such female (first) is found in a reputed house of prostitution or assignation; or is willfully disobedient to parent or guardian, and is in danger of becoming morally depraved; or (second) is a prostitute, or is of intemperate habits and who professes a desire to reform and has not been an inmate of the penitentiary, such magistrate may judge that it is for the welfare of such female that she be placed in a reformatory, and may thereupon commit such female to one of the following reformatory institutions, viz: The Protestant Episcopal House of Mercy, New York, the Roman Catholic House of Good Shepherd, foot of 89th

Street, or the Magdalen Female Benevolent Asylum and Home of Fallen Women, which said institutions are hereby severally authorized to receive and hold females committed under this act.

LAWS OF 1903, CHAP. 436

Whenever any female over the age of 12 years shall be brought by the police or shall voluntarily come before any court or a committing magistrate in the city of New York, and it shall be proved to the satisfaction of such court or magistrate by the confession of such female, or by competent testimony, that such female (first) is found in a reputed house of prostitution or assignation; or in company with, or frequenting the company of thieves or prostitutes, or is found associating with vicious and dissolute persons; or is wilfully disobedient to parent or guardian, and is in danger of becoming morally depraved; or (second) is a prostitute or is of intemperate habits, and has not been an inmate of the penitentiary or (third) is convicted of petit larceny and is over 16 years of age and has not been an inmate of the penitentiary, such court or magistrate may judge that it is for the welfare of such female that she be placed in a reformatory, and may thereupon commit such female to one of the following reformatory institutions, namely, The Protestant Episcopal House of Mercy, New York, Roman Catholic House of Good Shepherd, in the city of New York, or the New York Magdalen Home, which said institutions are hereby severally authorized to receive and hold females committed under this act.

LAWS OF 1922, CHAP. 547, AS AMENDED BY LAWS
OF 1924, CHAP. 477 AND 478: THE CHILDREN'S
COURT ACT (EXCERPTS)

Any child actually or apparently under the age of sixteen years who is found:

1. To be neglected; or
2. To be delinquent; or
3. To come within any of the descriptions of children mentioned in section four hundred and eighty-five of the penal law.

Must be brought before a proper court which, unless other disposition shall be made of the case as provided by law, may commit the child to any incorporated charitable reformatory, or other institution, and when practicable, to such as is governed by persons of the same religious faith as the parents of the child.

. . . .

The word "delinquent" shall include any child over seven and under sixteen years of age (*a*) who violates any law of this state or of the United States or any municipal ordinance or who commits any act which if committed by an adult would be a crime not punishable by death or life imprisonment; (*b*) who is incorrigible, ungovernable or habitually disobedient and beyond the contral of his parents, guardian, or other lawful authority; (*c*) who is habitually traunt; (*d*) who, without just cause and without the consent of his parent, guardian or other custodian, deserts his home or place of abode; (*e*) who engages in any occupation which is in violation of law; (*f*) who begs or solicits alms or money in public places under any pretense; (*g*) who associates with immoral or vicious persons; (*h*) who frequents any place the existence of which is in violation of law; (*i*) who habitually uses obscene or profane language; or (*j*) who so deports himself as wilfully to injure or endanger the morals or health of himself or others.

. . . .

A parent, guardian or other person having custody of a child actually or apparently under sixteen years of age, who omits to exercise reasonable diligence in the control of such child to prevent such child from becoming guilty of juvenile delinquency as defined by statute, or from becoming adjudged by a children's court in need of the care and protection of the state as defined by statute, or who permits such a child to associate with vicious, immoral or criminal persons, or to grow up in idleness, or to beg or solicit alms, or to wander about the streets of any city, town or village late at night without being in any lawful business or occupation, or to furnish entertainment for gain upon the streets or in any public place, or to be an habitual truant from school or to habitually wander around any railroad yard or tracks, to enter any house of prostitution or assignation, or any place where gambling is carried on, or any gambling device is operated, or any policy shop, or to enter any place where the morals of such child may be endangered or depraved or may be likely to be impaired, and any such person or any other person who knowingly or wilfully is responsible for, encourages, aids, causes or connives at, or who contributed to the conditions which cause such child to be adjudged guilty of juvenile delinquency, or to be in need of the care and protection of the state, or to do any of the acts hereinbefore enumerated, shall be guilty of a misdemeanor.

LAWS OF 1923, CHAP. 868, AS AMENDED BY LAWS
OF 1925, CHAP. 389, LAWS OF 1929, CHAP. 196,
AND LAWS OF 1935, CHAP. 707: THE WAYWARD
MINORS' ACT, TITLE VII—A

Sec. 913-a: Wayward minor defined.—Any person between the ages of sixteen and twenty-one who either (1) is habitually addicted to the use of drugs or the intemperate use of intoxicating liquors, or (2) habitually associates with dissolute persons, or (3) is found of his or her own free will and knowledge in a house of prostitution or assignation or ill fame, or (4) habitually associates with thieves, prostitutes, pimps or procurers or disorderly persons, or (5) is wilfully disobedient to the reasonable and lawful commands of parent, guardian or other custodian and is morally depraved or is in danger of becoming morally depraved may be deemed a wayward minor.

Sec. 913-b: Person may be adjudged wayward minor; summons; warrant.—Such person, where the charge is established upon competent evidence upon a hearing, may be so adjudged by any magistrate, other than a justice of the peace, where an information is laid before him on the complaint of a peace officer, parent, guardian, or other person standing in parental relation or being the next of kin, or by a representative of an incorporated society doing charitable or philanthropic work. Such magistrate may issue a summons and where such summons is not obeyed may issue a warrant for the appearance of any such wayward minor, in the same manner as provided by the code of criminal procedure and such minors shall have all the rights secured by law to defendants in proceedings under this title.

Sec. 913-c: Probation; commitment.—Any person adjudged a wayward minor before commitment to an institution shall, so far as practicable, be placed on probation for a period not to exceed two years, and in no event during any part of the last year of his or her minority, subject to the provisions of law applicable to persons placed on probation. If such minor, by reason of previous delinquency or other adequate reason, is not a fit subject for probation, he or she shall be committed to any religious, charitable, or other reformative institution authorized by law to receive commitments of persons over the age of sixteen years. Such commitment, irrespective of the age, at time of commitment, of the person committed, shall be for an indeterminate period not to exceed three years and if to a religious institution, so far as practicable, to one that is governed by persons of the same religious faith as such minor.

Sec. 913-d: Release, parole, transfer or other disposition.—Any person committed under the provisions of this title may be released or paroled in the manner provided by law with respect to adult and other offenders. Any person so committed who is in the opinion of the responsible head of the institution where committed incapable of benefiting by the training and discipline thereof or whose conduct is prejudicial to the good order thereof, may be returned to the committing magistrate or to the magistrate sitting in his stead and transferred for the remainder of his or her term to any other institution to which such minor might have been committed in the first instance, or may be committed to a parent or guardian or be otherwise disposed of in accordance with the provisions of this act.

LAWS OF 1943, CHAP. 549: YOUTHFUL OFFENDER LAW

Sec. 252-a: Definition of term "youth."—"Youth" means a minor over 16 and under 19 years of age.

Sec. 252-b: Definition of term "youthful offender."—"Youthful offender" means a youth who has committed a crime not punishable by death or life imprisonment, as determined under section 252-c.

Sec. 252-c: Determination of certain minors as youthful offenders.—In any case where a grand jury has found an indictment and where it shall appear that the defendant is between the ages of 16 and 19 years, the grand jury or the district attorney may recommend to the court for which the grand jury was drawn, or the court of its own motion may determine, that the defendant be examined, investigated, and tried to determine whether he should be adjudged a youthful offender, provided the defendant consents to such examination, investigation and trial without a jury. If the defendant consents to such examination, investigation and trial and the court approves the recommendation, the filing of the indictment shall be held in abeyance and no further action shall be taken in connection with such indictment against the defendant until an examination and investigation is made of the defendant and his conduct as the court may direct. After such examination and investigation, the court, in its discretion, may direct that the defendant be tried in order to determine whether the defendant is a youthful offender. If the court does not approve the recommendation of the grand jury or the district attorney, or should not determine that the defendant should be tried as a youthful offender, then the indictment shall be deemed filed as of the date the grand jury voted the indictment regardless of whether or not the grand jury has been discharged or be still in session. If the court should determine that the defendant be adjudged or tried as a youthful offender, the indictment shall not be filed and no further action should be taken thereon. In the event the court should order a hearing, then the youth shall be tried and be either acquitted of the charge or adjudged a youthful offender. After an indictment has been found and during the pendency of such examination and investigation, and before a final determination by the court, the court shall have the same powers and jurisdiction over the defendant as though the indictment had been filed.

Sec. 252-d.—No statement, admission or confession made by a defendant to the court or to any officer thereof during the examination and investigation referred to in section 252-c shall ever be admissible as evidence against him or his interest, except that the court may take such statement, admission or confession into consideration at the time of sentencing such defendant, after the defendant has been found guilty of a crime or adjudged a youthful offender.

Sec. 252-e.—All of the proceedings in connection with the determination of youthful offenders may be private and shall be conducted in such parts, terms of court or judge's chambers as shall be separate and apart from the other parts or terms of court which are held for the trial of adults charged with crimes. However, such parts or terms of court used by the court in connection with the trial of adults charged with crimes, may also be used in connection with the proceedings for youthful offenders if at the time of such use such parts or terms of court are not then being used for the trial of adults. In the event such defendant shall be committed while such examination and investigation is pending, before trial, during trial, or after judgment, and before sentence, then it shall be the duty of those persons in charge of the place of detention to segregate such defendant from defendants over the age of 19 years charged with crime.

Sec. 252-f: Probation; commitment.—Any person adjudged a youthful offender may be placed on probation for a period not to exceed three years, but if not a fit subject for probation, shall be committed to any religious, charitable or other reformative institution authorized by law to receive commitments of persons over the age of sixteen years. Such commitment shall be for a period not to exceed three years. Whenever a youthful offender is committed by the court to any duly authorized religious, charitable or other institution, other than an institution supported or controlled by the state or a subdivision thereof, such commitment must be made, when practicable, to a religious, charitable, or other institution under the control of persons of the same religious faith or persuasion as that of the youthful offender. If a youthful offender is committed by the court to any institution other than an institution supported or controlled by the state or a subdivision thereof, which is under the control of persons of a religion or persuasion different from that of the youthful offender, that court shall state or recite the facts which impel it to make such disposition, and such statement shall be made a part of the minutes of the proceedings.

Sec. 252-g: Adjudication not to serve as a disqualification.—No determination made under the provision of section 252-c shall operate as a disqualification of any youth subsequently to hold public office, public employment, or as a forfeiture of any right or privilege or to receive any license granted by public authority; and no youth shall be denominated a criminal by reason of such determination, nor shall such determination be deemed a conviction.

Sec. 252-h.—The records of any youth adjudged a youthful offender, including fingerprints and photographs, shall not be open to public inspection. However, the court in its discretion, in any case, may permit the inspection of any papers or records. Any duly organized institution to which a youth is committed may cause an inspection of any of the records to be had.

This act shall take effect September first, 1943.

B: OFFENSES IN BROOKLYN ADOLESCENT COURT

	1938	*1939*
Felonies	247	287
Burglary	139	175
Attempted burglary	15	9
Robbery	4	1
Forgery	2	2
Grand larceny	52	72
Extortion	1	..
Felonious assault	9	7
Receiving stolen goods	2	8
Possession of burglar's tools	1	4
Rape	11	11
Incest	1	1
Sodomy	5	1
Miscellaneous	5	..
Misdemeanors	182	137
Petit larceny	124	88
Unlawful entry	10	11
Malicious mischief	11	10
Assault in third degree	5	1
Possession of guns	8	4
Impairing morals	4	4
Indecent exposure	4	9
Other sex violations	..	..
Possession of policy slips	2	1
Failure to pay fare	12	4
Possession of slot machine	2	1
Summary Jurisdiction	73	66
Disorderly conduct	13	27
Vagrancy	28	21
Wayward minors	32	23
Miscellaneous	...	1
Total	1004	986

C: WAYWARD MINOR STATUTE (1945)

BILL NO. 1938 TO AMEND THE NEW YORK CITY CRIMINAL
COURTS ACT, IN RELATION TO THE PROCEDURE IN THE
WAYWARD MINOR COURT FOR GIRLS (ENACTED IN
APRIL, 1945)

Article IX-B. P. 149: Procedure to be followed in the Wayward Minor Court for girls.—1. The procedure to be followed in the wayward minor court for girls in the city of New York created by the chief magistrate, pursuant to the provisions of section one hundred of the New York City criminal courts act, shall be as prescribed in this article.

2. Upon arraignment on a sworn complaint of any girl alleged to be a wayward minor and after a preliminary hearing, the magistrate may discharge the alleged wayward minor or, pending the final disposition of the case, may release her on bail, or parole her in the custody of a parent, guardian, probation officer or other person, or, if upon such preliminary hearing, it shall appear to the magistrate to the best interests of the minor, he may remand her to the custody of any duly authorized agency, association, society or institution designated by him. If remanded, or paroled in the custody of a person other than the parent or legal guardian, the minor shall be remanded, or paroled, when practicable, to an institution governed by persons, or in the custody of a person, of the same religious persuasion as the minor. In the event that the alleged wayward minor is remanded, such period of remand shall not exceed fifteen days; however, such period may be extended by the magistrate with the consent of said minor for an additional period not to exceed fifteen days. The magistrate may direct that a probation officer make a preliminary investigation into the habits, surroundings, conditions and tendencies of the alleged wayward minor. No statement, admission or confession made by the alleged wayward minor to the court or to any officer thereof during such examination and investigation shall ever be admissible as evidence against her or her interest, except that the court may take such statement, admission or confession into consideration at the time of sentencing such wayward minor after she has been adjudged a wayward minor.

3. Upon the completion of the investigation, the magistrate shall

proceed to hear and determine the case with due regard for the legal rights of the alleged wayward minor. Where the charge is established by competent evidence upon a hearing, such person shall be adjudged a wayward minor and the magistrate, having before him the report of the probation officer in addition to the results of such examinations as he may have ordered, shall impose sentence as follows:

a) Suspend judgment.

b) Place the wayward minor on probation for a period not to exceed two years.

c) If such minor, by reason of previous delinquency or other adequate reason, is not a fit subject for probation, she shall be committed to any religious, charitable, or other reformative institution authorized by law to receive commitments of persons over the age of sixteen years. Such commitment, irrespective of age, at the time of commitment, of the person committed, shall be for an indeterminate period not to exceed three years, and if to a religious institution, so far as practicable, to one that is governed by persons of the same religious faith as such minor.

d) Remand such minor for a period of thirty days to the custody of any duly authorized agency, association, society or institution designated by the magistrate pending a further investigation by a probation officer. At the expiration of said period such minor shall be brought before the magistrate and sentence shall be then imposed.

P. 149-a: Examinations.—At any time after a preliminary hearing, or before, during, or after a trial, if it shall appear to the magistrate that there is reasonable ground to believe that a physical or mental examination is necessary, he may remand the alleged wayward minor to be examined physically or mentally by the department of hospitals of the city of New York for a period not to exceed thirty days. No information obtained through a physical examination of the alleged wayward minor shall ever be admissible as evidence against her or her interest, except that the court may take such information into consideration at the time of sentencing such minor after she has been adjudged a wayward minor. Whenever any minor shall have been committed for mental examination, if the qualified psychiatrists who have examined such minor, report that she is a mental defective, the magistrate may commit her to a state school of mental defectives.

P. 149-b: Result of conviction.—All persons arraigned in the wayward minor court for girls shall have all the rights secured by law to defendants at every stage of the proceedings. An adjudication that a girl is a wayward minor shall not operate to disqualify her from holding public office, from qualifying for civil service, from entering any profession, or as a forfeiture of any right or privilege or from receiving any license granted by public authority, and no such person shall be denominated a criminal by reason of such adjudication, nor shall such adjudication be deemed a conviction.

P. 149-c: Records to be confidential.—All records in each case must be deemed to be confidential records of the court and shall not be open to inspection by anyone except persons duly authorized by law or upon order of a court.

P. 149-d: Invalidity of a provision.—If any provision of this article is held by any court to be invalid such decision shall not affect the validity of any other provisions.

BILL NO. 1939 TO AMEND THE CODE OF CRIMINAL PROCEDURE, IN RELATION TO PROCEEDINGS RESPECTING WAYWARD MINORS

Section 1.—Sections nine hundred thirteen-*a* and nine hundred thirteen-*c* of the code of criminal procedure are hereby amended to read, respectively, as follows:

913-a: Wayward minor.—Any person between the ages of sixteen and twenty-one who either (1) is habitually addicted to the use of drugs or the intemperate use of intoxicating liquors, or (2) habitually associates with dissolute persons, or (3) is found of his or her own free will and knowledge in a house of prostitution, assignation or ill fame, or (4) habitually associates with thieves, prostitutes, pimps, or procurers, or disorderly persons, or (5) is wilfully disobedient to the reasonable and lawful commands of parent, guardian or other custodian and is morally depraved or is in danger of becoming morally depraved, or (6) who without just cause and without the consent of parents, guardians or other custodians, deserts his or her home or place of abode, and is morally depraved or is in danger of becoming morally depraved, or (7) who so deports himself or herself as to wilfully injure or endanger the morals or health of himself or herself or of others, may be deemed a wayward minor.

913-c: Probation of wayward minors.—Any person adjudged a wayward minor before commitment to an institution shall, so far as practicable, be placed on probation for a period not to exceed two years, subject to the provisions of law applicable to persons placed on probation. If such minor, by reason of previous delinquency or other adequate reason, is not a fit subject for probation, he or she shall be committed to any religious, charitable or other reformative institution authorized by law to receive commitments of persons over the age of sixteen years. Such commitment, irrespective of the age, at time of commitment, of the person committed, shall be for an indeterminate period not to exceed three years and if to a religious institution, so far as practicable, to one that is goverened by persons of the same religious faith as such minor.

Bibliography

Abrahamsen, David. Crime and the Human Mind. New York, 1944.

Addams, Jane, and others. The Child, the Clinic and the Court. New York, 1925.

Aichorn, August. Wayward Youth. New York, 1935.

Alexander, Franz, and William Healy. Roots of Crime. New York, 1935.

Alexander, Franz, and Hugo Staub. The Criminal, the Judge, and the Public. New York, 1931.

Alper, Benedict S. Young People in the Courts of New York State. Legislative Document No. 55. New York, 1942.

American Law Institute. Youth Correction Authority Act. Philadelphia, 1940.

—— Youth Court Act. Philadelphia, 1934.

American Law Reports Annotated.

American Prison Association. Report of the Committee on Crime Prevention. October, 1942.

Arnold, Thurman. "Law Enforcement; an Attempt at Social Dissection," Yale Law Journal, XLII (Nov., 1932), 1–24.

Barnes, Harry E., and Negley K. Teeters. New Horizons in Criminology. New York, 1943.

Beard, Belle Boone, Juvenile Probation. New York, 1934.

Belden, Evelina. Courts in the United States Hearing Children's Cases. United States Children's Bureau Publication No. 65. Washington, D.C., 1920.

Blanshard, Paul. The Adolescents' Court Problem in New York City. New York, 1941.

Blanshard, Paul, and Edwin J. Lukas. Probation and Psychiatric Care for Adolescent Offenders in New York City. New York, 1942.

Breckinridge, Sophonisba P. (ed.). Social Work and the Courts. Chicago, 1934.

Breckinridge, Sophonisba P., and Edith Abbott. The Delinquent Child and the Home. New York, 1912.

Brill, Jeanette G., and E. George Payne. The Adolescent Court and Crime Prevention. New York, 1938.

Bromley, Dorothy Dunbar, and Florence Haxton Britten. Youth and Sex. New York, 1938.

Brooklyn Adolescent Court. Annual Report. Brooklyn, 1938.

Bruce, Andrew A. The American Judge. New York, 1924.

Burtt, Harold E. Legal Psychology. New York, 1931.

Butterfield, Oliver McKinley. Love Problems of Adolescence. New York, 1939.

Cairns, Huntington. Law and the Social Sciences. New York, 1935.

Callendar, Clarence N. American Courts; Their Organization and Procedure. New York, 1927.

Cardozo, Benjamin. The Nature of the Judicial Process. New Haven, 1921.

—— The Paradoxes of Legal Science. New York, 1928.

Carr, Lowell J. Delinquency Control. New York, 1940.

Cobb, W. Bruce. "Social and Legal Aspects of the Children's Court." Address delivered on February 6, 1945, before a joint meeting of the committees of the Court of Domestic Relations, of the Association of the Bar, and the County Lawyers Associations. (Mimeographed.)

Cohen, Morris R. Law and the Social Order. New York, 1933.

Commission on Criminal Courts in New York. The Adolescent Offender. New York, 1923.

Cooley, Edwin J. Probation and Delinquency. New York, 1927.

Cooper, Courtney Ryley. Designs in Scarlet. Boston, 1939.

—— Here's to Crime. Boston, 1937.

Davis, Katherine B. Factors in the Sex Life of Twenty-two Hundred Women. New York, 1929.

del Vecchio, George. "The *Homo Juridicus* and the Inadequacy of Law as a Norm of Life," *Tulane Law Review,* XI (June, 1937), 503–26.

Dession, George. "Psychiatry and the Conditioning of Criminal Justice," *Yale Law Journal,* XLVII (Jan., 1938), 319–40.

—— "The Role of Penalties in Criminal Law," *Yale Law Journal,* XXXVII (June, 1928), 1048–69.

Dickinson, John. "Legal Rules; Their Function in the Process of Decision," *University of Pennsylvania Law Review,* LXXIX (May, 1931), 833–69.

Dickinson, Robert L., and Laura Beam. The Single Woman. Baltimore, 1934.

Dimock, H. S. Rediscovering the Adolescent. New York, 1937.

East, W. Norwood. The Adolescent Criminal. London, 1942.

Ernst, Morris L., and Alexander Lindley. The Censor Marches On. New York, 1940.

Ernst, Morris L., and William Seagle. To the Pure. New York, 1928.

Everson, George. "The Human Element in Justice," *Journal of Criminal Law and Criminology*, X (May, 1919), 90–99.

Flexner, B., R. Oppenheimer, and K. Lenroot. The Child, the Family, and the Court. United States Children's Bureau Publication No. 193. Washington, D.C., 1929.

Fosdick, Raymond. American Police Systems. New York, 1920.

Frank, Jerome. Law and the Modern Mind. New York, 1930.

Frank, L. K. "Social Problems," *American Journal of Sociology*, XXX (1925), 462–68.

Gans, B., (ed.). Concerning Parents. New York, 1926.

Gaudet, F. J., G. S. Harris, and C. W. St. John. "Individual Differences in the Sentencing Tendencies of Judges," *Journal of Criminal Law and Criminology*, XXIII (Jan., 1933), 811–18.

Genz, Herta N. An Analytical and Comparative Study of Treatment of Women Offenders Passing Through the Department of Correction in the City of New York. Unpublished doctoral dissertation, New York University, 1941.

Glueck, Sheldon. Crime and Justice. Boston, 1936.

—— Probation and Criminal Justice. New York, 1933.

Glueck, Sheldon, and Eleanor T. Glueck. Criminal Careers in Retrospect. New York, 1943.

—— 500 Criminal Careers. New York, 1930.

—— Five Hundred Delinquent Women. New York, 1934.

—— Juvenile Delinquents Grown Up. New York, 1940.

—— Later Criminal Careers. New York, 1937.

—— One Thousand Juvenile Delinquents. Cambridge, 1934.

—— (eds.). Preventing Crime. New York, 1936.

Goldsmith, I. I. Legal Evidence in the New York Children's Court. New York, 1933.

Goldstein, Jonah J. The Family in Court. New York, 1934.

Hall, Jerome. "Criminology and a Modern Penal Code," *Journal of Criminal Law and Criminology*, XXVI (May–June, 1936). 1–16.

—— Readings in Jurisprudence. Indianapolis, 1938.

—— Theft, Law and Society. Boston, 1935

Harrison, Leonard V. Chaos in Sentencing Youthful Offenders. Committee on Youth and Justice of the Community Service Society. New York, 1943.

—— Correctional Treatment of Youth Offenders. Committee on Youth and Justice of the Community Service Society. New York, 1944.

—— Preventing Criminal Careers. Committee on Youth and Justice of the Community Service Society. New York, 1941.

—— Prisons Cost Too Much. Committee on Youth and Justice of the Community Service Society. New York, 1942.

Harrison, Leonard V. and Pryor M. Grant. Youth in the Toils. New York, 1938.

Healy, William. Mental Conflicts and Misconduct. Boston, 1917.

Healy, William, and Benedict S. Alper. Criminal Youth and the Borstal System. New York, 1941.

Healy, William, and Augusta Bronner. Delinquents and Criminals, Their Making and Unmaking. New York, 1926.

—— New Light on Delinquency and Its Treatment. New Haven, 1936.

Healy, William, Augusta Bronner, Edith Baylor, and J. P. Murphy. Reconstructing Behavior in Youth. New York, 1929.

Kross, A. M. Procedures for Dealing with Wayward Minors in New York City. New York, 1936. (Mimeographed.)

Kross, A. M., and H. Grossman. "Magistrates' Courts of the City of New York," *Brooklyn Law Review,* VII (1937), 133–79, 295–341, 411–58.

Law and Contemporary Problems, Vol. IX, Autumn, 1942. Issue on Youth Correction Authority.

Lindner, Robert. Rebel without a Cause. Washington, 1944.

Lindsey, Benjamin B., and Wainwright Evans. Companionate Marriage. New York, 1927.

Llewellyn, Karl N. The Bramble Bush. New York, 1930.

—— "Horse-Trade and Merchant's Market in Sales; a Conflict of Institutional Ideology," reprint from *Harvard Law Review,* LII (March and April, 1939), 725–47, 873–905.

—— "Legal Tradition and Social Science Method," in Essays on Research in the Social Sciences. New York, 1931.

—— "The Normative, the Legal, and the Law-Jobs; the Problem of Juristic Method," *Yale Law Journal,* XLIX (June, 1940), 1355–1400.

—— "On Reading and Using the New Jurisprudence," *American Bar Association Journal,* XXVI (May, 1940), 418–25.

—— "On the Good, the True, and the Beautiful in Law," *Chicago Law Review,* IX (Feb., 1942), 2: 224–65.

Llewellyn Karl, and E. Adamson Hoebel. The Cheyenne Way. Norman, Okla., 1941.

Lou, Herbert H. Juvenile Courts in the United States. Chapel Hill, N.C., 1927.

Marsh, Marguerite. Prostitutes in New York City; Their Apprehension, Trial and Treatment. New York, 1941 (Mimeographed.)

May, Geoffrey. Social Control of Sex Expression. New York, 1930.

Michael, Jerome, and Mortimer Adler. Crime, Law and Social Science. New York, 1933.

Michael, Jerome, and Herbert Wechsler. Criminal Law and Its Administration; Cases, Statutes, and Commentaries. Chicago, 1940.

—— "A Rationale of the Law of Homicide," *Columbia Law Review,* XXXVII (Dec., 1937), 701–62, 1261–1325.

National Commission on Law Observance and Enforcement (Wickersham Commission). No. 4. Report on Prosecution. Washington, D.C., 1931.

National Probation Association. Cooperation in Crime Control. Year book. New York, 1944.

—— Coping with Crime. Year book. New York, 1937.

—— Dealing with Delinquency. Year book. New York, 1940.

—— Delinquency and the Community in Wartime. Year book. New York, 1943.

—— The Offender in the Community. Year book. New York, 1938.

—— Probation and Parole Progress. Year book. New York, 1941.

—— Social Defenses against Crime. Year book. New York, 1942.

—— Trends in Crime Treatment. Year book. New York, 1939.

—— Year book. New York, 1930.

Ness, Elliot. "Sex Delinquency as a Social Hazard," in Proceedings of the National Conference of Social Work. New York, 1944.

New York City Magistrates' Courts. Annual Reports. New York, 1935–45.

New York City Magistrates' Courts. Probation Bureau. "The Wayward Minors' Court." New York, 1939. (Mimeographed.)

New York City Magistrates' Courts. "The Wayward Minors' Court; an Evaluative Review of Procedures and Purposes, 1936 to 1941." New York, 1941. (Mimeographed.)

New York (City). Report of the Joint Committee on Maladjustment and Delinquency. The Psychological and Sociological Implications of Maladjustment and Delinquency. New York, Board of Education, 1938.

New York (State). Interdepartmental Committee on Delinquency. Interim Report. Preventing Juvenile Delinquency; Proposal for a State Program. Albany, N.Y., Dec., 1944.

—— Laws of 1882, Chap. 410, sec. 1466.

—— Laws of 1886, Chap. 353, sec. 1466, subd. 1.

—— Laws of 1903, Chap. 436.

—— Laws of 1910, Chap. 659, sec. 77.

—— Laws of 1918, Chaps. 418 and 419.

—— Laws of 1922, Chap. 547.

—— Laws of 1924, Chaps. 447 and 478.

—— Laws of 1933, Chap. 482.

—— Penal Law and the Code of Criminal Procedure.

New York County District Attorney's Office. Annual Reports, 1943–45.

New York *Journal-American.* Issue of July 24, 1944.

New York Law Society. The Forgotten Adolescent. New York, 1940.

New York *Post.* Issues of March 19, 1945, and November 24, 1943.

New York *Times.* Delinquency and Court Topics, 1935–45.

Pigeon, Helen D. Probation and Parole in Theory and Practice. New York, 1942.

PM. Issue of October 8, 1943.

Polier, Justine Wise. Everyone's Children, Nobody's Child. New York, 1941.

Pound, Roscoe. Criminal Justice in America. New York, 1930.

—— Law and Morals. Chapel Hill, N.C., 1926.

—— Social Control through Law. New Haven, 1942.

Prison Association of New York. Ninety-eighth Annual Report, 1942. Legislative Document No. 32. New York, 1943.

Radzinowicz, L., and J. W. C. Turner (eds.). Mental Abnormality and Crime. London, 1944.

—— The Modern Approach to Criminal Law. London, 1945.

Reckless, Walter C. The Etiology of Delinquency and Criminal Behavior. Social Science Research Council Bulletin No. 50. New York, 1943.

Reckless, Walter C., and Mapheus Smith. Juvenile Delinquency. New York, 1932.

Rogers, Carl R. The Clinical Treatment of the Problem Child. New York, 1939.

Ross, Edward Alsworth. Social Control. New York, 1901.

Seabury, Samuel. Report of the Joint Committee on Probation in New York City. New York, 1942.

Sellin, Thorsten. The Criminality of Youth. Philadelphia, 1940.

—— Culture Conflict and Crime. Social Science Research Council Bulletin No. 41. New York, 1938.

Shaw, Clifford. Delinquency Areas. Chicago, 1929.

—— The Jack-Roller. Chicago, 1930.

—— The Natural History of a Delinquent Career. Chicago, 1931.

Shaw, Clifford, and Henry McKay. Social Factors in Juvenile Delinquency. Vol. II, No. 13, of Reports on the Causes of Crime. National Commission on Law Observance and Enforcement. Washington, D.C., 1931.

Shaw, Clifford, and others. Brothers in Crime. Chicago, 1938.

Shulman, Harry M. A Statistical Study of Crime among the 16–20 Year Group in New York City, 1931. Report of the Subcommission on Causes and Effects of Crime. The Youthful Offender. Legislative Documents, Vol. XXI, No. 114, 1931.

Sullenger T. Earl. Social Determinants in Juvenile Delinquency. New York, 1936.

Tappan, Paul W., "The Nature of Law as a Process of Social Control," *Journal of Legal and Political Sociology,* II (April, 1944), 123–36.

—— "Treatment without Trial," *Social Forces,* XXIV, No. 3 (March, 1946), 306–12.

Taylor, Katherine. Do Adolescents Need Parents? New York, 1938.

Terman, Lewis M., and others. Psychological Factors in Marital Happiness. New York, 1938.

Thom, D. A. Guiding the Adolescent. Washington, D.C., 1933.

Thomas, W. I. The Unadjusted Girl. Boston, 1923.

Thomas, W. I., and Dorothy Thomas. The Child in America. New York, 1928.

Topping, Ruth. Women's Misdemeanants Division of the Municipal Court of Philadelphia. Philadelphia, 1932.

Tulin, Leon A. "The Role of Penalties in Criminal Law," *Yale
Law Journal*, XXXVII (June, 1928), 1048–69.

Ulman, Joseph N. A Judge Takes the Stand. New York, 1933.

United States Children's Bureau. The Child, the Family and the
Court. United States Children's Bureau Publication No. 193.
Washington, D.C., 1933.

—— Children in the Courts. United States Children's Bureau
Publication No. 250. Washington, D.C., 1940.

United States Department of Justice. Attorney General's Survey
of Release Procedures. Vol. I. Probation. Washington, D.C.,
1939.

United States Federal Bureau of Investigation. Uniform Crime
Reports. Washington, D.C., 1935–45.

—— Proceedings of the Attorney General's Conference on Crime.
Washington, D.C., 1934.

Van Waters, Mirian. The Child, the Clinic and the Court. New
York, 1925.

—— Youth in Conflict. New York, 1925.

Waite, E. F. "How Far Can Court Procedure Be Socialized without Impairing Individual Rights?" *Journal of Criminal Law
and Criminology*, XII (Nov., 1921), 339–47.

Waite, John B. Criminal Law in Action. New York, 1934.

—— The Prevention of Repeated Crime. Ann Arbor, 1943.

Waller, Willard. "A Deterministic View of Criminal Responsibility," *Journal of Criminal Law and Criminology*, XX (May,
1929), 88–101.

—— The Family; a Dynamic Interpretation. New York, 1938.

Warner, Sam Bass, and Henry B. Cabot. Judges and Law Reform.
Cambridge, 1936.

White House Conference. The Adolescent in the Family. New
York, 1934.

—— The Delinquent Child. New York, 1932.

—— The Young Child in the Home. New York, 1936.

Wile, Ira S. The Challenge of Adolescence. New York, 1939.

—— (ed.). The Sexual Life of the Unmarried Adult. New York,
1934.

Williams, Frankwood E. Adolescence; Studies in Mental Hygiene.
New York, 1930.

Williamson, Margaretta. The Social Worker in the Prevention and Treatment of Delinquency. New York, 1935.

Willoughby, W. F. Principles of Judicial Administration. Washington, 1929.

Witmer, Helen L. Psychiatric Clinics for Children with Special Reference to State Programs. New York, 1940.

Worthington, George. Men's Misdemeanants Division of the Municipal Court of Philadelphia. Philadelphia, 1932.

Worthington, George, and Ruth Topping. Specialized Courts Dealing with Sex Delinquency. Philadelphia, 1925.

Young, Kimball. Personality and Problems of Adjustment. New York, 1940.

Young, Pauline V. Social Treatment in Probation and Delinquency. New York, 1937.

Zachry, Caroline B. Emotions and Conduct in Adolescence. New York, 1940.

Index

Behavior problems (*Continued*)
  disparity between disposition
  and conduct, 158, 159, 165; cases,
  188; social agency should deal
  with, 205; *see also* Sex behavior
Bellevue Hospital, facilities for
  diagnosis and treatment: mental
  hygiene clinic, 83; psychiatrist
  needed in Court to aid in selection of cases requiring observation at, 141, 199, 204
Bentham, Jeremy, 103
Biological science, judiciary's lack
  of training in, 68
"Bobby socks Victory girls," 126
Borstal system, 217
Brancato, Peter J., quoted, 78n
Brill, J. G., and E. G. Payne,
  quoted, 112
Brooklyn, night court for women,
  41
Brooklyn, Adolescent Court, dispositions, 149, 150; offenses, *tab.*,
  238; principle of adjudication in,
  177, 188, 218, 224
Brooklyn Training School, 82

California, council system, 210;
  Youth Correction Authority law,
  216
Case work, *see* Social case work
Catholic Charity Societies, 28
Catholic Houses of the Good
  Shepherd, Brooklyn, 83
Cedar Knolls, 83
Character diagnosis, adjudication
  on basis of, 115
Child placement, 59
Children, protection from parents,
  186
Children's Bureau, 125n
Children's Court, 43-56; Wayward
  Minor Court's kinship to, 40;
  Family Court combined with, to
  create Domestic Relations court,
  44; practices criticized, 53; Ad-
  justment Bureau, 54; jurisdic-
  tion over errant parents, 54;

probation investigation and report prior to adjudication abandoned, 55; coöperation with social agencies needed, 74; deficient servicing, 80n; pre-trial
  investigation in, 113; procedure,
  129; clinical investigation, 197;
  handicapped by practices of institutions, 202
Children's Court Act, 43, 47, 202
City Hospital, 84
Civil service requirement for probation workers, 43
Classification institutions, 217
Clinical diagnosis, 112, 113
Clinical treatment and rehabilitation, ideal of in ascendency, 106;
  values ignored, 68
Clinics, mental hygiene, 83, 104;
  pre-sentence, 215
Cobb, W. Bruce, 55, 140n; quoted,
  53, 109n, 113
Code of Criminal Procedure, fine
  for contempt on refusal to obey
  summons, 130; right of Court to
  adjourn on remand, 135; sanction for pre-adjudication conference, 139; excerpt, 140n; probation and commitment provision, 146
Commitment, 57; facilities for, 77-
  85, 102; indeterminate, 82, 90,
  167; Westfield, in terms of race,
  151; changes needed in provisions, 209; institutional should
  be made only in rarest cases,
  225; *laws, text*, 234, 237
Committee on Institutions, 202
Community Organization Society,
  28
Community services, ignorance of,
  210
Community Service Society, 28, 84
Complainants, 125-27
Complaints, 129-30
Conduct problems, *see* Behavior
  problems
Consent procedures, dangers, 135,
  180, 183; technique, 197

Conviction, adjudication not deemed a (*law, text*), 241

Conviction rate, 15n, 16, 17, 147

Correction, Department of, House of Detention, 82

Correctional agencies, use for prevention of delinquency deprecated, 102 ff.

Corruption during institutional confinement, 193

Councils, coördinating, 210, 212, 217

Counsel, representation by, *see* Defense attorney

County courts, 30

County youth courts, 218, 219

Course of conduct, and preventive treatment, 98-106; cases which should be court processed, 104; *see also* Behavior problems

Court of Appeals, civil service requirement for probation workers, 43

Court of Special Sessions, children's court division, 43; probation department, 43

Courts, adolescent, endure only by year-to-year permissive legislation, 219; use for prevention of delinquency deprecated, 102 ff.; power should be clearly defined, 110; expansionist drives for extralegal treatment, 136; preventive function impossible to essay, 211; unified court with a part for girls, 218-23; similarity in procedure, 219; sociological approach, 226-30; *see also* Adolescent courts; Children's Court; County courts; General Sessions Court; Juvenile courts; Magistrates' courts; Night courts

Court systems need coördinated planning, 60, 220

Crime Prevention Bureau, 85, 222

Crimes, causation, 100; against common decency, 125n; doctrine of equating penalties to, aban-

doned, 167; Court should hear cases of girls who have committed, 224

Criminal behavior, deterring effect of legal penalties, 92; multiple-correlational analysis needed, 101

Criminals, antisocial patterns developed during youth, 2, 9; cost to society, 11

Criminogenetics, research in, with use of control groups, 101

Curran, Chief Magistrate, 220

Decision, *see* Adjudication

Defendant, social investigation (*q.v.*), 38, 196; situation which surrounds: personality, as determinants of disposition, 63, 173, 174, 180; court procedures and her rights should be explained to, 110, 138, 200; confined on remand during investigation, 111; pre-arraignment appearance, 130; punitive treatment of, compared with that of prostitutes, 147 ff.; attorney rarely represents, 172 (*see also* Defense attorney); civil and legal rights should be assured, 192; unaware of her legal rights, 192; right of due process vested in, 194 ff.; basic protections, 195; entitled to presumption of innocence, 196; ignorant of evidence by which adjudged, 196; need for a friend in court, 200 f.; right to explain her side of case, 200; effect of meeting new judge, 201; effect of remand without prior adjudication, 203; information that should not be brought out in presence of, 207; *see also* Wayward minor; Youthful offender

Defense attorney, 107 ff., 191 ff., 226; defendant rarely represented by, 172

Official attitudes, 12

Oppenheimer, R., B. Flexner, and, 70

Organizations, *see* Agencies; Institutions

Page Commission, night courts attacked, 40; children's court division of special sessions resulted from criticism by, 43

Parents, disobedience to commands of, 32, 33, 36, 46, 48, 171, 182; conflict between child and, 95; child and, submitted to jurisdiction of one court, 97; complaint and testimony of, often limit effectiveness of court, 122; as source of complaint, 126, 171; children to be protected from unreasonable, 186; complaint or consent necessary to prove waywardness, 186; Court lacks jurisdiction over, 186; summons misused by, 191; accusations of mother psychologically undesirable, 199; misdemeanor (*law, text*), 233; *see also* Family conflict

Parole, 56, 205; and remand, 57; during period when case is adjourned, 136; after adjudication and before sentence, 225

Payne, E. G., J. G. Brill and, quoted, 112

Penalties, deterring effect of legal, 92; *see also* Disposition; Punishment

People v. Brewster, 184, 200

People v. Harris, 197

People v. Lewis, 184

Personality diagnosis and treatment, basis of approach, 63; clinical values in, ignored, 68

Personnel, social action limited by, 11

Personnel, court: biases among, 122; quality of work of Court depends upon, 201; altered perspective imperative, 226

—— institutional: religio-moralistic and punitive correctional attitudes, 81

Police, referrals by, 124

Police Athletic League, 85

Police precinct councils, 213

Polier, Justine, 71; quoted, 74

Politicians, deadwood appointments of, 11; conservatism, 12; probation work removed from influence of, 43

Pound, Roscoe, quoted, 59, 74, 94n

Pre-adjudication investigation, *see* Social investigation

Pre-delinquents, noncriminal but incorrigible adolescents, 103; need for specialized assistance, 103 ff.; stigmatizing devices of court treatment unjustified, 104, 105; courts may irreparably harm, 105

Pregnancy not determinative of disposition, 157

Premarital relationship, 35

Prevention, social tribunal's goal, 37, 38; preventive therapy, 51; course of conduct and preventive treatment, 98-106; facilities of Court should be adequate, 102 ff.; coördinating council's emphasis upon, 211

Prison colony, 11

Prison farm, 11

Prison system, Federal: classification system, 217

Probation, 30, 150-51, 188; cost of reformative treatment by, service, 11; preferred form of treatment, 46; official, 57; supervisory function, 109, 111; relations of private social agencies and, 123; for constructive guidance, 188; use in final disposition, 207; extent of use, 225; *laws, text,* 234, 237, 242

Probation Court, 29

Probation investigation, 38, 168, 180, 206; when girl should not

PATTERSON SMITH REPRINT SERIES IN
CRIMINOLOGY, LAW ENFORCEMENT, AND SOCIAL PROBLEMS

1. Lewis: *The Development of American Prisons and Prison Customs, 1776-1845*
2. Carpenter: *Reformatory Prison Discipline*
3. Brace: *The Dangerous Classes of New York*
4. Dix: *Remarks on Prisons and Prison Discipline in the United States*
5. Bruce *et al: The Workings of the Indeterminate-Sentence Law and the Parole System in Illinois*
6. Wickersham Commission: *Complete Reports, Including the Mooney-Billings Report*. 14 Vols.
7. Livingston: *Complete Works on Criminal Jurisprudence*. 2 Vols.
8. Cleveland Foundation: *Criminal Justice in Cleveland*
9. Illinois Association for Criminal Justice: *The Illinois Crime Survey*
10. Missouri Association for Criminal Justice: *The Missouri Crime Survey*
11. Aschaffenburg: *Crime and Its Repression*
12. Garofalo: *Criminology*
13. Gross: *Criminal Psychology*
14. Lombroso: *Crime, Its Causes and Remedies*
15. Saleilles: *The Individualization of Punishment*
16. Tarde: *Penal Philosophy*
17. McKelvey: *American Prisons*
18. Sanders: *Negro Child Welfare in North Carolina*
19. Pike: *A History of Crime in England*. 2 Vols.
20. Herring: *Welfare Work in Mill Villages*
21. Barnes: *The Evolution of Penology in Pennsylvania*
22. Puckett: *Folk Beliefs of the Southern Negro*
23. Fernald *et al: A Study of Women Delinquents in New York State*
24. Wines: *The State of the Prisons and of Child-Saving Institutions*
25. Raper: *The Tragedy of Lynching*
26. Thomas: *The Unadjusted Girl*
27. Jorns: *The Quakers as Pioneers in Social Work*
28. Owings: *Women Police*
29. Woolston: *Prostitution in the United States*
30. Flexner: *Prostitution in Europe*
31. Kelso: *The History of Public Poor Relief in Massachusetts: 1820-1920*
32. Spivak: *Georgia Nigger*
33. Earle: *Curious Punishments of Bygone Days*
34. Bonger: *Race and Crime*
35. Fishman: *Crucibles of Crime*
36. Brearley: *Homicide in the United States*
37. Graper: *American Police Administration*
38. Hichborn: *"The System"*
39. Steiner & Brown: *The North Carolina Chain Gang*
40. Cherrington: *The Evolution of Prohibition in the United States of America*
41. Colquhoun: *A Treatise on the Commerce and Police of the River Thames*
42. Colquhoun: *A Treatise on the Police of the Metropolis*
43. Abrahamsen: *Crime and the Human Mind*
44. Schneider: *The History of Public Welfare in New York State: 1609-1866*
45. Schneider & Deutsch: *The History of Public Welfare in New York State: 1867-1940*
46. Crapsey: *The Nether Side of New York*
47. Young: *Social Treatment in Probation and Delinquency*
48. Quinn: *Gambling and Gambling Devices*
49. McCord & McCord: *Origins of Crime*
50. Worthington & Topping: *Specialized Courts Dealing with Sex Delinquency*